中華廚藝

Chung Wah Chu Ngai

THE WISDOM OF THE CHINESE KITCHEN

CLASSIC FAMILY RECIPES FOR CELEBRATION AND HEALING

GRACE YOUNG

楊玉華

SIMON &
SCHUSTER
EDITIONS

SIMON & SCHUSTER EDITIONS

Rockefeller Center

1230 Avenue of the Americas

New York, NY 10020

DESIGNED BY *Vertigo Design, NYC*

MANUFACTURED IN THE UNITED STATES OF AMERICA

LIBRARY OF CONGRESS CATALOGING-IN-PUBLICATION DATA

Young, Grace

    The wisdom of the Chinese kitchen : classic family recipes for celebration and
healing / Grace Young.

       p. cm.

    Includes index.

    1. Cookery, Chinese.   I. Title.

TX724.5.C5Y598   1999

641.5951—dc21   98-48815

                                   CIP

ISBN 0-684-84739-6

All photographs by Alan Richardson except for the photographs on pages 17, 29, 153, 155,
157, 159, 161, and 163 by Lisa Koenig, and on pages xix, 3, 20, 33, 47, 73, 100, 105, 123, 140,
170, 191, and 226 from the Young and Fung family collection.

For Mama and Baba
and, of course,
Michael

ACKNOWLEDGMENTS

Ancestor worship has been a tradition in China for thousands of years. Its practice is based on the belief that homage to one's ancestors recognizes their influence on one's existence. I have thought countless times that this cookbook is a modern-day act of filial piety. For in trying to record the recipes and family stories from my parents, aunties, and uncles, I honor our past for future generations. I wish to acknowledge the rich legacy not just of my grandparents or great-grandparents but of those relatives no longer with us. The list to whom I am indebted for their help and instruction in crafting this book is a long one. I offer my deep-felt thanks to the following family and friends and so many more: I would like to thank first and foremost Mama and Baba for this book owes its existence solely to them. They have bestowed upon me an enormous gift, answering questions, teaching me, and searching for information on my behalf. I know this project has been exhausting for my parents, and I thank them for their many sacrifices. The publication of this book coincides with their fiftieth anniversary, and I intend this as a fitting and auspicious tribute to them.

I am deeply indebted to my aunties and uncles who have shared recipes, generously taught their secrets for home cooking, recounted family stories and imparted their wisdom to me:

Samuel Fung, who read the stories and provided valuable insights. I am thankful for his patience in translating the Cantonese and his efforts to educate me in Chinese culture.

Katheryn Louie, who meticulously read the stories, confirmed the Chinese characters, and offered her expert counsel.

Margaret Lee, who gave the book its Chinese name and advised on many questions.

Anna Kwock, whose unconditional support and encouragement is always a blessing.

Auntie Lily (Mrs. K. L. Woo), who shared her wise expertise in Chinese cooking.

Lily and Philip Woo, who taught me so many of their recipes and willingly answered my many questions.

Many thanks to Young Shee Jew (Yee Gu Ma), Donald and Lulu Young, Elaine Ho, Herbert and Ivy Fung, Helen Fung, Bertha Jew, William and Lillian Jew, Roy and Betty Yim, Sherman and Frances Young, Shirley Jew, and Calvin and Bernice Jew.

Many thanks to my cousins who have been so helpful:

Fred "Maquire" Chow, whose encouragment and incredible belief in this book made an enormous difference.

Katherine Jew Lim, whose willingness to help in any way and friendship have always been a treasure.

Cindy Jew Fun, who supported this project from the beginning, sharing her recipes and answering my incessant questions.

With thanks to Sylvia Jew Chow, Jeanette Wong, Loretta Lee Seeley, Gloria Lee, and Craig Morita. And to Dorie Yim Song who wanted to contribute more.

Special thanks to my grandmother, Fung Tong Lai Lan, and my brother Douglas Young.

Yu Zhen Chen Mei taught me incredible lessons beyond cooking. It was a privilege to learn to shop and to cook by her side. She was a fountain of wisdom and culinary knowledge and I shall always treasure our sessions together.

I have been blessed to have many friends who offered their expertise in this cookbook:

This book began with the beautiful images my dear friend Alan Richardson photographed during my family's Chinese New Year's celebration. The photographs were the inspiration that helped me to visualize the possibility of this becoming a cookbook. My profound thanks to Alan for contributing his artistry and genius.

I am grateful to have Janice Easton as my editor. With her partially Chinese soul she has understood this book from the beginning. Heartfelt thanks for making this book a reality through her outstanding editorial guidance.

Martha Kaplan, my agent, recognized the potential of this book in its "raw" proposal stage and helped me to refine the proposal and find the perfect editor.

Special thanks to Laura Cerwinske, who gave invaluable advice and critique to the stories, and helped me to find my writing voice.

Kate Slate, who was instrumental in getting the recipes in shape (and to Julien for making this possible).

Evie Righter, whose insightful feedback and masterful guidance helped to elevate this book. My deepest gratitude for her exacting eye in reading the recipes and stories.

Liz Trovato, who created the exquisite cover design and has been an incredible friend throughout. I am ever appreciative.

Ray Furse, for bringing the book to Frankfurt when I was close to giving up, and for his graciousness in always answering my questions on all things Chinese.

Lisa Koenig, for her generosity in rephotographing my family's old photographs and for the exceptional how-to photographs.

Dr. Jacqueline Newman, who has been a wonderful friend to call upon for her expertise in Chinese cooking and who provided some of the nutritional information on Chinese vegetables. I am grateful for the existence of her publication *Flavor and Fortune*, whose purpose is to further the advancement of the science and art of Chinese cuisine.

Pamela Thomas, for her encouragement and help in writing the proposal at the beginning.

Special thanks to Kam Toa Miu and Professor Luke Hongzhi Yang, L.Ac., for their consultation on Chinese herbs.

Special thanks to Art Directors Katy Riegel and Jackie Seow, Production Editor Philip Metcalf, Senior Production Manager Peter McCulloch, and Publicist Mary Ellen Briggs for their help and guidance.

Generous thanks to: Stevie Bass, Barbara Chan, Grace Choi, Gerald Couzens, Neil Crumley, Andrea DiNoto, Alex Fatalevich, Chris and Jim Di Filippo, Larry Frascella, Rodney Friedman, Joan Golden, Scott Hunt, Zina Jasper, Tom Keane, H. T. King, Kathy Farrel Kingsley, Teresa Lam, Alessandra Mortola, Brad Paris, Kim Park, Marjorie Poore, Elizabeth Rice, Linda Russo, Bonnie Slotnick, Julia Stambules, Susie and P. C. Tang, Richard F. Ting, and Betty Tsang.

With thanks to everyone at Vertigo Design for the brilliant interior design. Thanks to David Goodrich at Bird Track Press for the Chinese calligraphy.

And last, but not least, to my husband, Michael Wiertz, who has been supportive throughout, taking endless walks to Chinatown, tasting every dish, good-naturedly doing the dishes, and making perceptive suggestions to the manuscript. It has been a long road, and I thank him for teaching me that patience is everything. Words cannot adequately express my thanks and appreciation.

In memory of Ruth Oppenheimer Weiss and Scott Frederick Riklin. Your light still shines brightly.

Contents

THE ART OF CELEBRATION

INTRODUCTION

In Chinese cooking, every ingredient and dish is imbued with its own brilliance and lore. When I was a young girl growing up in a traditional Chinese home in San Francisco, this knowledge was passed on to me through a lifetime of meals, conversations, celebrations, and rituals. I felt every food we ate in our home had a story. "Eat rice porridge, *jook*," Mama would say, "so you will live a long life." Or, "Drink the winter melon soup to preserve your complexion and to cool your body in the summer heat." Early on, my brother Douglas and I observed that the principles of yin and yang—a balance of opposites—were integrated into our everyday fare. For example, vegetables considered cooling, such as bean sprouts, were stir-fried with ginger, which is warming. Or stir-fried and deep-fat fried dishes were eaten with poached or steamed dishes in the same meal to offset the fatty qualities of the fried dishes. After a rich meal special nourishing soups were served to restore balance in the body.

Today, the brilliant harmony of Chinese cooking is gaining recognition. Chinese cuisine uses spare amounts of protein and a minimum of oil. Carbohydrates comprise essentially 80 percent of the diet and, in Southern China, this is primarily vegetables and rice, a nonallergenic complex carbohydrate that is one of the easiest foods to digest. Herbs and foods like ginseng, soybeans, gingko nuts, and ginger, which the Chinese have integrated into their diet for thousands of years, are now being accepted by the West as particularly beneficial for health. Many of the vegetables in the Chinese diet, especially greens like bok choy, are rich in beta carotene, other vitamins, phytochemicals, and minerals, and the favored technique of stir-frying preserves the vegetables' nutrients.

My parents have impressed upon me their love of food as they had learned it in China. I grew up to appreciate every aspect of cooking, from shopping to preparation to the rituals of eating. This lifelong influence led me to my career as a food stylist and recipe developer. My father, Baba, often warned Douglas and me about certain foods. Chow mein and fried dim sum, he said, were too warming, *yeet hay*, or toxic, if eaten in excess. On the other hand, most vegetables and fruits were cooling, *leung*, and therefore especially good to eat during the summer. He never actually explained to us precisely what "too warming" or "too cooling" meant but, somehow, we accepted it and allowed that he was right.

Still, my brother and I listened to our parents' stories with only half an ear. When Mama served Dried Fig, Apple, and Almond Soup (page 213) and reminded us that it was "soothing for our bodies, *yun*," we didn't really care. Instead, we could hardly wait to sink our teeth into a pizza, a hamburger, or a Swanson chicken pot pie, foods that we somehow knew were *yeet hay*, but were too much a part of the all-American life we led outside our home that we craved them anyway.

Both my parents brought from China the traditions of food and cooking as they had practiced them in their homeland. To this day, they maintain one of the few traditional Chinese households among the members of our extended family in America, which numbers well over two hundred relatives. Although some of my relatives eat more pasta than rice, my parents and the older uncles and aunties take pride in their expertise in classic Chinese cooking. They still center their diet around the principles of Chinese nutrition.

My family's kitchen was often fragrant with the aroma of homemade chicken broth simmering on the back burner of the stove. Invariably, bok choy was draining in a colander, while a fresh chicken hung on a rod over the counter to air-dry briefly before it was braised or roasted. Instead of boxes of commercial cereals, our kitchen cupboards were filled with jars of indigenous Chinese ingredients like lotus seeds, dried mushrooms, various soy sauces, cellophane noodles, and curious-looking herbs like ginseng, red dates, and angelica, or *dong quai*. Instead of milk and butter (dairy products are not part of Chinese cuisine), our refrigerator shelves were more likely to have tofu, ground bean sauce, ginger, and lotus root. In the pantry sat a 100-pound sack of rice.

Like many first-generation Americans, I didn't give my culinary heritage much thought until I was well into adulthood. Growing up in San Francisco, I ate Cantonese home-style food every day. These were not dishes found on restaurant menus, but rich, savory dishes with pure, simple flavors that are the hallmark of a home cook. Whether it was a simple weeknight supper or a more elaborate weekend meal, my parents wanted us to know why, in all of China, the Cantonese were considered to be the best cooks. Their cuisine is the most highly developed—it has the broadest range of flavors, yet the subtlest of tastes. Later I would learn that the concept of foods having "warming" and "cooling" characteristics is especially revered by the Cantonese and manifests itself in their cooking. All the special soups we drank for nourishing and harmonizing our bodies came from a distinctly Cantonese tradition, one not found in any other part of China.

Only recently have I realized that I had taken my marvelous Cantonese culinary heritage for granted. Even members of my extended family have, like me, expanded their diets far beyond Cantonese fare. My cousin tells me that his wife is an excellent Italian cook. When it comes to Chinese food, however, she cannot surpass the quality of their local take-out. While the cousins of my generation and their children enjoy Chinese traditions, only a few of them seem to have maintained the knowledge of the traditional recipes they were raised with. Who has time to learn the family recipes and digest their meaning and importance? My Auntie Bertha, who cooked countless memorable meals for me when I was a child, tells me she has forgotten most of her Chinese dishes; she says it is easier to cook simple American-style meals.

On my visits to San Francisco, Mama's delicious cooking stirred my taste memory, and I began to notice how much healthier I felt after several days of home cooking. As I began to record my family's recipes, I realized there were huge gaps in my knowledge, having learned

Chinese cooking only through casual observation and not from formal study. Even with my professional cooking experience and natural familiarity with Chinese cuisine, it required energetic detective work to decipher and understand some of the recipes. For Chinese cooking is as ancient as its culture, with layers of meaning and wisdom that cannot be easily explained. No one member of my family could teach me every recipe or answer all my questions. I acquired most of my knowledge from my parents, but relatives and family friends all offered little bits of information that I pieced together. The power and wisdom of Chinese cooking goes far beyond simply mastering the more complex cooking techniques or even knowing the ingredients. For me, the principles that govern Chinese cooking and nutrition are far more intriguing than the Western notions of nutrition, with its focus on cholesterol, vitamins, minerals, fiber, carbohydrates, protein, and fats in the diet. It is a cuisine based on opposites, the yin-yang principles of cooking. This philosophy is so instinctively ingrained in my family that it was hard for them to articulate it verbally. I recognized that if I didn't begin questioning my parents, grandmother, aunts, and uncles, the wisdom of their diet and the lore of our culinary heritage would be irretrievably lost. It became clear that I needed to look to the past to understand the present.

I recorded my family's recipes without Americanizing the ingredients. There are those who offer substitutes for traditional Chinese ingredients, but this fails to acknowledge the genius of Chinese cooking. There is a reason for thousands of years of reverence for certain combinations. Recipes that offer, for example, Kentucky string beans as a substitute for Chinese long beans fail to grasp the Chinese nutritional perspective. While both vegetables have a similar crunchiness and might seem comparable, the Chinese long bean is the only vegetable the Cantonese consider neutral, neither too yin, "cooling," nor too yang, "warming," and is the only vegetable women are allowed to eat after giving birth. Cantonese believe most vegetables and fruits are "cooling" and, therefore, dangerous for a new mother, especially in the first month after she gives birth.

The recipes in this book include some that do not require exotic Chinese ingredients. Not every dish needs a specialty ingredient or labor-intensive chopping and shredding but, in all truthfulness, if you genuinely desire to cook Chinese dishes, you will need exotic ingredients, along with the time to properly prepare them. Some cooks will suggest using canned water chestnuts in place of fresh, but it is my feeling that if fresh are not available, the recipe is not worth making. For me, using canned water chestnuts is like using canned potatoes. In some areas, I've simplified recipes by calling for the food processor to puree ingredients. But, overall, I have tried to preserve the traditional ingredients and techniques as much as possible, preferring to hand-shred ginger and vegetables rather than feed them through a food processor.

The recipes reflect the range of mastery of the Cantonese home cook. The rich flavors of home-style cooking include basic stir-fry recipes, steamed recipes, rice dishes, braises, and soups; my family cooked these on most weeknights. Also included are the auspicious and more elaborate foods connected with New Year's and special occasions. Some of these recipes have an old-world quality about them, reflecting an era when people had more time to cook. Finally, the healing remedies are intended to restore harmony and strength to the body for proper yin-yang balance.

Chinese culinary healing, while essentially overlooked in the West, remains vital to Cantonese culture. To restore the natural balance in our bodies, my family countered the rich and delicious foods we ate regularly with what I call *yin-yang concoctions,* or special soups made according to a more than thousand-year-old tradition. I have written these recipes and explained their health benefits as my family practices them. All the recipes were eaten in moderation, and never considered a substitute for professional medical attention. Sometimes, the recipes or stories behind them vary slightly from family to family, and from village to village. I offer them here as they were taught to me.

My parents' approach to cooking is Zen-like: attentive to detail and masterful. They are not formally trained in cooking, yet they share a passion for food that is common among many Chinese. They have great esteem for the meaning and symbolism of food as well as respect for age-old remedies. The everyday rituals of properly selecting produce, slicing meat, washing rice, and presenting a meal, which I have inherited from my family, have given me an aesthetic insight into life. The slow emergence of these truths has allowed me to see the meaning of my own cooking as a metaphor for life.

The rinsing, soaking, and washing of ingredients is very common in Chinese cooking. What follows are particular points I would like to clarify for home cooks.

Chinese cooking is unique in its use of so many dried ingredients. Many times, a dried ingredient is much more valuable than its fresh counterpart. Good-quality dried scallops are about four times the price of fresh, and are much more concentrated in flavor and aroma. The technique of handling dried ingredients is more or less the same for all ingredients. What will vary is the amount of soaking liquid, the length of time the ingredient needs to be soaked depending on the quality of the ingredient, and whether the soaking liquid can be used in cooking. All dried ingredients must be rinsed. If you have traveled in the Far East, you will have seen ingredients drying on fields or on the sides of roads. Ingredients are air-dried under the sun and, as you can imagine, it is natural that dirt becomes lodged in the ingredients. It is, therefore, always advisable to rinse dried ingredients. Different cookbooks instruct that ingredients can be soaked in cold, tepid, or hot water. My family always soaks dried ingredients in cold water.

The soaking liquid of ingredients like mushrooms, scallops, and oysters, for example, is extremely flavorful and should be saved for cooking. When using this liquid, never use the last teaspoon or so, as dirt or sediment that is not removed by rinsing often settles in the soaking liquid. The soaking liquid for cloud ears, wood ears, lily buds, lily bulbs, and red dates can be discarded.

Rice is another ingredient that is always rinsed. Once the proper amount of water has been added for cooking, some cooks will let the rice sit in the water until ready to cook. This soaking softens the rice so that it cooks faster and will be more tender. Those who like their rice to be firmer never let it soak, but cook it immediately after it's been rinsed. The length of soaking will vary according to how soft you prefer your rice. You need to experiment with different soaking times to discover what suits you best.

The poultry recipes often call for washing poultry with salt, rinsing it under cold water, and then allowing it to air-dry. This is the traditional Chinese way to treat poultry. The air-drying should always be done in a cool and breezy room to avoid any spoilage. Air-drying is believed to remove excess moisture and allow the poultry to better absorb flavors. These two steps can be omitted but I believe that if the cook has time to do them, the poultry will be more flavorful. It is also the custom in Chinese cooking to chop poultry before or after it is cooked into bite-sized pieces; this is the traditional way of serving food, never offering large pieces of meat. Chopping through the bone takes special skill with a meat cleaver ("Shreds of Ginger Like Blades of Grass," page 47). I often simply disjoint the poultry or cut chicken parts with small bones into bite-sized pieces with poultry shears.

Pork or pork bones are typically used when making soups. There are two different methods for cleaning pork. In the traditional method, the liquid is brought to a boil, the pork is added for one minute, and then drained in a colander, rinsed under cold water, and returned to the pot. The second method is a shortcut, and only requires bringing the cold water and pork to a boil and removing the scum that rises to the surface. Traditional cooks insist that pork must be "cleaned" before being made into stock.

When preparing to stir-fry vegetables, the vegetables should be washed several hours before the meal, so that they will have time to air-dry before stir-frying. Do not be alarmed if the vegetables appear slightly limp by the time they are cooked. This is preferable to wet vegetables. If the vegetables are wet, they will not stir-fry in the pan but will instead immediately begin steaming.

Traditional cooks always peel ginger before slicing because they prefer the taste and appearance and they feel it is cleaner, but there are also those who cook ginger unpeeled. When peeling ginger, use a paring knife to scrape off the skin. A slice of ginger is an ingredient that is needed in countless recipes. The ginger should be about ⅛-inch thick and roughly the diameter of a quarter.

If you have questions about any of the ingredients called for, check the Glossary (page 246). A complete description of each ingredient is provided along with shopping and storing tips. Also, use the identification photographs to help recognize ingredients (see "Chinese Staples," "Foods with Medicinal Attributes," "Fresh Vegetables," and "Fresh Foods" in the photo insert) and equipment (page 244), and read "Shopping Like a Sleuth" (page 241).

Cornstarch is commonly used to marinate meats and thicken sauces. My family has certainly used cornstarch, but prefers tapioca starch, which is available in Chinese supermarkets. Tapioca starch is a pure root and therefore more stable than cornstarch and makes a better sauce. If tapioca starch cannot be purchased, cornstarch can be used as a substitute. I list cornstarch in the recipes because it is more readily available.

Peanut oil has traditionally been the favorite oil in Chinese cooking. However, for years, my family used vegetable oil, preferring its lighter taste. In recent years, many Chinese have converted to olive oil for stir-frying because of the added health benefits of cooking with an oil rich in monounsaturated fats. Curiously, I've seen more and more Chinese markets stock extra virgin and extra light olive oil. My family prefers light olive oil, which has none of the distinctive fruity flavor of extra virgin olive oil, but still may protect against cancer and heart disease. It is excellent for high-heat cooking, such as stir-frying or deep-fat frying, as it is stable at high temperatures and coats food rather than being absorbed.

Homemade Chicken Broth (page 234) will always enhance the flavor of your dishes and soups. Whenever I have time, I make a big pot of chicken broth and freeze it into one-quart containers, so that I will always have it on hand. Homemade broth is a secret to achieving full-flavored dishes; canned chicken broth can be used, but the flavor will always be inferior to that of homemade.

There are two kinds of rice flour sold in Chinese grocery stores: rice flour and glutinous rice flour. They are never interchangeable, and produce distinctly different tastes and textures.

For stir-fries, meat should always be cut a scant ¼-inch thick. If it is difficult to cut such thin pieces, freeze the meat for twenty to thirty minutes, so that the meat is slightly firmer before slicing.

The Chinese consider many of their foods to have medicinal attributes. In this regard, Chinese herb shops stock many of the same foods (such as tangerine peel, wood ears, dried yam, wolfberries, and ginseng) that are found in Chinese grocery stores. In other words, what is found in a Chinese herb shop does not comply with the strict definitions of an herb in the West.

The recipes in this book should serve four to six people as part of a multicourse meal, unless otherwise indicated. As a general rule, Chinese families always prepare three dishes, a soup, and rice for four people—one less dish than diners. More dishes can be prepared, but this is the rough Chinese formula used to determine how much to cook.

Despite the lengthy cooking times for some of the soups in the section "Acheiving Yin-Yang Harmony," the Chinese typically eat the vegetables, meat, and herbs from the soup in addition to drinking the broth. And for recipes that call for large amounts of ginger, such as Rock Sugar Ginger Chicken (page 58) or Chicken Wine Soup (page 236), the ginger not only is used to flavor the dish but is eaten as well.

The Chinese vocabulary in the text is based on the Cantonese dialect. As a help to the reader I have supplied the phonetic Cantonese pronunciation, which appears alongside the Chinese calligraphy.

Three generations of the Young family. Canton, China, circa 1934.

念中
Nan Chung

REMEMBER CHINA, NAN CHUNG

MY OLDER BROTHER, DOUGLAS, WAS born in San Francisco just after the Communists took control of China. My grandfather, Gunggung, who lived in Shanghai, gave Douglas his Chinese name, Nan Chung, which means "Remember China." Grandfather was intent that this first grandchild, born in a foreign land, would never forget his family in China, and always reflect on his family's long history and tradition. Indeed, none of his grandchildren would be born in China. Growing up in America, Douglas and I behaved more like American children than Chinese. Our taste, our interests, our goals were all American. It is only now, after nearly fifty years, that I have begun to heed Gunggung's instruction to "Remember China."

Nothing can more powerfully transport me across time and geography to the intimacy of my childhood home than the taste or smell of Cantonese home cooking. I naively set about

xix

writing my family's recipes with the thought that this project would be solely about cooking. But with each question about a recipe came a memory from my parents and, with each memory, I was led into a world I hadn't realized belonged to me. I listened to Mama reminisce about the weeks of preparation at her grandmother's kitchen in Hong Kong before the New Year's feast, about the servants hand-grinding rice to make flour for all the special cakes. My relatives also discovered photographs they had forgotten existed. One was a fragile sepia portrait of my great-grandmother, her feet bound. I studied the image trying to grasp my blood relationship to this woman, separated by only three generations. Another elegant studio portrait shows Baba's family in Canton, in 1934. In it I see the young faces of my father, my uncles, my aunts. Who were these innocent souls before they carved their life paths? Few photographs survived that other life, making its reality ever more ephemeral. This glimpse into my own history was but one of the treasures uncovered in the process of collecting my family's recipes.

A remarkable chapter opened in my relationship with my parents when I began recording our family's culinary heritage. Despite their unfathomable reticence to talk about themselves, eventually, as I persisted in my questions, they slowly responded to my desire to learn. "Show me how *you* choose bok choy, how *you* prefer to stir-fry. Describe for me how it was in Shanghai and Canton when you were little. Did the water chestnuts taste like this or were they sweeter, the lotus root smaller, the tea more fragrant?" My parents, each in his or her own way, came to enjoy teaching me. Baba, whose routine is to monitor the stock market while drifting in and out of catnaps, suddenly had a list of cooking lessons. Mama, ever the matriarch, was only too happy to instruct me on her highly specific principles for produce shopping, or to confer with my aunties on recipes I requested. I, in turn, was grateful for this new relationship. We talked not only about cooking but also of their recollections of life in China and in San Francisco's Chinatown at mid-century. Flattered by my interest, they stretched their memories to unearth stories and reclaim their forgotten past. Baba mentions to me one day that he had owned a restaurant in Chinatown in the 1940s called the Grant Cafe, on the corner of Bush and Grant Avenues, which served Chinese and American food. But when I ask for details, it is difficult to get him to elaborate. His reluctance to talk about what he considers private tempers how much I learn about his past.

On one visit Auntie Margaret and Auntie Elaine describe the thrill of being driven by my Yee Gu Ma (second-eldest aunt) in her Packard in 1937, when Grant Avenue was a two-way street. Few Chinese women drove in those days, but my uncle, George Jew, was a "modern man" who wanted my aunt to drive. Baba wonders aloud about whether it was a Buick or a Packard, but I am lost in thought imagining my petite aunt wielding a big car down Grant Avenue, on her way to Market Street with her younger sisters and brother.

The San Francisco Chinatown of my youth is barely evident in the Chinatown of today. In the 1960s it was a charming, intimate community inhabited by legions of old-timers, known as *lo wah kue*, and locals. On any given day I would see Uncle Kai Bock sitting on a stoop on

Washington Street; run into Auntie Margaret at her restaurant, Sun Ya, or stop to see Auntie Anna or Uncle Roy at Wing Sing Chong market. My Auntie Anna knew everyone who came into her store, and I was convinced she was Chinatown's honorary mayor. To this day you can barely walk two steps with Auntie Anna without someone greeting her. Every Friday night my family went out to eat. Whichever restaurant it was, Sai Yuen, Far East Cafe, or Sun Hung Heung, Baba would stroll into the kitchen to order our food. This was no small feat. Restaurant kitchens were off-limits to everyone but staff, but Baba sold liquor to all the Chinese restaurants, and often the owner was the chef. Rejoining us, he would tell us which dishes were the freshest and best to eat that day. I still believe he must have observed many professional cooking secrets during these visits, and I can't recall ever eating in a restaurant where Baba didn't know the chef or owner. Baba seemed to know everyone.

In those days, Chinatown was the safest neighborhood in all of San Francisco. My cousins Cindy and Kim stayed with their grandparents in Chinatown on weekends and Gunggung would take them for a late-night snack, *siu ye,* of won ton noodles, chow mein, or rice porridge, *jook*, at two or three in the morning. Their paternal great-grandfather, Jew Chong Quai, was one of the wealthiest merchants in Chinatown in the early 1920s. San Francisco had a thriving bay shrimp industry for more than eighty years, and he had a shrimp cannery in Hunter's Point in addition to being an importer and exporter of bean sauce (*fu yu*).

I have warm memories of standing on Grant Avenue for the Chinese New Year's parade and watching for my glamorous Auntie Katheryn on the Pan Am float and my cousin Carol who led the St. Mary's drum corp. Today, Chinatown is still the vital center of the Chinese community, but the purity of its Cantonese soul is lost amidst the Wax Museum, McDonald's, Arab merchants hawking cameras on Grant Avenue, and the mixture of non-Cantonese Asian immigrants who have since moved in. Still, a few sights remind me of the Chinatown of old: the Bank of America on Grant Avenue with its classical Chinese architecture, the creation of my Uncle Stephen, an architect, as is the Imperial Palace Restaurant on Grant Avenue and the Cumberland Church on Jackson Street; my Uncle Larry's medical practice on Clay Street, one of the oldest original practices remaining; and, until recently, my Uncle William and Aunt Lil's family's restaurant, Sun Hung Heung, the oldest Chinese restaurant owned by one family, in operation since 1919. Another remaining point of pride is the Kong Chow Benevolent Association and Temple on Stockton Street, which my Uncle Donald was instrumental in building. This association serves the overseas Cantonese from two counties in China: Sunwui (where Baba's family was born) and Hokshan (where Mama's family was born).

When I think of the delicious food of my childhood beyond my own family's influences, I think of my beloved Uncle Tommy. He was an artist and a natural cook who had a special gift in the kitchen. His early death left an enormous void in the family. As a child, I enjoyed many a meal at Uncle Tommy and Auntie Bertha's home. I well remember the intoxicating aromas that would come from their kitchen, and the taste of the food Uncle Tommy cooked.

It was out of this world. I have asked my cousins Sylvia, Kathy, and David for their father's recipes but, sadly, neither Auntie Bertha nor my cousins ever recorded them. Alas, they are but a sweet memory for all of us. We partook of his specialties without ever thinking there would come a time when we couldn't taste the pleasure of his cooking and company. A great cook's recipes are as unique as fingerprints.

My brother and I did not grow up sitting on our grandparents' laps, hearing tales of their youth. And it was not my parents' custom to speak much about their life in China. They came to America for economic and political reasons, to seek a better future. I once asked Mama a simple question about her parents, and was surprised that she couldn't answer me. "In China, we only knew what our parents told us. We never asked personal questions out of respect for our elders." Occasionally, my parents would share a story but, for the most part, they rarely divulged their remembrances. Perhaps, too, Mama and Baba weren't ready to speak of their former life and we were too young to care, or to know what to ask.

The year 1999 marks the 150th anniversary of the Gold Rush and the first major immigration of the Chinese people to America. Despite a century and a half of transplantation, Chinese cuisine remains alive and virtually unchanged—testimony to the strengh of its traditions. The recipes my parents prepare today are not dramatically different from those of their parents and grandparents in China. Yet the Chinese of my generation stand at a crossroads: We maintain the desire to preserve our culinary heritage yet, like most Americans, have precious little time for cooking and honoring the old ways. We risk the loss of our great cooking rituals and along with them their spiritual enrichment. I have yet to find the web site for wisdom.

The time I have spent cooking with my parents, listening to their stories, and receiving their wisdom has allowed me to claim something of my cultural identity and heritage. To master Chinese cooking requires a lifetime of study, and I offer this book as an example of one family's culinary devotion. A knowledge of cooking passed from generation to generation offers a gift to the soul, one that appeals to all of the senses and affirms our deepest connection to life.

THE FOLLOWING ARE EVERYDAY RECIPES that my parents have always cooked for family meals. They demonstrate the fundamental techniques of Cantonese cooking, from rice dishes to stir-fries to simple soups and steamed and braised dishes. This section also includes three rice-pot dishes ranging from the classic to the extraordinary. These recipes reflect the level of mastery a typical Cantonese home cook of my parents' generation has attained and what, in turn, my generation considers Cantonese comfort food. Some recipes are very basic, others more advanced. All are considered family fare.

Mastering the Fundamentals

米者糧也

Mai Tzat Leung Ya

THE MEANING OF RICE

Mama, Auntie Katheryn, Uncle Norman, and Uncle Sam. Shanghai, China, circa 1937.

ON THE SHELF IN MY KITCHEN IN New York, I used to have a canister filled with rice that sat next to similar containers filled with flour and sugar. For years, I thought nothing of my storage methodology. Then, my parents came to visit. As Mama was making tea one morning, she came across the canister of rice. "Where is the rest of the rice?" she asked, her face fixed with concern.

I was single at the time, and a pound of rice was all I ever needed. But, in that moment, I realized how far I had journeyed from my Chinese roots. I suddenly pictured the 100-pound sack that always sat in my parents' pantry, representing a kind of savings account or retirement fund. It served myriad practical purposes as well; whenever fruit wasn't quite ripe, we'd bury it in the sack overnight and the heat of the rice would ripen it. Once, when we ran out of glue, Baba calmly mashed a little cooked rice with water to make a thin paste. This, he informed me, was stronger than Elmer's, and what an ingenious use for leftover rice. I also learned from Baba that in villages, when the rice pot was cleaned, the leftover rice and water was given to the pigs for food. For the Chinese, the value of rice far exceeds its primary role as a carbohydrate. For my parents, rice is the ultimate symbol of prosperity, and my little canister was a painful symbol of an impoverished life. Beggars had more rice than I did.

Rice's importance to Chinese culture is reflected in the language. The Cantonese, for example, have two words for rice: *mai,* which is the raw rice, and *fan,* the cooked grains. *Fan* also just means "food," as in the common, everyday greeting, *"Nay sik zaw fan may?"* The literal translation is "Have you had your rice yet?," but *fan* in this sentence symbolizes all food. If the answer is no, a popular reply is, *"Gnaw chang nay sik bien fan,"* or "I will invite you for a casual bit of rice." Financial security is also described in terms of rice. A woman seeking a wealthy mate is said to be coveting a long-term rice ticket or a diamond rice bowl. To have a well-paying job is to "have a golden rice bowl," and to be fired from your job is "to lose your rice bowl." A famous Chinese proverb about respect teaches, "Whether (eating) a bowl of rice porridge or cooked rice, one should remember the trouble it has cost to produce it." Nothing compares to the importance of rice. If all else fails, there is hopefully always rice.

When I first went to China in 1979, I was astonished at how foreign I felt. The fields of sorghum, soybeans, and lotus were all so new to me—as was a lush, green vegetation I could not identify. I asked the local guide what it was and his jaw dropped. In disbelief, he said, "Rice . . ." As a Chinese woman, I immediately felt ashamed of my ignorance of my own culture's most revered staple. How could I explain to him that rice doesn't grow in foggy San Francisco? That the Chinese born abroad are a different breed?

Mama used to tell us how precious rice was in China during the war. My grandfather, Gunggung, would buy rice whenever it was available, hoarding it as long as he could to feed his family of seven. Throughout the war years, they always ate the old, stale-tasting rice, fearing they might not be able to buy more. After the war, the family's first wish was to have several bowls of steaming fresh rice, to be able to relish the taste of the new rice crop. Likewise, whenever my family returned home from a vacation, my own father's fondest wish was for a bowl of hot rice served with a few simple dishes. Tasting this, he would declare contentedly that now he was home.

The Chinese consider a strong appetite for rice to be a sign of good health and fortune. It's common for wives and mothers to brag of their husband's or children's ability to eat three or four bowls of rice at a sitting. Baba, like many Cantonese men, will insist that he does not feel right until he has eaten rice. Cooks are happy to see their guests *teem fan,* that is, get another helping of rice. It indicates that their vegetable dishes, cooked with a little meat, poultry, fish, or tofu, must be delicious enough to inspire such an appetite.

The traditional Cantonese diet is in fact the diet advised by today's nutrition experts in the new food pyramid: primarily complex carbohydrates, vegetables, legumes (mainly soybeans), and scant amounts of meat, fish, or poultry cooked in a little oil, complemented with fresh fruit. Tea, a rich source of the antioxidant called *polyphenol,* is the favorite beverage. The only component missing is dairy, which more and more nutritionists believe is difficult for the body to digest and not a necessity. For the Cantonese, carbohydrates make up 80 percent of the diet; the dishes are the accompaniment to the rice, not the focal point. Sauce can be spooned on rice, but rice is never doused with soy sauce. Rice is enjoyed for its pure, natural flavor and its singular texture, and accounts for three-fourths of the meal. (This is definitely not how Americans eat Chinese food!)

In sickness, health, and celebration, the Cantonese look to rice for nourishment. Tender cooked rice is the first food a baby is given when old enough to eat. Rice porridge cooked for three or four hours is eaten when one is ill (it is believed that this hydrates the body and cleanses it of toxins). The Cantonese savor the same porridge for breakfast, preferring steamed rice for lunch and dinner. To the Chinese, rice is the most versatile ingredient, as it can be steamed, boiled, stir-fried, deep-fried, cooked as a porridge, or made into a dessert. The grain can also be made into vinegar or wine, ground into two different kinds of flour, or made into dried or fresh noodles. For New Year's celebrations, round rice cakes are prepared to symbolize unity and cohesiveness in the family (page 132). For the summer solstice, savory and sweet rice tamales (pages 152 and 154) are prepared. In autumn, sweet rice is cooked with Chinese sausage, barbecued pork, and mushrooms (page 8). And, in the winter, savory and sweet rice dumplings are made from rice flour to commemorate the winter solstice (pages 16 and 18). When paying respects to one's ancestors, cooked rice, food, and liquor are traditionally offered. One can live without nearly everything on earth and in heaven but rice.

The preparation of rice is also steeped in tradition. For example, rice is washed by stirring the raw grains in several changes of cold water until the water runs crystal clear. Recently, I discovered that in China this water is often saved for cleaning the traditional wok. Soap is *never* used to clean a cast-iron or carbon-steel wok, because it strips the wok of its natural seasoning; simply soak the dirty wok in the rice-washing water, then scrub the wok with a soft bristle brush. This remarkable starchy rice water removes all traces of grease, and prevents the wok from ever rusting, eliminating the need for constantly reseasoning the wok, as described in most Chinese cookbooks.

As rice cooks it should be covered at all times. Modern recipes for cooking steamed rice often call for boiling the rice uncovered until the water is almost completely evaporated. For old-fashioned Chinese cooks boiling rice uncovered is a foolish release of the *fan hay,* or rice breath. According to my mother, rice should be covered at all times to preserve the special rice energy. However, as she told me, this is not practical for most cooks, as it requires a large pot to cook the rice, so that the water will not boil over. In China, rice was cooked in a covered sandpot or wok, which has a capacity of about five quarts, and with its wide surface it was impossible for the water to boil over even on high heat.

In the 1960s, when health food first became popular, my brother and I tried to teach or enlighten Mama about how bad it was to wash rice, because it also washed away the nutrients. "Don't you know that studies prove how bad it is to do that?" we'd say. But it would just fall on deaf ears, as Mama would shake her head and say matter-of-factly, "The rice is dirty and it must be washed!" Having witnessed the wisdom of so many other aspects of Chinese cooking, I anticipate that sooner or later someone will discover that simply rinsing rice eliminates toxins. It wouldn't surprise me at all.

In China, there is an old saying that rice is one of the seven necessities of life. Along with oil, wood for cooking, salt, soy sauce, vinegar, and tea, rice is all one needs in order to begin a home. My family ate rice every day and never got tired of it. It gave everyone a sense of well-being and, before each meal, the blessing I was taught to say to my elders was "Baba, Mama, Gege [older brother], *sik fan,*" encouraging each person at the table to "eat rice."

Steamed Rice

The Chinese do not measure rice cooking water with a liquid measuring cup but simply add enough water so that when the tip of the middle finger sits gently on the surface of the leveled rice, the water just reaches the first crease of the middle finger, or a depth of about one inch. I have seen dozens of people with completely different hand sizes do this and, in spite of the differences, this always works. If you feel too nervous to trust this method, add not quite double the amount of water to the amount of rice being cooked.

Some Chinese cooks soak rice for a while before cooking to soften it so that it cooks faster and to render the grains more tender. Those who like their rice to be firmer never soak it, but cook it immediately after rinsing. If you'd like, experiment with different soaking times to discover what suits you best. Never stir rice as it cooks, because it will make the rice "gluey"; ideally the grains should be separate and fluffy.

When washing rice, remember to save the water if you plan on stir-frying in a traditional wok. The starchy water is the best cleanser you'll ever use for a cast-iron or carbon-steel wok.

2 cups long grain rice

Place the rice in a 3-quart saucepan. Wash the rice in several changes of cold water until the water runs clear. Drain the rice. Level the rice, and add enough cold water to cover the rice by 1 inch of water. (Or add 3¼ cups of water.) Bring to a boil, covered, over high heat, never stirring. Reduce heat to low and simmer, covered, 15 to 17 minutes, or until all of the water is absorbed. Turn off the heat and let sit 5 minutes before serving.

Makes 6 cups. Serves 4 to 6 as part of a multicourse meal.

Naw Mai Fan

Flavored Sweet Rice

Auntie Frances and Uncle Sherman are famous in my family for their *Naw Mai Fan,* a dish that is mainly served at Chinese banquets. If there is a family potluck gathering, it is assumed that they will bring the rice. I have taken an informal survey of my cousins, and *Naw Mai Fan* is the one dish almost all of them wished they knew how to make. It is unbelievably rich because the ingredients—dried scallops, shrimp, Chinese mushrooms, Chinese sausage, and barbecued pork—infuse the sweet rice with incredible flavor. And it is sweet rice, also known as *glutinous, wax,* or *sticky rice,* that is used here. Available mainly in Asian markets, this type of rice has short, plump grains that, when cooked, become sticky and glutinous. If you prefer less meat, add more dried mushrooms, scallops, or shrimp. However you combine the ingredients, the sum total of flavoring ingredients should be about 1 cup or so.

¼ cup Chinese dried scallops (*gawn yu chee*)

1 cup sweet rice

½ cup long grain rice

2 tablespoons Chinese dried shrimp

4 Chinese dried mushrooms

1 Chinese sausage (*lop chong*)

4 ounces Chinese Barbecued Pork, store-bought or homemade (page 176)

1 teaspoon vegetable oil

1½ teaspoons thin soy sauce

1¼ cups Homemade Chicken Broth (page 234)

2 teaspoons black soy sauce

2 teaspoons oyster flavored sauce

⅓ cup chopped scallions

⅓ cup chopped cilantro

In a small bowl, soak the dried scallops in about ⅓ cup cold water for 2 hours, or until softened. In a medium-sized bowl, wash all the rice in several changes of cold water until the water runs clear. Soak the combined sweet and long grain rices for 1 hour in enough cold water to cover. Place the shrimp and mushrooms in separate bowls. Pour about ¼ cup cold water over each ingredient, and soak for about 30 minutes, to soften.

When softened, drain all the ingredients except the rice, discarding the shrimp water and reserving the scallop and mushroom liquids. Remove the small hard knob from the side of the scallops and discard. Finely shred the scallops with your hands. Chop shrimp if larger than ¼ inch. Drain and squeeze dry mushrooms. Cut off and discard stems and finely chop the caps.

Finely chop sausage and barbecued pork and set aside separately.

Meanwhile, heat a 14-inch flat-bottomed wok or skillet over high heat until hot but not smoking. Add oil and Chinese sausage, and stir-fry 30 seconds. Add scallops and stir-fry another 30 seconds. Add the shrimp, mushrooms, and barbecued pork, and stir-fry 1 minute. Add thin soy sauce, stir to combine, remove from heat, and set aside.

Drain rice and place in a 2-quart saucepan. Add chicken broth and enough of the reserved scallop and mushroom liquids to measure ¼ cup, and bring to a boil over high heat. Reduce heat to low, cover, and cook 10 minutes. Uncover and quickly scoop Chinese sausage mixture onto top of rice. Immediately cover and continue cooking the rice 25 to 30 minutes, or until broth is completely absorbed and rice is tender. Let stand 5 minutes. Add the black soy sauce, oyster sauce, scallions, and cilantro, and stir to combine. Serve immediately.

Makes about 6 cups. Serves 6 to 8 as part of a multicourse meal.

炒飯

Chow Fan

Fried Rice

My family only made this dish when there was leftover rice, and as a ploy to get us to eat more rice as children. Fried rice is an authentic Cantonese dish, and makes a quick dish for weeknight meals. My own favorite way of cooking fried rice is to use brown rice, because I prefer the texture, and it is delicious with any combination of vegetables. The traditional recipe is made, though, with cooked long grain rice. XO Sauce is a relatively new condiment, made from dried scallops, shrimp roe, chili peppers, garlic, and spices. It is a popular ingredient Hong Kong chefs now add to fried rice to enhance the flavor.

2 large eggs

2 teaspoons plus 1 tablespoon vegetable oil

6 ounces Chinese Barbecued Pork, store-bought or homemade (page 176)

3 cups cooked brown rice, cooled

1 cup frozen peas, thawed

⅓ cup finely minced scallions

1 tablespoon thin soy sauce

1 teaspoon XO Sauce, optional

¼ teaspoon salt

¼ teaspoon ground white pepper

Lightly beat eggs. Heat a 14-inch flat-bottomed wok or skillet over medium-high heat until hot but not smoking. Add 2 teaspoons oil and beaten eggs, and cook 1 to 2 minutes, tilting the pan so that the egg covers the surface as thinly as possible to make a pancake. When the bottom is just beginning to brown and the pancake is just set, transfer to a cutting board. Allow pancake to cool slightly, then cut into ¼-inch-wide, 2-inch-long strips. Cut barbecued pork into ¼-inch dice to make about 1¼ cups.

Add remaining 1 tablespoon oil and rice to wok, and stir-fry 2 to 3 minutes, breaking up the rice to separate the grains, until it is lightly coated with oil. Add the diced pork, peas, scallions, and egg strips, and continue stir-frying 3 to 4 minutes, or until rice is beginning to brown slightly. Add soy sauce, XO Sauce if desired, salt, and pepper, and stir-fry 1 more minute, or until well combined. Serve immediately.

Serves 4 to 6 as part of a multicourse meal.

滑
鷄
飯

Tender Chicken on Rice

Proving that the foundation of a meal is rice, the Cantonese are famous for their one-pot rice dishes, *gook fan.* A pot of rice is cooked and, 5 minutes or so before the rice is done, a stir-fried dish that hasn't been completely cooked through is placed on top of the rice and finishes cooking from the rice's steam heat.

Wat Gai Fan, or Tender Chicken on Rice, is a classic home-style combination of smoky ham, chicken, and Chinese mushrooms. The rich sauce, accented with ginger, melts into the rice. I like this even better when prepared with chicken on the bone, chopped into bite-sized pieces, but it takes expertise to chop the chicken and the steaming time will increase. An enameled cast-iron pot is best for this dish, because it not only conducts heat well but is colorful enough to present at the table.

If Smithfield ham is not available, Black Forest ham can be substituted; there is no need to boil it. Add the julienne ham with the mushroom liquid.

2 ounces Smithfield ham

8 Chinese dried mushrooms

8 ounces skinless, boneless chicken breast or thigh

2 tablespoons finely shredded ginger

1 tablespoon Shao Hsing rice cooking wine

1 tablespoon thin soy sauce

1½ teaspoons black soy sauce

1½ teaspoons cornstarch

½ teaspoon sesame oil

¼ teaspoon sugar

⅛ teaspoon ground white pepper

1 cup long grain rice

2 tablespoons vegetable oil

1 scallion, finely julienned

Rinse ham in cold water. In a small saucepan, bring 1 cup of cold water to a boil over high heat. Add ham and return to a boil. Reduce heat to medium–low, cover, and simmer 20 minutes. Drain ham, and set aside until cool enough to handle. Slice the ham into paper-thin slices. Stack a few slices at a time, and cut into julienne strips to make about ½ cup.

In a small bowl, soak mushrooms in ½ cup cold water for about 30 minutes, to soften. When softened, drain and squeeze mushrooms dry, reserving the mushroom liquid. Cut off and discard stems and thinly slice the caps.

Cut chicken into scant ½-inch-thick slices, place in a medium bowl. Add mushrooms, ginger, rice wine, thin soy sauce, black soy sauce, cornstarch, sesame oil, sugar, and pepper, and mix with your hands to combine.

Place the rice in a 2-quart saucepan. Wash the rice in several changes of cold water until the water runs clear. Drain the rice. Level the rice, and add enough cold water to cover by 1 inch. (Or add 1¾ cups of water.) Bring to a boil, covered, over high heat, never stirring the rice. Reduce heat to low and simmer, covered, 7 to 10 minutes or until the water almost completely evaporates.

Meanwhile, stir 1 tablespoon vegetable oil into the chicken mixture and combine thoroughly. Heat a 14-inch flat-bottomed wok or skillet over high heat until hot but not smoking. Add the remaining 1 tablespoon vegetable oil to the wok, and carefully add chicken mixture, spreading it in wok. Cook undisturbed 1 minute, letting chicken begin to brown. Then, using a metal spatula, stir-fry 1 minute, or until chicken is lightly browned on all sides but not cooked through. Add mushroom liquid and ham, and cook, stirring, 30 seconds.

Uncover rice and quickly spread chicken mixture and scallions over it. Immediately re-cover rice and cook 5 to 10 minutes more, or until chicken is just cooked through and rice is tender. Bring the pot to the table and serve immediately.

Serves 4 to 6 as part of a multicourse meal.

Tender Beef on Rice

My Uncle Sam remembers that his mother, my grandmother, Popo, would prepare Tender Beef on Rice as a restorative food for her children after they had been sick, or whenever she felt they were weak. The combination of beef and rice is said to be strengthening. I learned from Baba that an old-fashioned Cantonese way to serve this dish is to crack an egg over the hot beef and to cook the egg until it is just firm but soft on the inside. Today, with health concerns about salmonella, this is no longer recommended.

8 ounces flank steak, well trimmed

¼ teaspoon baking soda

2 tablespoons finely shredded ginger

2 teaspoons Shao Hsing rice cooking wine

1½ teaspoons thin soy sauce

1½ teaspoons cornstarch

½ teaspoon sesame oil

¼ teaspoon ground white pepper

1 tablespoon oyster flavored sauce

1 cup long grain rice

2 teaspoons plus 1 tablespoon vegetable oil

2 medium scallions, finely shredded

Halve the flank steak with the grain into 2 strips. Cut each strip across the grain into ¼-inch-thick slices. Place slices in a shallow bowl, and sprinkle baking soda over the beef; stir to combine. Add ginger, rice wine, soy sauce, cornstarch, sesame oil, and pepper, and stir to combine.

In a small bowl, combine oyster sauce and 2 tablespoons water.

Place the rice in a 2-quart saucepan. Wash the rice in several changes of cold water until the water runs clear. Drain the rice. Level the rice and add enough cold water to cover by 1 inch. (Or add 1¾ cups of water.) Bring to a boil, covered, over high heat, never stirring the rice. Reduce heat to low and continue simmering, covered, for 10 to 15 minutes, or until the water almost completely evaporates.

Stir 2 teaspoons oil into the beef mixture. Heat a 14-inch flat-bottomed wok or skillet over high heat until hot but not smoking. Add remaining 1 tablespoon oil to the wok and carefully add the beef, spreading it in the wok. Cook, undisturbed, 1 minute, letting the beef begin to brown. Then, using a metal spatula, stir-fry 30 seconds, or until beef is browned but still rare. Swirl in oyster sauce and scallions.

Uncover the rice and quickly spread beef mixture over it. Immediately re-cover rice and cook 3 to 5 minutes more, or until beef is just cooked through and rice is tender. Bring the pot to the table and serve immediately.

Serves 4 to 6 as part of a multicourse meal.

Gai Jook

Chicken Porridge

Rice porridge, also known as *congee* or *jook,* is eaten for breakfast, lunch, and late-night snacks. There are two other porridge recipes in this book: Turkey Porridge (page 188) and Gingko Nut Porridge (page 222). This first one is closest in taste to the porridge served in restaurants, but the flavor is much richer if the dish is made with a good homemade broth. The porridge can be cooked in water or broth and served with bite-sized pieces of cooked chicken, beef, duck, or fish as well as a variety of condiments. The favorite condiment served with rice porridge is finely chopped Sichuan preserved vegetable, which adds heat and spice to the quiet flavors of the porridge. Mama likes to soak the rice the night before in cold water with a little oil to make the rice more tender, but many cooks omit this step. The slow cooking transforms the rice into a creamy, thick comfort soup.

½ cup long grain rice

¼ teaspoon plus 1 tablespoon vegetable oil

1 quart Homemade Chicken Broth (page 234)

2 ounces Sichuan preserved vegetable

8 ounces White Cut Chicken, store-bought or homemade (page 110)

1 cup finely shredded iceberg or romaine lettuce

Cilantro sprigs

Wash the rice in several changes of cold water. In a 2-quart saucepan, soak the rice overnight, at room temperature, in 3 cups cold water with ¼ teaspoon vegetable oil. Add the chicken broth and bring to a boil over high heat. Reduce heat to low, cover, and simmer 2 to 3 hours, stirring occasionally, until the porridge is almost smooth.

Rinse the Sichuan preserved vegetable in cold water until the red chili paste coating is removed, and pat dry. Finely chop to make about ⅓ cup and place in a small heatproof bowl. In a small skillet, heat the remaining 1 tablespoon oil over high heat until hot but not smoking. Carefully pour hot oil over the preserved vegetable. The oil will make a crackling sound as it hits the vegetable.

Chop the chicken into bite-sized pieces. Divide the lettuce among 4 large soup bowls. Ladle the porridge into bowls. Top with the chicken and sprinkle with the preserved vegetable and oil. Garnish with cilantro sprigs and serve immediately.

Serves 4 as part of a multicourse meal.

Stir-Fried Frog on Rice

This is Cantonese rice-pot cooking at its highest art form. The ingredients here are more exotic, and the method more involved. But frog, which is normally so sweet and delicate, becomes sublime when cooked with finely shredded tangerine peel, salted turnip (*chung choy zack*), sweet Chinese dried red dates, ginger, and Chinese mushrooms. Of the three rice-pot dishes I include in this chapter, Stir-Fried Frog on Rice has a wonderfully complex combination of sweetness, piquance, spiciness, a little fruitiness, and saltiness. For me, this is one of the recipes I am so pleased to have finally learned from Baba. The beginner cook should not attempt this too soon. It is a recipe one should grow into; Baba and I made it many times before I finally understood how to prepare it.

Many Chinese believe frog is a restorative food. It has very little or no fat. Baba never buys frogs that are more than 1 pound, feeling that these are too old, but neither should you buy frogs that are less than ¾ pound each. Most fish markets in Chinatown carry live frogs, and the markets will kill them and skin them for you. Some gourmet fish markets carry frog legs but not whole frogs; the legs are the meatiest part of the frog, so the dish will be even more luxurious. The salted turnip, or *chung choy zack*, is very salty, so it needs to be soaked in water before cooking. See Glossary (page 259) for purchasing information.

1 dried tangerine peel (*guo pay*), about 3 inches wide

4 Chinese dried mushrooms

1 piece salted turnip (*chung choy zack*)

3 Chinese dried red dates

½ Chinese sausage (*lop chong*)

2 medium frogs, skinned, about 1 pound

2 tablespoons finely shredded ginger

Place the tangerine peel, mushrooms, salted turnip, and red dates in separate bowls. Pour about ¼ cup cold water over each ingredient, and allow to soak for about 30 minutes, to soften. When softened, drain all the ingredients, discarding all the water except for the mushroom liquid (reserve for use in soups). Finely shred the hard tangerine peel to make about 1 tablespoon. Drain and squeeze mushrooms dry. Cut off and discard stems, and thinly slice the caps to make about ½ cup. Rinse the turnip and cut into fine shreds. Remove pits from the dates and discard; cut dates into fine shreds. Cut the Chinese sausage into thin slices.

Wash the frogs in several changes of cold water, removing any visible intestines, and allow to thoroughly drain in a colander. Cut off and discard feet. Separate each frog at the joints, and cut into bite-

- 1 tablespoon plus 2 teaspoons Shao Hsing rice cooking wine
- 1 tablespoon thin soy sauce
- 1 1/2 teaspoons black soy sauce
- 1 1/2 teaspoons cornstarch
- 1 cup long grain rice
- 3 tablespoons vegetable oil

sized pieces. Place the frog pieces in a medium bowl and add the tangerine peel, mushrooms, turnip, dates, Chinese sausage, ginger, rice wine, thin soy sauce, black soy sauce, and cornstarch, and mix with hands to combine.

Place the rice in a 2-quart saucepan. Wash the rice in several changes of cold water until the water runs clear. Drain the rice. Level the rice and add enough cold water to cover by 1 inch. (Or add 1¾ cups water.) Bring to a boil, covered, over high heat, never stirring the rice. Reduce heat to low and continue simmering, covered, 7 to 10 minutes, or until the water almost completely evaporates.

Meanwhile, drain the frog mixture from the marinade, reserving the marinade. Heat a 14-inch flat-bottomed wok or skillet over high heat until hot but not smoking. Add oil to the wok and carefully add the frog mixture, spreading it in the wok. Cook undisturbed for 1 minute, letting frog begin to brown. Then, using a metal spatula, stir-fry 1 to 2 minutes, or until frog is lightly browned on all sides but not cooked through. Add reserved marinade and bring to a boil, stirring constantly over high heat until sauce is just thickened, about 30 seconds.

Uncover the rice, spread the frog mixture over the rice, and immediately re-cover rice. Cook 5 to 10 minutes more, or until frog is just cooked through and rice is tender. Bring the entire pot to the table and serve immediately.

Serves 4 to 6 as part of a multicourse meal.

Savory Rice Dumplings

In old China, the Festival of the Winter Solstice was an important holiday and family members would return home. *Tong yuen,* glutinous rice dumplings, are eaten during the winter solstice to fortify the stomach for the winter. The roundness of the dumpling signifies family unity and completion. The dough, which is made from glutinous rice flour, is both tender and chewy; filled with the robust flavors of minced shrimp, pork, mushrooms, and scallions, and served with a rich chicken broth, the dumplings are heavenly. In cold weather, *tong yuen* are a Chinese comfort food to warm the soul.

To make this dough correctly, the water must be boiling; the hot water cooks the rice flour and gives the dough the proper consistency. Be careful as you begin to work the mixture because it is hot enough to burn your hands. This means that you will only be able to work the mixture a few seconds at a time. Do not let this prevent you from working the dough while it is still hot; if you let it cool, the dough will not work. Add enough water to make the dough hold its shape but still be slightly sticky. Make sure you use glutinous rice flour and not rice flour for the following two recipes! Rice flour makes a completely different dough, which is not edible.

2 Chinese dried mushrooms

1 tablespoon Chinese dried shrimp

4 ounces ground pork butt, about ½ cup

1 tablespoon finely minced scallions

¾ teaspoon thin soy sauce

¾ teaspoon black soy sauce

¼ teaspoon sesame oil

¼ teaspoon salt

⅛ teaspoon ground white pepper

3 cups glutinous rice flour, plus additional for kneading

1½ quarts Homemade Chicken Broth (page 234)

In a small bowl, soak the mushrooms in ¼ cup cold water for 30 minutes, or until softened. Drain and squeeze dry (reserving soaking liquid for soups). Cut off and discard stems and mince caps. In a small bowl, soak the dried shrimp in 3 tablespoons cold water for 30 minutes, or until softened. Drain shrimp and finely mince.

In a medium bowl, combine the pork, mushrooms, shrimp, scallions, thin soy sauce, black soy sauce, sesame oil, salt, and pepper, and stir to combine. Loosely cover and set aside.

Place the rice flour in a large bowl. Make a well. Add about 1¼ cups boiling water and stir until well combined. Lightly dust your hands with rice flour and work the mixture for a few seconds at a time, as the mixture will be very hot, to form a dough. If the dough is dry, add more boiling water a tablespoonful at a time. Knead until dough is smooth, slightly sticky, and still hot to the touch, about 1 to 2 minutes.

Dust hands with additional flour and divide dough into thirds. Roll each third into a thick rope, about 12 inches long and 1 inch in di-

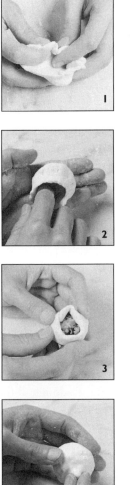

ameter. Cut the ropes into 1-inch pieces to make a total of about 36 pieces. Loosely cover the dough with a kitchen towel to prevent it from drying out. Roll each piece into a ball and flatten to make a scant ¼-inch-thick 2-inch round. Using the thumbs and index fingers from both hands, pleat the edges of the dough to form a small cup (photo 1). Place the cup in the palm of your hand, and use your index finger to gently press the dough into your palm on all sides of the cup to create a smooth, even surface, making the dough even thinner (photo 2).

Spoon about 1 teaspoon of the pork mixture into the cup, using a ¼-teaspoon measure. (A larger spoon will not fit into the cup.) Gently pack the filling down. Gather edges of dough over the filling and again pleat until hole is about ½ inch in diameter (photo 3). Squeeze together the dough, pressing to seal securely (photo 4). Roll between palms to form a ball. Loosely cover with a kitchen towel, and continue making more cups and filling them with pork mixture.

In a 3-quart saucepan, bring chicken broth to a boil over high heat. Add half the dumplings, return to a boil, and cook, gently stirring to separate, until they float to the surface. Gently turn the dumplings over and over until they are fat and plump, 3 to 4 minutes. Transfer to individual bowls with a little of the broth. Repeat with remaining dumplings. Serve immediately.

Makes 36 dumplings. Serves 4 to 6 as part of a multicourse meal.

Peanut Rice Dumplings

My cousins Jeanette, Loretta, and Gloria have fond memories of making rice dumplings, *tong yuen,* with my Auntie Margaret when they were children. The dumplings can be made without any filling at all or filled with a small slab of brown candy, which is a type of Chinese sugar. Another simple filling is this one: fragrant wok-roasted peanuts ground with sugar. This sweet, filled dumpling is enjoyed as an afternoon snack or as a dessert. Read the introduction for Savory Rice Dumplings (page 16) for special dough instructions.

⅓ cup raw, skinless peanuts, about 2 ounces

¼ cup sugar

2 cups glutinous rice flour, plus additional for kneading

Heat a small wok or skillet over high heat until hot but not smoking. Add peanuts and stir-fry 30 seconds. Reduce heat to medium, and stir-fry 3 to 5 minutes, or until peanuts are golden and fragrant. Cool thoroughly.

Place the cooled peanuts in a mini–food processor and process until finely ground but not to the peanut-butter stage, 30 seconds to 1 minute. Add sugar and process 5 seconds, or just until combined.

Place the rice flour in a large bowl. Make a well. Add about ¾ cup boiling water and stir until well combined. Lightly dust your hands with rice flour and gently work the mixture for a few seconds at a time, as the mixture will be very hot, to form a dough. If the dough is dry, add more boiling water a tablespoonful at a time. Knead until dough is smooth, slightly sticky, and still hot to the touch, about 1 to 2 minutes.

Dust hands with additional flour and divide dough in half. Roll each half into a thick rope, about 12 inches long and 1 inch in diameter. Cut the ropes into 1-inch pieces to make a total of about 24 pieces. Loosely cover the dough with a kitchen towel to prevent it from drying out. Roll each piece into a ball and flatten to make a scant ¼-inch-thick 2-inch round. Using thumbs and index fingers from both hands, pleat edges of the dough to form a small cup (photo 1, page 17). Place cup in palm of your hand and use your index finger to gently press dough into your palm on all sides of cup to create a smooth, even surface, making the dough even thinner (photo 2, page 17).

Spoon about 1 teaspoon of the ground peanut mixture into the cup, using a ¼-teaspoon measure. (A larger spoon will not fit into the cup.) Gently pack the filling down. Gather the edges of dough over the filling and again pleat until hole is about ½ inch in diameter (photo 3, page 17). Squeeze together the dough, pressing to seal dough securely (photo 4, page 17). Roll between palms to form a ball. Loosely cover with a kitchen towel and continue making more cups and filling them with the peanut mixture. You will have about ⅓ cup of peanut mixture left over. Set it aside.

In a 2½-quart saucepan, bring 1½ quarts of cold water to a boil over high heat. Add half the dumplings, return to a boil, and cook, gently stirring to separate, until the dumplings float to the surface. Gently turn the dumplings over and over until they are fat and plump, about 3 to 4 minutes. Transfer to individual bowls with a little of the cooking liquid and sprinkle with reserved peanut mixture. Repeat with the remaining dumplings and serve immediately.

Makes 24 dumplings. Serves 4 to 6 as part of a multicourse meal.

鑊
氣

Wok Hay

THE BREATH
OF A WOK

Baba. Canton, China, circa 1935.

ALL MY LIFE I HAVE HEARD BABA speak about *wok hay*, the *breath* of a wok. No matter whether he is in a restaurant or his own home, when a stir-fried dish comes to the table, the sight of the heat rising from the food always causes him to smile and say, "Ahhh, *wok hay*." I know that many people dislike piping-hot food and prefer their food to cool before eating it, but most Chinese are just the opposite—the hotter, the better.

Wok hay is not simply hot food; it's that elusive seared taste that only lasts for a minute or two. It reminds me of the difference between food just off the grill and grilled food that has been left to sit. *Wok hay* occurs in that special moment when a great chef achieves food that nearly, but not quite, burns in the mouth. For the Chinese, if the dish doesn't have the prized taste of the wok's aroma, it isn't an authentic stir-fry.

As a child, I clearly understood that when dinner was announced there was no excuse for tardiness. It was totally unacceptable to explain that you wanted to see the last five minutes of a television show, finish a phone conversation, or even do a few more minutes of homework. Hot food was serious business, and the idea of missing the *wok hay* was unthinkable. The dishes were choreographed for completion at the moment we sat at the table and the piping-hot rice arrived. I always imagined *wok hay* as a special life force that, when consumed, provided us with extra energy, *hay.* Some readers may be familiar with the Mandarin word for *hay,* which is *qi,* as in *qigong. Qi* (pronounced "chee") is the Chinese concept of vital energy that flows through the body.

When my parents entertained, they cooked in tandem, bringing out each dish as it was stir-fried. Douglas and I were left to "entertain" the guests, and I recall thinking how uncomfortable we and our American friends felt. Our guests seemed more intent on socializing and, although they enjoyed the food, they couldn't comprehend my parents' refusal to eat one morsel until all the food was on the table. It puzzled them to see my parents cook one dish at a time, disappearing into the kitchen and not sitting until everything was done. When Chinese friends came over, however, they would agree, after politely refusing to eat, that sacrificing the *wok hay* was inappropriate and they would gladly eat dish by dish with gusto. Forgoing their own enjoyment of *wok hay* was my parents' gift to their guests.

Even today, whenever my family attends a Chinese banquet, I can guarantee that shortly after the dinner my parents will comment first on the crispness of the Peking duck, then on the amount of shark's fin in the shark's fin soup (versus the filler ingredients), and, finally, on the *wok hay* of the stir-fried dishes. Later the same evening, the critique will continue by telephone with a few of my uncles and aunts. The discussion will be brief, but no one in the family can resist commenting on the quality of the food. If the dishes were outstanding, then the evening was memorable. I have heard my family fondly recall meals from years ago where the shark's fin was extra thick or abalone was prepared particularly well. Baba likes to sit closest to the kitchen when we go to a restaurant, especially for dim sum. This way, he can get the freshest food the moment it leaves the kitchen. If there is no table available near the kitchen, Mama will occasionally ask one of us to go to the dim sum cart as it emerges to retrieve the piping-hot food ourselves. Why wait for the lifeless food that arrives by the time the waitress makes her way to us? My Uncle Sam reminds me that the family still laments the change in what was once a favorite restaurant. The establishment was so successful that it expanded to three floors, moving the kitchen to the basement. Same chefs, same cooking technique, but now the *wok hay* had disappeared, because the distance between the kitchen and the dining area was too far for the "breath" to last.

To achieve *wok hay,* it is necessary to learn a few secrets of successful stir-frying. Stir-frying, like sautéing, is cooking bite-sized pieces of meat or vegetables in a small amount of oil over high heat for a brief period of time. Stir-frying, especially, requires keeping the food in constant motion, tossing it with a metal spatula, to ensure that everything cooks evenly and quickly, preserving the vitamins and vibrancy of the ingredients. The wok must be sufficiently hot for the food to sizzle vigorously the moment it hits the oil. The ingredients must be dry, especially the vegetables. If there is any water left clinging to them after washing, the oil will splatter when the vegetables are added, and then they will steam, rather than stir-fry. For this reason, Mama washes vegetables early in the day to allow time for them to dry. It's best to have all the ingredients at room temperature and everything cut into uniform pieces to ensure the same cooking time. Some dishes, like Baba's Stir-Fried Butterfly Fish and Bean Sprouts (page 28) or Stir-Fried Squid (page 30), must cook in very small quantities because the home stove cannot produce the same amount of heat as a restaurant wok. Crowding food in the wok requires more heat and longer cooking time and results in braised food rather than stir-fried food.

My parents do not use a wok for stir-frying. They use an old fourteen-inch Farberware skillet or an eight-inch-wide, four-inch-deep metal pot that protects them from oil splatters. The traditional wok used in China was cast-iron, preferred because it adds iron to food and conducts heat well. Chinese cast-iron woks can be purchased in some cookware shops in Chinatown; they are thinner and lighter in weight than Western cast-iron pans. Today carbon-steel woks are more common; each time food is stir-fried the wok becomes seasoned, as the ingredients and oil leave a delicate varnish on the wok's surface. Unlike a cast-iron skillet that simply becomes black with use, a carbon-steel wok develops a rich mahogany patina after about six months of regular use. A well-seasoned cast-iron or carbon-steel wok is a Chinese chef's most treasured utensil, for the more you use it, the more it becomes like a nonstick pan, requiring less and less oil for stir-frying. Be sure never to use a well-seasoned wok for steaming, as the water will strip the wok of its seasoning. The important advice here is that fancy equipment is not necessary to stir-fry. Choose a twelve- to fourteen-inch skillet that conducts heat evenly on high heat, or a fourteen-inch flat-bottomed cast-iron, carbon-steel, or stainless-steel wok. (See photo, page 244.) Never use a nonstick or an electric wok. It's dangerous to heat most nonstick pans on high heat, and electric woks do not generate enough heat; without adequate heat the food cannot properly stir-fry. Also avoid the traditional round-bottomed wok popular in restaurants, because it is impossible to heat sufficiently on a household stove. A gas stove is always preferable to an electric one because the heat level can be regulated instantaneously; however, for years, my parents successfully cooked on an electric stove.

The time-honored way of seasoning a new cast-iron wok is to wash it with mild soap, rinse, and let dry. Warm the wok and lightly grease it with vegetable oil. Place in a 300-degree oven and season 40 minutes. To season a carbon-steel wok, wash it in mild, soapy, hot water to remove the protective coating of oil from the factory. Dry the wok thoroughly before heating it over high heat until hot but not smoking. Add two tablespoons of vegetable oil and stir-fry a bunch of Chinese chives, *gul choy,* and discard the vegetables after cooking. This onion-like vegetable miraculously removes the metallic taste from the wok. Wash the wok in hot water and never use soap again. Be sure to dry it thoroughly. To wash a cast-iron or carbon-steel wok after cooking, soak the wok in hot water or rice water (see "The Meaning of Rice," page 3), then wash with a soft bristle brush. Scrub it well, as any excess food or oil left in the wok will become rancid with time.

In my own family, the level of cooking tension escalates as the stir-frying begins. I always think of the Cantonese as the Italians of the Far East, and cooking certainly brings out their "Mediterranean" emotions. Voices rise as the drama of the cooking performance commences. My parents cook with a high degree of difficulty, ranked for Olympic competition. Sometimes I will cringe at the possible dangers. Their Chinese slippers offer no protection from hot spills, and Baba, who always wears a sports jacket, is equally formally attired when he cooks. One parent will precariously carry the steamer of boiling water from the stove to the sink, while the other stir-fries, often leaning over the front gas burner to tame a pot on the back burner. Their voices rise with urgency as they react to the demands of each moment, against the backdrop of the exhaust fan and the sound of a reporter discussing some world crisis on the *CBS Evening News.* Suddenly, Mama climbs the kitchen ladder to reach into the cabinet for a platter and Baba matches her exploit by pouring boiling water over the platter to heat it. (Hot food can never be served on a cold platter.) Miraculously, my parents arrive at the table unscathed, along with the stir-fried dish, rice, the steamed dish, and a piping-hot saucepan of soup. Within seconds, it seems, everything is on the table, masterfully executed. If more than one dish is to be stir-fried, the second is cooked after we have sampled these first dishes.

Timing is the most essential technique to master for stir-frying. Prepare carefully, and never try to chop or measure anything at the last minute, especially while you are stir-frying. The moment the wok is hot, turn on the exhaust fan, swirl in the oil, and immediately add the food. One of the secrets for preventing food from sticking in the wok is to have the wok hot, but the oil cool. Do not heat the oil but heat the wok. Stay calm as the first crackle is heard as the food touches the oil. Sometimes the oil smokes or sputters. If you feel anxious, simply pull the wok off the heat and regroup.

Stir-frying is full of life and energy, and requires quick reactions. Garlic, ginger, and vegetables require immediate stir-frying; but poultry, meat, and seafood should cook undisturbed for a minute or two, so that the ingredient sears slightly before stir-frying. If you immediately start stirring, the meat will surely stick and tear, yet too much hesitation will result in food that is overcooked. Always swirl sauce ingredients down the sides of the wok to prevent the temperature of the pan from dropping. Stay focused, pay attention, follow these tips, and you will master the art of stir-frying. Eventually, too, you will achieve *wok hay* and understand why the Chinese have for centuries revered the experience of food that still breathes its life force.

Chinese with Cashews

腰果炒鷄球

Yue Gwo Chow Gai Kul

Traditionally, the cashews for this stir-fry are deep-fried. My preference is to oven-roast the nuts. This brings out the flavor of the cashews: The results are equally delicious without the trouble of deep-frying.

6 Chinese dried mushrooms

12 ounces skinless, boneless chicken breast or thigh

2 tablespoons thin soy sauce

1 teaspoon Shao Hsing rice cooking wine

1 teaspoon cornstarch

¼ teaspoon sugar

¼ teaspoon salt

¾ cup raw cashew nuts, about 3 ounces

2 tablespoons vegetable oil

3 slices ginger

1 teaspoon finely minced garlic

1 red bell pepper, cut into 1-inch squares

In a medium bowl, soak the mushrooms in ⅓ cup cold water for 30 minutes, or until softened. Drain and squeeze dry, reserving the soaking liquid. Cut off and discard stems, and thinly slice the caps.

Preheat oven to 375 degrees.

Remove any visible tendons from the chicken. Cut chicken into 1-inch cubes. In a medium bowl, combine the chicken, 1 tablespoon soy sauce, rice wine, cornstarch, sugar, and salt. Stir to combine and set aside.

Place the cashews on a baking sheet, then place in the oven for 7 to 10 minutes, or until golden brown. Set aside to cool.

Heat a 14-inch flat-bottomed wok or skillet over high heat until hot but not smoking. Add 1 tablespoon vegetable oil and ginger, and stir-fry 30 seconds. Carefully add the chicken mixture, spreading it in the wok. Cook, undisturbed, 1 to 2 minutes, letting chicken begin to brown. Then, using a metal spatula, stir-fry 1 to 2 minutes, or until the chicken is browned on all sides but not cooked through. Transfer chicken to a plate and set aside.

Add remaining 1 tablespoon vegetable oil to the wok and then add garlic, mushrooms, and red pepper, and stir-fry 1 minute. Swirl in reserved mushroom soaking liquid and stir-fry until almost all the liquid has evaporated, about 1 minute.

Return the chicken to the wok with any juices that have accumulated, along with the cashews and the remaining tablespoon of soy sauce, and stir-fry 1 to 2 minutes, or until chicken is cooked through. Serve immediately.

Serves 4 to 6 as part of a multicourse meal.

Fan Ke Gnul Yok

Tomato Beef

One day I came home to find a message on the answering machine from my brother, Douglas, asking if I remembered to include the recipe for Tomato Beef in this book. It was my brother's and my own favorite dish as we were growing up. It is a wonderfully uncomplicated recipe that my parents used to make regularly during the week, when they had less time to devote to cooking. Thick wedges of tomato cook with oyster flavored sauce and beef that has been stir-fried with ginger to make a flavorful and delicious sauce to serve over rice. Oddly enough, this is amazingly good even when tomatoes are not in season.

8 ounces flank steak, well trimmed

¼ teaspoon baking soda

1½ teaspoons thin soy sauce

1½ teaspoons cornstarch

1 teaspoon Shao Hsing rice cooking wine

¼ teaspoon sesame oil

1¼ teaspoons sugar

5 tomatoes, about 2 pounds

1 teaspoon plus 1 tablespoon vegetable oil

6 slices ginger

3 tablespoons oyster flavored sauce

4 scallions, cut into 2-inch sections

Halve the flank steak with the grain into 2 strips. Cut each strip across the grain into ¼-inch-thick slices. Place slices in a shallow bowl and sprinkle with the baking soda; stir to combine. Add the soy sauce, cornstarch, rice wine, sesame oil, and ¼ teaspoon sugar. Stir to combine and set aside.

In a large pot, bring about 1½ quarts of water to a boil over high heat. Add the tomatoes and cook 1 to 3 minutes, or until the tomato skins just break. Remove tomatoes with a slotted spoon and, when cool enough to handle, peel skins. Core tomatoes and cut into ½-inch-thick wedges.

Meanwhile, stir 1 teaspoon vegetable oil into the beef mixture. Heat a 14-inch flat-bottomed wok or skillet over high heat until hot but not smoking. Add the remaining tablespoon vegetable oil and ginger, and stir-fry about 1 minute. Carefully add the beef, spreading it in the wok. Cook, undisturbed, 1 to 2 minutes, letting beef begin to brown. Then, using a metal spatula, stir-fry 1 to 2 minutes, or until beef is browned but still slightly rare. Transfer the beef to a plate and set aside.

Add the tomatoes and remaining teaspoon of sugar to wok, and stir-fry 1 minute on high heat until tomatoes begin to soften. Add the oyster sauce and ¼ cup cold water, cover, and cook 2 to 3 minutes, or until the tomatoes are just limp. Add the beef with any juices that have accumulated on the plate, and the scallions, and stir-fry 1 minute, or until just heated through. Serve immediately.

Serves 4 to 6 as part of a multicourse meal.

Stir-Fried Chicken with Baby Corn and Straw Mushrooms

The following recipe was given to me by my cousin Cindy, who grew up watching her grandfather, Lum Bo Fay, cook in his restaurant Sun Hung Heung. I am told that Cindy's grandfather was a very accomplished cook, having begun working in Chinese restaurants at the age of seven. My family often ate at Sun Hung Heung, especially for big family banquets. Even then, I was fascinated with the world of cooking and envied Cindy and her sister Kim as they went in and out of the kitchen, wondering what they got to see.

¾ pound skinless, boneless chicken breast or thigh

1 tablespoon thin soy sauce

1 tablespoon Shao Hsing rice cooking wine

1 tablespoon oyster flavored sauce

1 teaspoon cornstarch

¼ teaspoon sesame oil

One 15-ounce can whole baby corn, drained

One 15-ounce can straw mushrooms, drained

½ pound snow peas

¼ teaspoon salt

1 tablespoon vegetable oil

½ teaspoon red pepper flakes

¼ cup Homemade Chicken Broth (page 234)

2 scallions, cut into 2-inch sections

Remove any visible tendons from the chicken. Cut chicken into 1-inch cubes. In a medium bowl, combine the soy sauce, rice wine, oyster sauce, cornstarch, sesame oil, and chicken, and stir to combine. Set aside.

Cut any corn longer than 3 inches in half. Place the baby corn and straw mushrooms in a colander and rinse under cold water. Drain and set aside, leaving the vegetables in the colander. String the snow peas and rinse under cold water.

In a 2-quart saucepan, bring 1 quart of water to a boil over high heat. Add salt and snow peas, and blanch over high heat 1 minute, or until snow peas just turn bright green. Remove from heat and pour snow peas and boiling water over the baby corn and mushrooms in the colander; set aside to drain well.

Using a slotted spoon, remove chicken from marinade, reserving the marinade. Heat a 14-inch flat-bottomed wok or skillet over high heat until hot but not smoking. Add vegetable oil and carefully add chicken, spreading it in the wok. Cook, undisturbed, 1 to 2 minutes, letting chicken begin to brown. Then, using a metal spatula, stir-fry 1 to 2 minutes, or until chicken is browned but not cooked through. Add red pepper flakes, snow peas, baby corn, and straw mushrooms, and stir-fry 1 minute. Combine chicken broth and reserved marinade. Swirl broth mixture into the wok and stir-fry 1 to 2 minutes, or until chicken is cooked through and vegetables are hot. Stir in scallions and serve immediately.

Serves 4 to 6 as part of a multicourse meal.

Stir-Fried Eggs with Barbecued Pork

My cousins Sylvia, Kathy, and David reminded me of this favorite dish. The ingredients are inexpensive and the method is simple, but for us it evokes the best of homecooking as we remember it. As children it was hard to get us to eat much rice, but my Uncle Tommy slyly would put a little oyster sauce on the eggs and serve them over steaming hot rice, and the flavors would be so comforting that we would eat lots of rice—every Chinese parent's wish.

4 large eggs

½ teaspoon salt

4 ounces Chinese Barbecued Pork, store-bought or homemade (page 176)

3 teaspoons vegetable oil

1 scallion, finely chopped

Oyster flavored sauce

In a medium bowl, beat the eggs with the salt. Julienne the barbecued pork into thin strips. Heat a 14-inch flat-bottomed wok or skillet over high heat until hot but not smoking. Add 1 teaspoon vegetable oil and the barbecued pork, and stir-fry 30 seconds. Add remaining 2 teaspoons vegetable oil and beaten eggs, and stir-fry until eggs are just beginning to set, about 1 minute. Add scallion and continue stir-frying 1 minute, or until eggs are just set but still moist. Do not overcook. Serve immediately with oyster sauce.

Serves 4 to 6 as part of a multicourse meal.

Baba's Stir-Fried Butterfly Fish and Bean Sprouts

Baba says the secret to making this is only cooking a small portion of fish. The first time I made this, the fish was overcooked and dry. It takes practice to get a feeling for doing this. The timing is very fast. From the moment the fish enters the wok until it is removed, the total time is only about 1 minute. For an accomplished cook this is an easy weeknight recipe to prepare, but for a beginner I would set this as a goal for cooking after one has reached a level of mastery both in knife skills and stir-frying.

Remove any visible bones you see in the fillet. The butterflying cuts any hidden bones into scant 1/8-inch pieces, so they are of no danger. However, in order to do this, your knife needs to be razor sharp to make the thinnest possible slices on the diagonal. You will hear the bones as they are being cut.

My parents tell me that traditionally this dish has no bean sprouts, only stir-fried fish, but I like the contrasting textures and tastes of the fish and sprouts, and this is how my family cooks it. Rock cod is also known as rock-fish, and is widely available in California; if it is unavailable, use striped bass, snapper, or black sea bass.

8 ounces mung bean sprouts, about 4 cups

12 ounces skinless rock cod fillet

2 scallions, white portion only

1 tablespoon Homemade Chicken Broth (page 234) or water

1 tablespoon thin soy sauce

1 teaspoon Shao Hsing rice cooking wine

1 teaspoon cornstarch

1/2 teaspoon sesame oil

4 tablespoons vegetable oil

1/4 teaspoon salt

3 teaspoons shredded ginger

Early in the day, rinse the bean sprouts in several changes of cold water and drain thoroughly in a colander until dry to the touch.

Remove any visible bones from the fish. Halve fish lengthwise, along the deep natural crease of the fillet, into 2 strips roughly 2 inches wide. Using one strip at a time, make butterfly slices by first cutting a scant 1/8-inch-thick slice across the strip on a slight diagonal without cutting through (photo 1). Then, make a second scant 1/8-inch-thick slice, this time cutting through to make the complete butterfly (photo 2). (You will be cutting through bones.) Continue making butterfly slices.

Cut the scallions into 2-inch sections and finely shred them. In a small bowl, combine the chicken broth, soy sauce, rice wine, cornstarch, and sesame oil; set aside.

Heat a 14-inch flat-bottomed wok or skillet over high heat until hot but not smoking. Add 1 tablespoon vegetable oil, bean sprouts, salt, and 1½ teaspoons ginger, and stir-fry 1 minute. Transfer to a platter.

Wipe wok with paper towels, add remaining 3 tablespoons vegetable oil, and carefully add the fish, spreading it in wok with the remain-

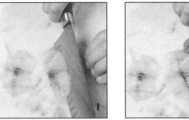

ing 1½ teaspoons ginger. Immediately swirl in the soy sauce mixture and scallions and, using a metal spatula, stir-fry gently, so as not to break up the fish, about 1 minute, until fish is just cooked but not browned. Place fish on top of the stir-fried bean sprouts and serve immediately.

Serves 4 as part of a multicourse meal.

Stir-Fried Asparagus with Shrimp

When local asparagus is available in the spring, it is often turned into a simple stir-fried dish for fancier occasions. I prefer asparagus stalks that are at least half an inch in diameter to pencil-sized ones. The natural sweetness of the shrimp and asparagus is the perfect counterpoint to the pungent flavors of the dried black beans, ginger, and garlic. This is my cousin Cindy's recipe.

2 tablespoons Chinese dried black beans (*dul see*)

2 tablespoons thin soy sauce

2 tablespoons Shao Hsing rice cooking wine

1 tablespoon finely minced garlic

1 tablespoon finely minced ginger

4 drops sesame oil

½ jalapeño pepper, seeded and finely chopped

1 pound asparagus

¼ teaspoon salt

2 tablespoons vegetable oil

1 pound large shrimp, shelled and deveined

Rinse the black beans in several changes of cold water and drain. In a small bowl, mash the black beans with the back of a wooden spoon. Stir in the soy sauce, rice wine, garlic, ginger, sesame oil, and jalapeño pepper; set aside.

Snap off the woody ends of the asparagus and discard. Cut asparagus on the diagonal into 2-inch pieces. In a medium saucepan, bring 2 cups water and ¼ teaspoon salt to a boil over high heat. Add asparagus and blanch 1 to 2 minutes, just until asparagus turns bright green. Drain well, rinse under cold water, and set aside.

Heat a 14-inch flat-bottomed wok or skillet over high heat until hot but not smoking. Add 2 tablespoons vegetable oil and the shrimp and stir-fry just until shrimp start to turn pink, about 1 minute. Remove shrimp to a plate and set aside. Add the soy sauce mixture to the wok. Cook, stirring, about 30 seconds, until mixture is fragrant. Add the asparagus, shrimp, and any juices that have accumulated on the plate, and stir-fry 2 to 3 minutes, or until shrimp are just cooked through. Serve immediately.

Serves 4 to 6 as part of a multicourse meal.

Stir-Fried Squid

Cantonese cooks love a stir-fry where only one ingredient is featured and a few simple seasonings are added to complement the flavor. Squid, if it is very fresh, can be stir-fried alone. But, because squid releases juices as it cooks, do not attempt to cook too much at one time. More than 12 ounces and the dish will become soupy. Scoring the squid makes it look more beautiful.

8 small squid, about 12 ounces

⅛ teaspoon salt

1 teaspoon thin soy sauce

1 teaspoon Shao Hsing rice cooking wine

½ teaspoon sesame oil

¼ teaspoon sugar

¼ teaspoon ground white pepper

2 scallions, white portion only

½ teaspoon cornstarch

1 tablespoon vegetable oil

1 tablespoon finely shredded ginger

Cut off and reserve the tentacles attached to the squid heads. Remove the internal cartilage and heads from squid bodies and discard. Peel off the purple membrane. Wash squid in several changes of cold water and allow to thoroughly drain in a colander. Cut each body in half lengthwise. Using a very sharp knife, lightly score the inside of the bodies in a crisscross pattern. Cut squid into 1½-inch squares. Place tentacles and squid pieces in a bowl and toss with salt. Add the soy sauce, rice wine, sesame oil, sugar, and pepper, and stir to combine. Marinate for 15 minutes. Remove the squid with a slotted spoon, draining well and reserving marinade. Cut the scallions into 2-inch sections and finely shred. In a small bowl, combine the cornstarch, 1 tablespoon cold water, and reserved marinade and set aside.

Heat a 14-inch flat-bottomed wok or skillet over high heat until hot but not smoking. Add vegetable oil and squid, and stir-fry 1 minute. Add scallions and ginger, and stir-fry 1 minute. Restir cornstarch mixture and swirl into the wok and bring to a boil, stirring, about 30 seconds, or until sauce is slightly thickened and squid is cooked through. Serve immediately.

Serves 4 as part of a multicourse meal.

Beef Chow Fun

I am very fond of Beef Chow Fun, but in Chinese restaurants it is often cooked with far too much oil. Use fresh broad rice noodles, *haw fun,* which are available in 1-pound slabs in Chinese markets; there are also small shops that specialize in selling the noodles. Broad rice noodles are steamed in big, lightly oiled jelly roll pans and they come folded several times, like a kitchen towel; they are sold unrefrigerated. Be sure to ask for *haw fun,* since *broad rice noodles* will not be a familiar term. Once the noodles have been refrigerated, they become hard, and although this recipe will still work, fresh noodles are preferable.

8 ounces mung bean sprouts, about 4 cups

8 ounces flank steak, well trimmed

¼ teaspoon baking soda

1 tablespoon thin soy sauce

1½ teaspoons cornstarch

1½ teaspoons Shao Hsing rice cooking wine

1 tablespoon Chinese dried black beans (*dul see*)

1 pound fresh broad rice noodles (*haw fun*)

3 tablespoons vegetable oil

3 slices ginger

2 teaspoons finely minced garlic

2 scallions, cut into 2-inch sections

2 tablespoons oyster flavored sauce

Rinse the bean sprouts in several changes of cold water and drain thoroughly in a colander until dry to the touch.

Halve the flank steak with the grain into 2 strips. Cut each strip across the grain into ¼-inch-thick slices. Place in a shallow bowl, sprinkle with baking soda, and stir to combine. Add the soy sauce, cornstarch, and rice wine, and stir to combine; set aside.

Rinse the black beans in several changes of cold water and drain. In a small bowl, mash the black beans with the back of a wooden spoon. Leaving the noodles as a slab, cut noodles crosswise into ¾-inch-wide strips.

Heat a 14-inch flat-bottomed wok or skillet over high heat until hot but not smoking. Add 1 tablespoon oil, ginger, and garlic to the wok, and stir-fry about 15 to 30 seconds, until fragrant. Carefully add the beef, spreading it in the wok. Cook, undisturbed, 30 seconds to 1 minute, letting the beef begin to brown. Add the mashed black beans and, using a metal spatula, stir-fry 1 to 2 minutes, or until beef is browned but still slightly rare. Transfer to a plate. Rinse the wok and dry it thoroughly.

Heat the wok over high heat until hot but not smoking. Add the remaining 2 tablespoons oil to the wok with the noodles, spreading them in the wok. Cook undisturbed for 1 minute, or until slightly crusty. Add the bean sprouts and stir-fry 1 to 2 minutes. Return the beef with any juices that have accumulated to the wok, add the scallions and oyster sauce, and stir-fry 1 to 2 minutes, or until heated through and well combined. Serve immediately.

Serves 4 to 6 as part of a multicourse meal.

Singapore Rice Noodles

In Singapore, it is common to catch the intoxicating aroma of curry in the air. Almost every restaurant serves *mai fun*—rice vermicelli or rice sticks—stir-fried with curry powder, baby shrimp, scallions, celery, and Chinese mushrooms, for this is one of Singapore's most famous dishes. The trick in preparing the dried noodles is to soak them in cold water until they soften before cooking them. When first placed in cold water they are hard and brittle but after twenty to thirty minutes they will feel as soft as if they've been cooked. Drain the noodles well before stir-frying.

4 Chinese dried mushrooms

8 ounces rice vermicelli (*mai fun*)

2 tablespoons thin soy sauce

1 tablespoon Shao Hsing rice cooking wine

1 1/2 teaspoons sugar

1/2 teaspoon salt

3 tablespoons vegetable oil

4 ounces small shrimp, shelled and deveined

1/2 cup finely shredded scallions

1 cup thinly sliced celery

2 teaspoons Madras curry powder

3/4 cup Homemade Chicken Broth (page 234)

4 ounces Chinese Barbecued Pork, store-bought or homemade (page 176), cut into julienne strips

In a medium bowl, soak the mushrooms in 1/4 cup cold water for 30 minutes, or until softened. Drain and squeeze dry, reserving soaking liquid. Cut off and discard stems and thinly slice the caps.

In a large bowl, soak the rice noodles in enough cold water to cover for 20 to 30 minutes, or until noodles are limp and softened. Drain in a colander and set aside. In a small bowl, combine the soy sauce, rice wine, sugar, and salt. Set aside.

Heat a 14-inch flat-bottomed wok or skillet over high heat until hot but not smoking. Add 1 tablespoon vegetable oil and the shrimp, and stir-fry 10 seconds. Add the scallions and stir-fry 30 seconds, or until shrimp have just turned orange but are not cooked through. Transfer the shrimp mixture to a plate and set aside.

Add the remaining 2 tablespoons vegetable oil, celery, and sliced mushrooms, and stir-fry 30 seconds. Add the curry powder and stir-fry 10 seconds, or until fragrant. Restir soy sauce mixture and swirl it into the wok. Add the chicken broth, reserved mushroom soaking liquid, and 1/3 cup cold water, and bring to a boil over high heat.

Add the drained rice noodles and return to a boil, stirring noodles to completely coat in curry mixture. Cover and cook over medium-high heat 2 to 3 minutes, stirring occasionally, until noodles are just tender. Add the shrimp and barbecued pork, and cook, stirring, 1 to 2 minutes, or until shrimp are just cooked through and liquid has been absorbed by the noodles. Serve immediately.

Serves 4 to 6 as part of a multicourse meal.

蒸煮食藝

Zing Chu Sik Ngai

THE ART OF STEAMING

Grandfather (Yeye) Young Suey Hay. Canton, China, circa 1902.

WHENEVER MY FAMILY THINKS OF comfort food, we picture steamed dishes. To us, they are the most flavorful and delicate. Mama says that stir-fried or pan-fried foods taste delicious to the mouth, but they are less healthy for the body. In fact, the Chinese say a steamed dish, whether for the elderly or for the young, is appropriate, or *lo siu, ping on*. It is for this reason that nearly every home-cooked meal includes a steamed dish. Countering stir-fried dishes with steamed dishes in the same meal creates balance. And, healthwise, steaming is considered the most neutral and harmonious, being clear and cleansing, or *ching, ching day*, neither too yin nor too yang. It is also healthful, because it requires very little oil. Tastewise, steaming accentuates the freshness and natural sweetness of the food. It intensifies flavor and ensures moistness for foods that are susceptible to being dry or tough. For Chinese epicureans, steaming creates the best flavor.

Although countless steamed recipes have appeared in any number of cookbooks, the art of steaming is seldom understood by the Western cook. For Americans, steaming is considered bland and dietetic, a limited method used exclusively for plain vegetables. A Chinese person would be puzzled by this image of steamed food. The range of possibilities in Chinese steam cooking is extraordinary, especially in the Cantonese repertoire, where chefs have taken steaming to a high art. Savory dishes, sweet cakes, and dumplings all benefit from this simple method of cooking. In classic French cuisine, chefs rely on the use of a water bath, or *bain marie*, to achieve tenderness in custards and timbales. In Chinese cooking, steaming produces equally tender and moist foods, and the Cantonese version of steamed custard rivals the French in tenderness. It is a technique suitable for marinated meats, fish, and chicken, especially when left on the bone, where the Cantonese feel the most intense flavor is hidden. Cooking protein in this way captures the succulence of an ingredient, and draws the natural juices and flavor from the bone.

Only the freshest ingredients can be used for steaming. Seasonings are never heavy, allowing the true flavor to come through. Mama says you cannot tell if pork is fresh when camouflaged in a curry sauce or cooked with hot spices, but once an ingredient is steamed, you cannot hide its age—its true quality is exposed. A recent misconception about Chinese food being not good for you was derived from American dietitians' analysis of Chinese restaurant food, where dishes are often deep fried or stir-fried with excessive oil, and steamed dishes are seldom served. In fact, Cantonese families rarely, if ever, eat deep-fat fry foods at home, preferring instead to have at least one steamed dish at every meal. Foods prepared by the steaming method are considered to have the purest flavor, or *chun may*.

There are two ways to steam foods in Chinese cooking. The first method is called *dun,* or double-steaming, and is used only by traditional cooks to bring out the most intense flavors, mainly for herbal soups, such as Double-Steamed Black Chicken Soup (page 235), Double-Steamed Papaya and Snow Fungus Soup (page 207), and Korean Ginseng Soup (page 232). For example, to make ginseng soup, chicken, ginseng, and cold water are placed in a Chinese-style tureen (see photo page 244) or a deep heatproof bowl (never use a Western-style tureen) and covered with an airtight lid. Some cooks tie a cloth around the rim of the lid to ensure the tightest seal. The bowl is then set on a rack in a very large pot (such as a canning kettle) and about two inches of cold water are added to the pot. The water both inside and outside the tureen must be cold, or else the tureen might crack. The covered tureen steams for at least three hours. The flavor is so concentrated that, when the lid of the bowl is lifted, a potent aroma of ginseng emanates. The Chinese believe all other styles of cooking allow flavor to escape through the vapors, but this method of steaming retains both flavor and nutrients. For herbal soups especially, this method extracts the most from the ingredients and is therefore the most healthful.

The second method—which steams food directly over boiling water—is the more common for home cooking. It was undoubtedly developed out of necessity, as an energy-efficient way of cooking. There are many different approaches with this method. There are bamboo steamers, which come in several sizes and can be stacked and covered with a bamboo lid. They are designed to sit in a wok over boiling water. The preferred size of a bamboo steamer for home cooking is about eleven inches in diameter. There are also inexpensive metal steamers—this is what I use—that come with a ten-and-one-quarter-inch-wide aluminum pot, two stackable steaming baskets, and a lid. This type of pot is safest for the novice cook, because at least three inches of boiling water can be used, thus it is less likely that the water will evaporate quickly. These are available in Chinese hardware shops and in some cookware shops. Another advantage to metal over bamboo is that the metal lid is more airtight. Keeping vapors in is critical for steaming. My parents improvise a steamer by setting a round cake rack in a twelve- to fourteen-inch skillet with a tight-fitting domed lid. Because the skillet is so shallow, they steam over only about half an inch of boiling water. Any more than that, and the water would spill into the food dish, diluting the flavors. However, with so little water, the pan must be carefully monitored to ensure that the water does not run out! Another way to jury-rig a steamer is to place a rack in a wok (instead of a skillet); this way you can steam over two inches of water. Traditional cooks never use their stir-fry wok for steaming (as the water strips the seasoning from a cast-iron or carbon-steel wok) but keep a separate wok, preferably stainless steel, just for steaming. Naturally, the wok must have a domed lid.

Whichever style you use, the food can be placed in the steamer in two different ways. In one, you steam the food in a shallow heatproof bowl with sloping sides or a Pyrex pie plate that will fit into your steamer *without touching the sides of the steamer!* Nearly every Chinese household uses the same shallow pale-blue bowls with sloping sides. These are available in any Chinatown in a variety of sizes, but the nine-inch with the painted blue fish is the most popular for steaming. First, bring the water in the steamer to a boil, then place the dish of food to be steamed onto the bamboo or metal steamer basket or onto the cake rack. In a second method, if dumplings are to be cooked, for example, first line the steamer basket or cake rack off the heat with Napa cabbage leaves and then place the dumplings directly on the leaves. Whichever method is used, once the food is added, the water must be either already at a rolling boil or simmering. Food should never be added to a steamer when the water is cold.

Even though steaming is a simple method of cooking, there is an art to doing it well. Some foods demand that the steam be created by a rolling boil on high heat, while others need to steam on a bare simmer. When making Steamed Egg Custard (page 39), for example, the steam should be gentle, so as not to toughen the eggs, but for Steamed Sole with Black Bean Sauce (page 43), medium-high heat is necessary for a brief amount of time. Then the fish continues cooking, off the heat, while still enveloped by the closed steamer's heat.

When I steam, I stay attuned to the sound the simmering or boiling water makes in the pot, to be sure that the water does not evaporate completely. Not only can this make for a completely ruined pot, it can also lead to an *explosion*! I listen for the sound of the steam and check the pot occasionally, keeping a kettle of boiling water ready to replenish with water as necessary—the water level should never fall below a depth of half an inch. Never replenish with cold water: It stops the steaming. Expert cooks, who use a bamboo steamer and wrap a cloth around the bamboo lid for a tighter seal, pour boiling water directly onto the cloth to replenish the steaming pot. This avoids any splashing, and prevents any flavor or aroma from escaping.

While caution is important, I discourage too much checking, because it allows the steam and flavor to escape. This also increases the cooking time. It is critical to develop an instinct for how much water to use and finely tuned ears to detect the sound of a pot that is about to lose its steam. Metal and bamboo stackable steamers are the easiest for monitoring the water level without disturbing the food.

Be advised that it is very easy for accidents to occur when removing the dish from the steamer; always turn off the heat before removing food to avoid steam burns. The shallow bowl the food cooks in should be about two inches smaller than the pot or steamer basket, so that there is room to grab the dish with potholders. There are special steamer plate lifters (see photo, page 244) that can be used to lift the dish out, but some of these lifters don't seem to grip very well, and the hot dish can fall onto the cook's feet! (My parents insist on wearing slippers in the house and, as they carry their fourteen-inch skillet filled with sloshing boiling water to the sink after steaming, my heart always skips a beat.)

If you learn how to steam foods, you will have mastered one if the most fundamental of Chinese cooking techniques. You will also encounter some of the purest flavors in the cook's repertoire. The technique is simple, but the results can be exquisite and complex. If a cook uses the freshest ingredients and masters the timing, the food will be delicate, sweet, and harmonious for the body.

蠔豉馬蹄蒸豬肉餅

Hoe See Ma Tai Zing Jew Yok Bang

Steamed Oyster and Water Chestnut Pork Cake

I remember Mama hand-chopping pork with a cleaver to make this dish when we were growing up. The hand-chopping creates a more *al dente* texture than grinding the meat does, and the difference is worth the effort (however, your arm begins to ache after only a few chops). This dish is still delicious made with ground pork, and is one of the most popular home-style recipes in the Cantonese repertoire. The flavor of the dried oysters is concentrated, but know that they require at least 2 hours of soaking to release sand and grit and to soften before they can be cooked.

2 Chinese dried oysters

6 Chinese dried mushrooms

8 fresh water chestnuts, about 6 ounces

8 ounces ground pork butt

2 tablespoons cornstarch

2 teaspoons thin soy sauce

1 teaspoon Shao Hsing rice cooking wine

1 teaspoon vegetable oil

1 teaspoon sesame oil

¼ teaspoon sugar

¼ teaspoon salt

Cilantro sprigs

Rinse the oysters in cold water. In a small bowl, soak the oysters in ¼ cup water for 3 to 4 hours or until soft. Drain and gently squeeze dry, reserving soaking liquid. Finely mince and set aside. In a medium bowl, soak the mushrooms in ½ cup cold water for 30 minutes or until softened. Drain and squeeze dry, reserving soaking liquid. Cut off and discard the stems and mince the caps.

Peel water chestnuts with a paring knife, then finely mince to make about 1 cup. In a 9-inch shallow heatproof bowl, mix pork, oysters, mushrooms, and water chestnuts. Add the cornstarch, soy sauce, rice wine, vegetable oil, sesame oil, sugar, and salt, and mix with hands until well combined. Add the reserved oyster liquid 1 tablespoon at a time, mixing between each addition.

Spread mixture evenly, poke meat with fingers making little dents, and add 2 tablespoons of the reserved mushroom liquid. Mix liquid into the meat with hands until absorbed. (Reserve remaining mushroom liquid for use in soups.) Spread mixture evenly to within 1 inch of the edge of the dish.

Bring water to a boil over high heat in a covered steamer large enough to fit the dish *without touching the sides of the steamer*. Carefully place dish into steamer, cover, and steam on high heat 5 minutes. Turn off the heat and let stand, covered, 15 minutes, without removing lid. Pork should be just done and no longer pink; if not, resteam 1 to 2 more minutes. Carefully remove dish from the steamer and sprinkle with cilantro sprigs. Serve immediately.

Serves 4 to 6 as part of a multicourse meal.

Steamed Pork Cake with Salted Duck Egg

This is a simple Cantonese village recipe best eaten with mounds of hot, steaming rice. The method is similar to the preceding recipe but, with the addition of salted duck eggs, the result is totally different. Salted duck eggs are cured in ash and brine. The shell is very hard and the egg white is cloudier than eggs as we know them in the West. The "raw" egg yolk resembles a soft cooked egg, being firm enough to cut. Because the eggs have been preserved in salt, no additional salt is needed in this recipe.

8 ounces ground pork butt

1 tablespoon plus 1 teaspoon cornstarch

2 teaspoons thin soy sauce

1 1/2 teaspoons Shao Hsing rice cooking wine

1 teaspoon vegetable oil

1 teaspoon sesame oil

1/2 teaspoon sugar

2 salted duck eggs (hom dan)

2 teaspoons finely chopped scallions

In a 9-inch, shallow, heatproof bowl, combine the pork, cornstarch, soy sauce, rice wine, vegetable oil, sesame oil, and sugar, and mix together thoroughly with hands. Crack open the eggs and add 1 egg white to the meat mixture (discard the second white), and mix with hands until well combined. Mix in 2 tablespoons cold water, making the mixture quite loose. Spread mixture evenly to within 1 inch of the edge of the dish. Cut yolks into 5 pieces each and press gently on top of mixture.

Bring water to a boil over high heat in a covered steamer large enough to fit the dish *without touching the sides of the steamer.* Carefully place the dish into the steamer, cover, and steam on high heat 5 minutes. Turn off heat and let stand, covered, 20 minutes, without removing lid. Pork should be just done and no longer pink; if not, resteam 1 to 2 more minutes. Carefully remove dish from the steamer and sprinkle with scallions. Serve immediately.

Serves 4 to 6 as part of a multicourse meal.

Steamed Egg Custard

This is one of the humblest of Cantonese dishes, and one of the noblest custards. My Auntie Betty learned to cook at the age of nine, and recalls that this was one of the first dishes she helped prepare for the family's evening meal.

Baba says that he used to measure the water for this recipe by using the empty cracked eggshells and refilling them with water, but has found that this old-timer's method is too much work. He now cracks the eggs into a rice bowl and then roughly measures the same amount of water into a second rice bowl before combining the two. For those who want to know precisely how much water to use, I have provided the exact amounts. There are several tips for making a perfect custard. Boiled water that has been cooled is one of the requirements for achieving a delicate, smooth custard. The water in the steamer should never be above a bare simmer, and be careful to remove the custard as soon as it sets. Heat that is too strong or overcooking results in a spongy texture.

2 tablespoons Chinese dried shrimp

4 large eggs

1 tablespoon thin soy sauce or oyster flavored sauce

1 tablespoon vegetable oil

Cilantro sprigs

Minced scallions

Bring ¾ cup water to a boil. Remove from heat, and allow to cool until tepid. In a small bowl, soak the dried shrimp in 3 tablespoons cold water for 30 minutes, or until softened. Drain, reserving soaking liquid. Roughly chop the shrimp if they are larger than ½ inch.

Crack the eggs into a medium bowl. Whisk until well beaten. Stir in the tepid water and reserved shrimp soaking liquid. Transfer the beaten eggs to a 9-inch shallow heatproof bowl, add the dried shrimp, and stir to combine.

Bring water to a boil over high heat in a covered steamer large enough to fit the dish *without touching the sides of the steamer.* Carefully place dish into steamer, cover, lower heat to medium, and steam 10 to 13 minutes, or just until custard is set and barely trembles when the dish is touched. Check the water level from time to time and replenish, if necessary, with boiling water. Carefully remove dish from the steamer.

Pour soy sauce or oyster sauce over the custard. In a small skillet, heat oil until hot but not smoking over high heat. Carefully pour hot oil over custard. The oil will make a crackling sound as it hits the sauce. Garnish with cilantro sprigs and scallions, and serve immediately.

Serves 4 to 6 as part of a multicourse meal.

Steamed Tangerine Beef

This is one of Baba's signature dishes. Quite a few of my uncles and aunties, wonderful cooks themselves, rave about his expertise in cooking this. Make sure the flank steak is at room temperature before marinating it. If the beef is too cold, the cooking time will increase by 2 to 3 minutes, and the beef will not cook evenly.

Mama says Baba likes to add dried tangerine peel, *guo pay,* to every dish. Although dried tangerine peel can be found in Chinese grocery stores, herb shops tend to carry better quality. There you will also find *chun pay,* which is tangerine peel that has been aged for at least one year and has even better flavor. It brings a lovely, mellow tangerine flavor to foods, but Baba cautions to never soak it for more than 30 minutes or the flavor will be lost. The tangerine peel will still be hard after a 30-minute soaking. If *chun pay* is unavailable, use *guo pay.* You can also dry tangerine peel yourself; remove the peel and allow it to air-dry under the sun several days, until it is dry and brittle.

1 dried tangerine peel (*chun pay*), about 3 inches wide

8 ounces flank steak, well trimmed

¼ teaspoon baking soda

2 teaspoons thin soy sauce

2 tablespoons finely shredded ginger

1 teaspoon cornstarch

In a small bowl, soak tangerine peel in ¼ cup water for 30 minutes. Drain and finely shred the hard tangerine peel to make about 1 tablespoon. Set aside.

Halve flank steak with the grain into 2 strips. Cut each strip across the grain into scant ¼-inch-thick slices. Place slices in a 9-inch shallow heatproof bowl. Add baking soda and mix lightly with hands until well distributed. Add soy sauce, mixing with hands, then set aside 5 minutes.

Add 2 teaspoons finely shredded tangerine peel, ginger, and cornstarch, and mix by hand. Add about 2 tablespoons of cold water and mix until well absorbed. Spread mixture evenly to within 1 inch of the edge of the dish. Sprinkle with remaining tangerine peel.

Bring water to a boil over high heat in a covered steamer large enough to fit the dish *without touching the sides of the steamer.* Carefully place dish into steamer, cover, and steam on high heat, 2 minutes. Uncover and redistribute meat, placing the rare pieces on the edges of the dish. Steam an additional 15 seconds to 1 minute, or until meat is medium rare. Carefully remove dish from the steamer. Serve immediately.

Serves 4 to 6 as part of a multicourse meal.

Steamed Spareribs with Black Bean Sauce

If you live near a Chinatown, it will be easy to get the correct spareribs for the next two recipes. There, the butchers will take a 1-pound slab of lean pork spareribs—not baby-back and not country-style—and use a huge electric machine to cut them across the bones into 1-inch-wide pieces. Once home, you can cut them between the bones into individual squares. It is important to wash the spareribs thoroughly to remove any tiny bones or splinters of bone.

Because the spareribs cook on medium-high heat for 30 minutes, it is critical that you monitor the water level in the steamer for both this recipe and the next. The spareribs are cooked through after 20 minutes, but generally are still tough. The additional cooking is to tenderize the ribs, so you should test the ribs from time to time, tasting them to see if they are tender enough for you. The cooking time will vary according to the quality of the spareribs and each cook's preference. Countless Cantonese families cook Spareribs with Black Bean Sauce, and this is my cousin Cindy's version.

1 pound lean pork spareribs, cut into bite-sized pieces

2 tablespoons Chinese dried black beans (*dul see*)

2 tablespoons thin soy sauce

1½ teaspoons cornstarch

1 teaspoon minced garlic

1 teaspoon minced ginger

½ jalapeño pepper, seeded and minced

3 drops sesame oil

2 squares firm tofu, rinsed, each square cut into 4 equal pieces

Wash the spareribs in several changes of cold water, and drain in a colander. Pat dry with paper towels.

Rinse the black beans in several changes of cold water and drain them. In a small bowl, mash the black beans with the back of a wooden spoon. Add the soy sauce, cornstarch, garlic, ginger, jalapeño pepper, and sesame oil, and stir to combine.

Place spareribs in a 9-inch shallow heatproof bowl, pour black bean mixture over spareribs, and stir to combine. Spread spareribs evenly to within ⅛ inch of the edge of the plate. Place the tofu on top.

Bring water to a boil over high heat in a covered steamer large enough to fit the dish *without touching the sides of the steamer.* Carefully place dish into steamer, cover, reduce heat to medium-high, and steam 20 minutes. Check the water level from time to time and replenish, if necessary, with boiling water. Uncover steamer and carefully stir spareribs and tofu to redistribute the sauce. Cover and continue steaming on medium heat 5 to 10 minutes or until spareribs are tender and sauce has formed. Carefully remove dish from the steamer. Serve immediately.

Serves 4 to 6 as part of a multicourse meal.

Steamed Spareribs with Plum Sauce

酸
梅
醬
蒸
排
骨

Shoon Moy Zheung Zing Pie Qwat

This is an old-fashioned Cantonese recipe that is a favorite of my father's. The plum sauce is generally shelved next to hoisin sauce and ground bean sauce in a Chinese market. Once it is opened, it must be refrigerated. If you like your spareribs a little more sour, add 1 teaspoon or more of the plum sauce. Note that the cooking times and heat levels in this recipe are different from those in Cindy's recipe for Steamed Spareribs with Black Bean Sauce. As I've said before, every family has a slightly different style of cooking. Read the introduction for Steamed Spareribs with Black Bean Sauce (page 41) for special instructions on purchasing the spareribs.

1 pound lean pork spareribs, cut into bite-sized pieces

1 teaspoon sugar

1 tablespoon plum sauce (*shoon moy zheung*)

2 teaspoons cornstarch

1½ teaspoons Shao Hsing rice cooking wine

1 teaspoon sesame oil

1 teaspoon thin soy sauce

¼ teaspoon salt

Wash spareribs in several changes of cold water and thoroughly drain in a colander until almost dry to the touch. Pat dry with paper towels. Place spareribs in a 9-inch shallow heatproof bowl, sprinkle with sugar, and marinate for 10 minutes. Pour off any excess liquid. Add plum sauce, cornstarch, rice wine, sesame oil, soy sauce, and salt, and stir to combine. Spread spareribs evenly to within 1 inch of the edge of the dish.

Bring water to a boil over high heat in a covered steamer large enough to fit the dish *without touching the sides of the steamer*. Carefully place dish into steamer, cover, and steam on high heat 30 minutes. Check the water level from time to time and replenish, if necessary, with boiling water. Reduce temperature to medium heat and cook 5 more minutes or until spareribs are tender and sauce is formed. Carefully remove dish from the steamer. Serve immediately.

Serves 4 to 6 as part of a multicourse meal.

Steamed Sole with Black Bean Sauce

One of the secrets of steaming sole is to season the fish just before cooking. If the fish sits too long with the seasonings, the salt will extract water from the fish and, consequently, the fish will be less juicy. Try to choose a fish not longer than 14 inches, so that it will hang over the plate by no more than 1½ inches on each end but will still fit into the steamer.

It is not necessary to purchase lemon sole for this recipe; just be sure the fish is very fresh and has the head and tail intact.

One 1¼-pound sole, cleaned and gutted, with head and tail intact

½ plus ⅛ teaspoon salt

2 teaspoons Chinese dried black beans (*dul see*)

2 teaspoons minced garlic

½ teaspoon sugar

¾ teaspoon sesame oil

¾ teaspoon Shao Hsing rice cooking wine

¼ teaspoon ground white pepper

1 tablespoon vegetable oil

1 tablespoon finely shredded ginger

1 scallion, finely shredded

1 tablespoon thin soy sauce

Thoroughly rinse the fish in cold water and pat dry. Sprinkle ½ teaspoon salt over the outside and into the cavity of the fish.

Rinse the black beans in several changes of cold water and drain them. In a small bowl, mash beans, garlic, and sugar with the back of a wooden spoon. Stir in sesame oil, rice wine, pepper, and ⅛ teaspoon salt.

Place fish in a 9-inch shallow heatproof bowl and spread black beans over fish on both sides and in cavity.

Bring water to a boil over high heat in a covered steamer large enough to fit the dish *without touching the sides of the steamer*. Carefully place dish into steamer, cover, and steam 5 minutes. Turn off heat and let stand, covered, 4 minutes. Test fish for doneness by poking the thickest part with a fork or chopstick; flesh should flake. If not, resteam 1 to 2 minutes or until fish just flakes. Carefully remove the dish from the steamer and pour off any liquid in the dish.

In a small skillet, heat oil until hot but not smoking over high heat. Sprinkle ginger and scallion over the fish. Drizzle the soy sauce over the fish, and carefully pour oil over fish. The oil will make a crackling sound as it hits the fish. Serve immediately.

Serves 4 to 6 as part of a multicourse meal.

Steamed Chicken with Lily Buds, Cloud Ears, and Mushrooms

This dish is one of the great wonders of steam cooking. After only 10 minutes of steaming, an intensely flavored sauce is formed that is impressive in its complexity of flavors. Baba expertly uses a meat cleaver to chop chicken through the bone into bite-sized pieces. If this is too intimidating for you, choose chicken breast on the bone and use poultry shears; drumsticks cannot be cut with poultry shears. For this dish, use a mixture of white and dark meat. The Chinese prefer the dark meat, because they feel the meat closest to the bone is the juiciest and most flavorful.

¹/₃ **cup cloud ears (*wun yee*)**

¹/₄ **cup lily buds (*gum tzum*)**

6 Chinese dried mushrooms

I pound mixed chicken parts, bone in

2 tablespoons cornstarch

I tablespoon thin soy sauce

2 teaspoons Shao Hsing rice cooking wine

I teaspoon sesame oil

I teaspoon vegetable oil

³/₄ **teaspoon sugar**

¹/₄ **teaspoon salt**

2 tablespoons slivered scallions

I tablespoon shredded ginger

Place the cloud ears, lily buds, and mushrooms in separate bowls. Pour about ½ cup cold water over each ingredient and soak for about 30 minutes, to soften. When softened, drain all the ingredients, discarding all the water, except for the mushroom liquid. Remove any hard spots from the cloud ears. Remove the hard end from the lily buds and tie each lily bud into a knot. Drain and squeeze the mushrooms dry. Cut off and discard stems and thinly slice the caps.

With a meat cleaver, chop chicken through the bone into 2-inch bite-sized pieces. In a 9-inch shallow heatproof bowl, combine the chicken, cornstarch, soy sauce, rice wine, sesame oil, vegetable oil, sugar, and salt, and stir to combine. Add the cloud ears, lily buds, and mushrooms, and stir to combine. Add 2 tablespoons of the reserved mushroom liquid, and mix until absorbed. (Reserve remaining mushroom liquid to flavor soups.) Spread mixture evenly to within ¼ inch of the edge of the dish. Sprinkle with scallions and ginger.

Bring water to a boil over high heat in a covered steamer large enough to fit the dish *without touching the sides of the steamer*. Carefully place dish into steamer, cover, and steam on high heat 10 minutes or until chicken is just cooked and juices have formed. Check the water level from time to time and replenish, if necessary, with boiling water. Carefully remove dish from the steamer. Serve immediately.

Serves 4 to 6 as part of a multicourse meal.

蒸石班

Zing Seck Ban

Steamed Rock Cod

For steaming a whole rock cod, it's best to use a cake rack set into a 14-inch skillet. Most oval platters large enough to hold the fish will not fit into a bamboo or metal steamer basket. The platter used for steaming should be heatproof and have slightly sloping sides, so that the juices that form during cooking do not spill over. Rock cod is known as seck ban in Cantonese, and has a delicate texture. It is widely available in California, where several species of rock cod, also known there as rockfish, are found along the Pacific Coast. Outside California, black sea bass, snapper, or small striped bass would be appropriate substitutes.

One 1½-pound rock cod, cleaned and gutted, with head and tail intact

1½ teaspoons salt

4 Chinese dried mushrooms

1½ teaspoons finely minced garlic

3 tablespoons finely shredded ginger

2 scallions, finely shredded

1 tablespoon Shao Hsing rice cooking wine

½ teaspoon sugar

2 tablespoons vegetable oil

2 tablespoons thin soy sauce

Cilantro sprigs

Thoroughly rinse the fish in cold water and drain. Gently rub the cavity and outside of the fish with salt and rinse again. Place fish on a rack and allow to air-dry. In a medium bowl, soak the mushrooms in ¼ cup cold water for 30 minutes, or until softened. Drain and squeeze dry. (Reserve remaining mushroom liquid to flavor soups.) Cut off and discard the stems, and thinly slice the caps.

Place the fish on a heatproof oval platter with sloping sides (be sure it fits in the skillet to be used for steaming *without touching its sides*). Trim the fish tail, if necessary, to fit the fish onto the platter. Evenly sprinkle mushrooms, garlic, ginger, and half the scallions on the fish. Drizzle with rice wine and sprinkle with the sugar.

Set a cake rack in a 14-inch skillet and pour in about ½ inch of water. Cover the skillet, and bring water to a boil over high heat. Carefully place the platter into the steamer, cover, and steam 13 to 15 minutes on high heat or until fish flakes when tested. Check the water level and replenish, if necessary, with boiling water. Test fish for doneness by poking the thickest part with a fork or chopstick; flesh should flake. If not, resteam 1 to 2 minutes, or until fish just flakes. Remove skillet from heat, and carefully remove the platter from steamer and pour off any liquid in the platter.

In a small skillet, heat oil over high heat until hot but not smoking. Sprinkle remaining scallions over fish and drizzle with the soy sauce. Carefully pour hot oil over fish. The oil will make a crackling sound as it hits the fish. Garnish with cilantro. Serve immediately.

Serves 4 to 6 as part of a multicourse meal.

The Art of Steaming   **45**

Steamed Sponge Cake

I thought Steamed Sponge Cake was probably a Chinese-American invention, as it is an interesting fusion of Western ingredients with the Chinese method of steaming. My Auntie Elaine reminds me that it is an authentic Chinese recipe; most homes in China did not have ovens, so it was natural that people would steam rather than bake a cake. This cake has a delicate crumb, resembling a *génoise,* and is not very sweet. Because it is steamed, it is very moist and will stay moist if kept in an airtight container for 2 to 3 days. For Western tastes it may seem a little plain and unusual, as the cake, obviously, does not brown. Neither is it frosted or served with cream. The Chinese prefer their cakes simple and unadorned. When I was a child, we always purchased this from one of the Chinatown bakeries, but I discovered recently that it was easy to make. When removing the lid after steaming, do it quickly to prevent water that has condensed under the lid from dripping onto the cake.

4 large eggs

1 egg white

³/₄ cup sugar

1 teaspoon vanilla extract

1 cup sifted cake flour

¹/₂ teaspoon baking powder

Line the bottom of an 8-inch-round, 2-inch-deep metal cake pan with parchment paper. In a large bowl, beat whole eggs, egg white, and sugar until thick and pale yellow, 3 to 4 minutes. Stir in the vanilla extract. In a small bowl, thoroughly mix the cake flour and baking powder. Using a rubber spatula, quickly fold in flour mixture, just until flour is no longer visible. Turn the batter into the prepared cake pan, filling the pan about ¾ full. Lightly tap pan to settle any air pockets.

Bring water to a boil over high heat in a covered steamer large enough to fit the cake pan *without touching the sides.* Place cake pan into steamer and cover with the lid. Reduce heat to medium and steam 20 minutes, or until a toothpick inserted into the center of the cake comes out clean. Check the water level and replenish, if necessary, with boiling water. Carefully remove cake pan from steamer. Immediately run a knife along the edge of the cake to loosen sides. Place an 8- to 9-inch rack over the cake pan and un-mold cake. Remove the parchment paper, flip cake right-side up onto another cake rack, and allow to cool. Serve warm or at room temperature.

Serves 6 to 8 as a dessert.

薑
絲
如
幼
茸

SHREDS OF GINGER LIKE BLADES OF GRASS

Grandfather (Gunggung) Fung Lok Chi with a younger
brother standing by him. Canton, China, circa 1920.

I ASK BABA TO TEACH ME TO MAKE A
few of his specialties. "First you must learn to
correctly shred ginger, before we cook anything," he admonishes. For Baba, it is mean-
ingless to cook unless you properly slice,
shred, chop, or mince your ingredients.

My arm sometimes aches as I shred a chunk of ginger, trying to control the
knife to make the thinnest slices. Baba, looking over my shoulder, says critically,
"So crude, *tai cho.*" I examine my shreds and think this is as fine as any I've ever

seen. Then Baba takes the cleaver, the traditional Chinese knife, and demonstrates. Indeed his shreds are like blades of grass, extraordinarily fine and delicate. Although he is elderly, his hands are steady as he cuts slices so thin that they curl off the cleaver. He compares his ginger to mine and observes that not only is his more beautiful but it will also taste better in the mouth. He tells me that a cook recognizes another cook the moment he sees him slice ginger.

When I was ten years old, our family made its first trip to the Far East. Even though I had eaten Chinese food my entire life, I had my first taste of the life of an epicure. In those days, Mama had said Chinese food in America was unrefined and, as we dined in Hong Kong, I finally understood what she meant. The dim sum were like jewels, studded with the tiniest pieces of vegetable—like slivers of bamboo shoots, finely minced water chestnuts, shreds of scallions—amazing to look at and more delectable to savor. Morsels so delicate they bore no resemblance to the big, clumsy things we called dim sum in San Francisco. These were works of art. This is what my parents meant when they said, "You must take heart to prepare." I understood, even then, that my lesson was not to return home and try to replicate the dishes, for these chefs were masters, and any comparison would be unrealistic. However, these masterpieces made a lasting impression on me of how superior food looks, smells, and tastes when created with heart.

When the food processor first entered the market, people commented on how great it would be for Chinese food. All the labor-intensive preparation would now take no time. Even Baba and Mama eagerly bought the machine. But, whether the vegetable was sliced or shredded, it looked haphazard and horrible to their practiced and discerning eyes. Each evening before the preparation of dinner in my parents' home, the kitchen is peaceful, a still life of plates lined along the counter, each delicately mounded with finely sliced or slivered ingredients. Soon the room will hum with the clanging of pots, the sizzling of stir-frying, and the deafening din of the exhaust fan. In the midst of this melee, I marvel at the beauty of their unsurpassable knife skills.

The refinement of the hand-cut slice, shred, or mince is one of the hallmarks of great Chinese food, and theirs is a superior model. Vegetable Lo Mein (page 97), for example, combines shreds of Chinese mushroom, carrots, Napa cabbage, scallions, and minced ginger. Mama shreds these ingredients so finely that every mouthful includes a taste of each ingredient. Drunken Chicken (page 52) is magnificent, partially because the chicken is never overcooked, but also because it is drizzled with a delicate ginger and scallion sauce. Until I studied Baba's technique, I shredded in the French style of scant one-eighth-inch-thick matchsticks, producing ginger and scallions that were slightly crunchy to the bite rather than feathery, with just a wisp of aromatic flavor. When my parents prepare Singapore Rice Noodles (page 32), the sweet scallions, Chinese mushrooms, and celery are so finely shredded that their flavors meld with the shrimp and provide texture without any one ingredient dominating in flavor.

I have been a professional in the cooking field for over twenty years, yet wielding a meat cleaver to chop chicken is for me an intimidating process. I have watched Chinese butchers swiftly chop, and I have watched my parents do it more slowly, but with as much control. I often wondered how Mama, who didn't learn to cook until she immigrated to America, and Baba, who was pampered with his mother's cooking until he married, ever learned this skill. My parents share a practical outlook on life. When cooking became a necessity, they simply learned, never stopping to think about their fears.

Rock Sugar Ginger Chicken (page 58) and Steamed Chicken with Lily Buds, Cloud Ears, and Mushrooms (page 44) are two of my all-time favorite dishes. Raw chicken is chopped straight through the bone with a sharp meat cleaver into bite-sized pieces and then marinated. The breast is not difficult to chop, since the bone is quite soft. The drumstick, however, with its thick bones, requires perfect technique to chop into three bite-sized pieces. As I perform this feat, I worry about how slippery the raw chicken skin is and how uneven my pieces are. I have questioned why the chicken needs to be chopped, although I know quite well that cooking chicken on the bone makes it more juicy and succulent. In addition, it is the Chinese custom not to eat big pieces of meat.

You must be swift and sure when chopping with a meat cleaver, employing the same unerring exactness a craftsman uses to hammer. Insufficient power and the knife will not cut through, producing bone splinters; trying to place the cleaver in the same spot twice can result in two half-cut incisions that are unattractive. However, if the move is too swift and inaccurate, the hand holding the chicken could . . . the thought turns me cold. Chopping with a meat cleaver is not my strength. I will confess that sometimes, in the name of my own safety, I skip the traditions and simply disjoint the chicken. I would advise novice cooks to do the same. The Chinese also chop cooked chicken, such as Soy Sauce Chicken (page 174), White Cut Chicken (page 110), and Salt-Roasted Chicken (page 173), which is frankly no easier than chopping raw chicken. For Western tastes, it is perhaps better to always disjoint a chicken. A chopped chicken can often have fine splinters from the bone, and I have observed that this creates unease for some eaters. Cutting slivers of scallions, slicing any vegetable into a roll-cut or shred does not daunt me. But to this day, I still wish I chopped effortlessly.

There are two types of cleavers (see photo, page 245). One has a more delicate appearance with a thinner cutting edge, and is sometimes called a *Chinese chef's knife* or *vegetable cleaver,* despite the fact that it can be used for boneless meats and chicken in addition to vegetables. The heavier cleaver, with a blunter edge, is known as a *meat cleaver,* and is better for chopping through chicken and fish bones. For most Chinese cooking, a hand-forged, European, high-carbon *stainless-steel* vegetable cleaver or high-quality eight-inch cook's knife is recommended. There are also fantastic "hollow ground" Japanese cook's knives, which have a super-fine edge for slicing but not for chopping. Avoid the high-carbon steel cleavers (which are the traditional

Chinese cleavers) because they corrode too easily and the quality of the blade is inferior. Carefully wash and dry the cleaver or cook's knife after each use, and never place it in the dishwasher. I prefer the vegetable cleaver over a cook's knife because of its versatility: The butt end of the cleaver's handle is often used to mash ingredients, the blade can be laid on its side to smash ginger or garlic, and the blunt edge of the cleaver blade is excellent for pounding meat for tenderizing. The broad surface of the blade also makes it a useful tool for gathering up ingredients.

As part of my quest to learn and perfect the preparation techniques so central to Chinese cooking, I asked Baba to cook Stir-Fried Butterfly Fish and Bean Sprouts (page 28), one of his specialties. "Well," he said smiling, "you know I'm still practicing—sometimes it works and sometimes it doesn't." Indeed, the first cooking demonstration Baba gave me was disappointing—the fish was slightly overcooked and fell apart. A few weeks later, though, he cooked it to perfection. I compared notes: The timing differed by about forty-five seconds, the most subtle of adjustments. Eighty-four years old and Baba is still practicing. His humility is an inspiration. It reminds me that mastery comes with perseverance. I will think of this the next time I feel I ought to be as good as the Chinatown butcher.

All Chinese recipes require mastery of knife skills, some more than others. The preceding recipes for rice, stir-fries, and steaming dishes demand expertise in knife skills as much as do the following recipes for panfrying, poaching, braising, and soups.

Fried White Fish

For a long time I used to think nothing could compare to the delicate flavor of steamed or poached fish. But this simple method of pan-frying fish until golden, and then drizzling it with a half-dozen seasonings infuses the fish with a sauce that is irresistible. White fish are small fish that are a little over 1 ounce apiece and are no longer than 7 inches in length.

10 small white fish (about 12 ounces), cleaned and gutted

½ teaspoon salt

1 scallion, white portion only

1 garlic clove, finely minced

1 tablespoon finely minced ginger

1 tablespoon thin soy sauce

2 teaspoons Shao Hsing rice cooking wine

1 teaspoon sesame oil

½ teaspoon sugar

¼ teaspoon ground white pepper

About 4 tablespoons vegetable oil

Cilantro sprigs

Wash the fish in several changes of cold water. Cut off heads and tails on the diagonal. Rinse fish and thoroughly drain in a colander. Gently rub the cavities and the outsides of the fish with salt.

Finely mince the scallion and place in a small bowl. Add the garlic, ginger, soy sauce, rice wine, sesame oil, sugar, and pepper.

Heat a 14-inch skillet over high heat, until hot but not smoking. Add 2 tablespoons oil and fish, and cook, undisturbed, 3 to 4 minutes on medium-high heat, letting fish fry until golden brown. Using a metal spatula, carefully turn fish, add 1 to 2 more tablespoons of oil, and reduce heat to medium. Fry until golden, about 4 to 5 minutes. Spoon sauce over all the fish, reduce heat to low, cover, turn off the heat, and let sit for 1 minute. Test fish for doneness by poking the thickest part with a fork or chopstick; flesh should flake. If not, gently warm fish on medium heat until just cooked through. Transfer fish to a platter and garnish with cilantro sprigs. Serve immediately.

Serves 4 to 6 as part of a multicourse meal.

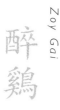

Drunken Chicken

Unlike the Western style of poaching chicken, this unusual method calls for vigorously boiling the chicken, then rapidly cooling the chicken down with ice water. This is done twice, which results in the chicken being succulent and juicy. The chicken is then scented and infused with Shao Hsing rice cooking wine and served with the classic ginger and scallion sauce. Rice wine is available in Chinese grocery and liquor stores for about two to five dollars. Choose a more expensive rice wine for this dish. A bonus of this recipe is the poaching liquid, which is a lovely light broth that can be reserved for soups.

One 4-pound broiler-fryer chicken

4¼ teaspoons salt

8 quarts ice water

1 cup Shao Hsing rice cooking wine

¼ cup finely shredded green scallions

¼ cup finely shredded ginger

3 tablespoons vegetable oil

Remove any fat pockets from the chicken. Rub chicken with about 2 teaspoons salt. Rinse the chicken under cold water and drain on a rack.

In a 6-quart pot, or a pot large enough to fit the chicken, bring 3 quarts cold water to a boil over high heat, covered. Carefully add chicken, breast-side up, adding more boiling water, if necessary, to completely cover chicken. Cover and return to a boil over high heat. When the broth returns to a rolling boil, boil vigorously over high heat, uncovered, 17 minutes, removing any scum that rises to the surface. Remove from heat. Using 2 heavy spoons, carefully transfer hot chicken to a colander in the sink. Slowly pour 4 quarts ice water over the chicken, until chicken is warm to the touch.

Return the chicken cooking liquid to a rolling boil over high heat. Again, carefully add the partially cooked chicken, breast-side up, adding more boiling water, if necessary, to completely cover chicken. Return to a boil over high heat, uncovered. When the broth returns to a rolling boil, boil vigorously over high heat, uncovered, 17 minutes, removing any scum that rises to the surface. Remove from heat. Using 2 heavy spoons, carefully transfer hot chicken to a colander in the sink. (The chicken should register 170 degrees when tested with a meat thermometer at the meatiest part of the thigh. If not, return to the pot and simmer several more minutes.) Slowly pour the remaining 4 quarts of ice water over the chicken in the colander, until chicken is warm to the touch. Save the chicken broth and reserve for soups.

Place the chicken on a rack and air-dry 30 minutes in a cool and breezy room. Sprinkle the entire surface of the chicken with ¾ teaspoon salt. With a meat cleaver, chop the chicken through the bone into bite-sized pieces, reserving any chicken juices (or disjoint into serving pieces). Place the chicken in a casserole dish and pour rice wine over the chicken. Cover and marinate 1 to 2 hours at room temperature, occasionally basting chicken with rice wine. Pour reserved juices back into the casserole.

Meanwhile, place scallions, ginger, and remaining 1½ teaspoons salt in a small heatproof dish. In a small skillet, heat oil over high heat until hot but not smoking. Carefully pour hot oil over scallions and ginger. The oil will make a crackling sound as it hits the scallions and ginger. Serve chicken with scallion-ginger sauce at room temperature.

Serves 4 to 6 as part of a multicourse meal.

Braised Beef

It took me so long to find out that the English name for the cut of beef used in this recipe is outside flank. Every Chinese butcher shop carries this, for it is a popular item, but there it is known by its Cantonese name, *gnul nam.* I found a few Chinese markets that had signs calling it beef rough flank or beef outside flank; but finally Tom Keane, of J.A.W.D. meat wholesalers in New York City, told me it is outside flank, *not* to be confused with flank steak. In the trade it is called katilius trunk eye or rosetti. Flank steak is popular for stir-frying, but the outside flank is a tougher cut that must be braised in order to tenderize it. It is doubtful you'll find this in an American butcher shop, but if you have a helpful butcher, ask for outside flank. The beef is about a scant ½ inch thick with a thin layer of silver skin on top. This cut is delicious, especially when cooked for this classic home-style Cantonese stew, a popular item found in noodle shops, where it is served with Chinese egg noodles and braised lettuce. For the Chinese the real prize in this dish is the beef tendon, *gnul gun.* It is an ingredient that may surprise Westerners. As the tendons cook, they become gelatinous and so rich in texture they almost melt in your mouth. Firm, white beef tendons are sold in Chinese butcher shops.

1½ pounds outside flank (*gnul nam*)

1 pound beef tendons (*gnul gun*)

1 tablespoon light brown sugar

2 tablespoons thin soy sauce

1 tablespoon black soy sauce

2 tablespoons Shao Hsing rice cooking wine

½-inch-thick slice fresh ginger

3 pieces dried ginger (*sa geung*)

2 star anise (*bot guok*)

1 Chinese white turnip, about 3 pounds

In a 3-quart pot, bring about 1 quart cold water to a boil over high heat. Add outside flank and beef tendons, and return to a boil. Drain beef and tendons in a colander and rinse under cold water. Remove any excess fat with a paring knife. Cut the beef into 2-inch squares, using a very sharp meat cleaver or knife, as it will be difficult to cut. Cut the tendons into 1-inch pieces; this will feel like you're cutting through bone.

Heat a 14-inch flat-bottomed wok or skillet over high heat, until hot but not smoking. Add the beef and tendons without any oil, and stir-fry 4 minutes; the meat will stick a little. Add the brown sugar, thin and black soy sauces, and rice wine, and cook, stirring, 2 minutes. Add 3½ cups cold water, fresh ginger, dried ginger, and star anise, and bring to a boil over high heat. Cover, reduce heat to low, and simmer 3 hours. Increase heat to high and bring to a boil.

Meanwhile, peel the turnip and cut into ¾-inch-thick pieces. When stew comes to a boil, add turnip and return to a boil. Cover, reduce heat to low, and simmer 30 to 45 minutes, or until the turnip is tender when pierced with a knife. Serve immediately.

Serves 6 to 8 as part of a multicourse meal.

Braised Sweet and Sour Spareribs

甜酸排骨 *Teen Shoon Pie Qwat*

This is one of the simplest recipes to make, yet it produces spareribs that taste much more complex than one would expect from such ordinary ingredients. No one ingredient dominates in flavor, but the results are delicious and the spareribs are tender to the bone. If Chinese red rice vinegar, *zun gong cho,* is not available, red wine vinegar would be an adequate substitute. The spareribs must be well trimmed or the sauce will be too fatty (at least 4 ounces of fat can usually be removed). These ribs are even better if made the day before serving.

2 pounds lean pork spareribs, cut into single ribs

3 tablespoons sugar

2 tablespoons thin soy sauce

1 tablespoon black soy sauce

1 tablespoon Chinese red rice vinegar

1 tablespoon ketchup

1 tablespoon Shao Hsing rice cooking wine

Trim excess fat from the spareribs. Rinse in cold water and pat dry with paper towels until almost dry to the touch. Place spareribs in a 3-quart saucepan. Sprinkle them with sugar and toss to combine. Marinate 30 minutes. Pour off excess liquid.

Add thin and black soy sauces, vinegar, ketchup, rice wine, and ½ cup cold water, and stir to combine. Bring to a boil over high heat, covered. Reduce to medium-low and simmer, stirring occasionally to make sure the sauce does not dry up (add a little water if necessary), for 1 hour, or until the spareribs are tender when pierced with a knife and the sauce is thick enough to lightly coat a spoon. Transfer to a plate and skim excess fat from the sauce. Pour sauce over the spareribs. Serve immediately.

Serves 4 to 6 as part of a multicourse meal.

Nom Yu Spareribs

This is a completely different style of braised spareribs than the Braised Sweet and Sour Spareribs (page 55), but equally superb. If you live near a Chinatown, buy the wet bean curd, and you will be gratified by how it enriches the taste of the spareribs. Wet bean curd, also known as fermented bean curd, comes in at least two different styles, and although the labels are not differentiated in English, you'll notice some with cubes of curd that are beige colored, *fu yu*, and some that are red, *nom yu*. It is the red version that you want for this recipe.

2 pounds lean pork spareribs, cut into single ribs

3 teaspoons vegetable oil

I tablespoon finely minced garlic

I tablespoon finely minced ginger

3 cubes red wet bean curd (*nom yu*)

I tablespoon thin soy sauce

I tablespoon sugar

I tablespoon Chinese red rice vinegar

I cup Homemade Chicken Broth (page 234)

Trim excess fat from the spareribs. Rinse spareribs in cold water and drain in a colander. In a 4-quart pot, bring 2 quarts water to a boil over high heat. Add the spareribs, return to a boil, and cook 30 seconds. Drain spareribs in a colander and rinse under cold water. Allow the spareribs to air-dry.

Heat a 14-inch flat-bottomed wok or skillet over high heat until hot but not smoking. Add 2 teaspoons vegetable oil, garlic, and ginger, and stir-fry 20 seconds. Add the remaining 1 teaspoon vegetable oil and spareribs, and cook until spareribs are lightly browned, 3 to 4 minutes, turning ribs on all sides. Add the bean curd, soy sauce, sugar, vinegar, and chicken broth, mashing the bean curd and stirring until well combined. Bring to a boil over high heat. Cover, reduce heat to low, and simmer 45 minutes to 1 hour, stirring occasionally, until the spareribs are tender. Serve immediately.

Serves 4 to 6 as part of a multicourse meal.

Lemongrass Pork Chops

Lemongrass, *heung mal,* is found in Thai markets as well as in most Chinese produce markets. Choose stalks with thick bottoms that are flexible and pale green. As the lemongrass ages, it becomes dry, brittle, and paler in color. After all the outer leaves have been peeled away, the tender core, about two to three inches long, is the part of the lemongrass added to the marinade to infuse the pork with flavor and to tenderize the chops.

Do not discard the tough outer leaves of the lemongrass. Instead, make a fragrant tea by cutting the leaves into two-inch pieces and boiling them in water, covered, for fifteen minutes. Lemongrass is thought by the Chinese to be good for arthritis. My mother-in-law, Hildegarde, who suffers from painful arthritis, says her condition has improved after drinking lemongrass tea, which she now drinks daily.

4 blade rib pork chops, ½ inch thick, about 1 pound

4 fresh stalks lemongrass

2 teaspoons thin soy sauce

1½ teaspoons Shao Hsing rice cooking wine

¾ teaspoon sesame oil

½ teaspoon sugar

¼ teaspoon salt

¼ teaspoon ground white pepper

1 teaspoon vegetable oil

2 tablespoons finely sliced scallion

Place the pork chops on a cutting board and, using the blunt side of a cleaver blade or a meat pounder, pound the meat portion of the chops in a crisscross pattern for about 10 minutes. Turn the chops over and continue pounding until they are ¼ inch thick.

Peel away the outer leaves of the lemongrass until only the tender core remains. Finely mince the core to equal about ¼ cup. Place lemongrass in a large shallow bowl. Add the soy sauce, rice wine, sesame oil, sugar, salt, and pepper, and stir to combine. Press both sides of pork chops into the mixture, until chops are well coated. Loosely cover with plastic wrap and marinate 2 hours, turning chops after 1 hour. Remove the pork chops from the plate, reserving any marinade—there will be very little left in the plate.

Heat a 14-inch skillet over high heat until hot but not smoking. Add vegetable oil and pork chops, reduce the heat to medium-high, and pan-fry undisturbed for 4 to 5 minutes, until they are golden brown. Turn pork chops over, pour reserved marinade, if any, into skillet, and continue frying on medium heat until pork chops are golden brown and cooked through, about 5 minutes. Sprinkle with scallion. Serve immediately. The typical Chinese style for serving pork chops is to cut them into bite-sized pieces.

Serves 4 to 6 as part of a multicourse meal.

Rock Sugar Ginger Chicken

冰
糖
焗
薑
鷄

Bing Tong Gook Geung Gai

One of my parents' oldest friends, Lady Ivy Fung, taught Mama this typical Cantonese village recipe. You can use more or less ginger, depending on your taste. The traditional technique for cooking this is to brown the ginger and chicken in an extra-large wok, cover it with the lid, and then pour the marinade down the sides of the pan. Some of the marinade can get caught on the lid cover, so I have simplified the method by just lifting the lid to add the marinade quickly. It is also easier to use a 14-inch skillet rather than such a large wok. Because the chicken and ginger finish cooking in a covered pan, when the lid is finally removed, the room becomes fragrant with ginger. The authentic method is to chop up the chicken, but whole, bone-in legs or chicken breast halves can also be cooked, in which case the braising time will increase by 5 to 10 minutes. I have experimented with using 2 tablespoons of granulated sugar in place of the rock sugar; the result is fine, but I prefer rock sugar.

2 pounds mixed chicken parts, on the bone

1/2 cup Homemade Chicken Broth (page 234)

2 tablespoons black soy sauce

2 ounces rock sugar, about 1/4 cup

2 teaspoons vegetable oil

1 1/2 cups sliced ginger, about 6 ounces

1/2 teaspoon salt

With a meat cleaver, chop the chicken through the bone, into 2-inch pieces, or disjoint into serving pieces.

In a small saucepan, combine the chicken broth, 1/2 cup water, soy sauce, and rock sugar. Bring to a simmer over medium heat and cook until the sugar is completely dissolved, about 5 minutes. Set aside.

Heat a 14-inch skillet over high heat until hot but not smoking. Add oil and ginger, and stir-fry until ginger is lightly browned, about 1 minute.

Bring the ginger to the sides of the skillet. Reduce heat to medium, and carefully add the chicken, skin side down, spreading it in the skillet. Cook, undisturbed, 3 to 4 minutes, adjusting heat between medium and medium-high to let the chicken brown. Then, using a metal spatula, turn the chicken over and pan-fry 3 to 4 minutes, or until chicken is browned on the other side, but not cooked through. Pour off any excess fat, redistribute the ginger, and sprinkle the chicken with salt. Quickly drizzle chicken broth mixture down the sides of the skillet, and immediately cover. Cook, covered, on medium heat 4 minutes. Turn the chicken, reduce heat to low, and cook 3 to 4 minutes, or until chicken is cooked through. Serve immediately.

Serves 4 to 6 as part of a multicourse meal.

Lemon Chicken

My parents have made this recipe for over twenty years, as it was taught to Mama by her friend Anna Loke. The traditional method is to marinate the chicken with the lemon and seasonings before browning it. For the novice cook, however, the wet chicken and lemon wedges can cause the oil to splatter, and the honey can make the chicken burn. I adapted the recipe slightly, but it still results in a golden brown chicken with a rich lemon sauce. The chicken can also be cooked with whole pieces of breast or leg instead of the chopped chicken, but the cooking time must be increased by 5 to 10 minutes.

2 pounds mixed chicken parts, on the bone

1 tablespoon Shao Hsing rice cooking wine

1 tablespoon thin soy sauce

1 tablespoon honey

1 lemon

1 tablespoon vegetable oil

3 slices ginger

¹/₂ teaspoon salt

With a meat cleaver, chop the chicken through the bone into 2-inch pieces, or disjoint into serving pieces. In a medium bowl, combine the rice wine, soy sauce, and honey.

Shave ⅛ inch off both ends of the lemon. Halve the lemon crosswise and cut each half into 4 wedges. Remove any visible seeds.

Heat a 14-inch skillet over high heat until hot but not smoking. Add the oil, lemon wedges, and ginger, and stir-fry 1 to 2 minutes until lemon and ginger are lightly browned. Be careful, as wet lemon wedges will cause oil to splatter. Transfer lemon and ginger to a plate.

Carefully add chicken, skin side down, spreading it in the skillet. Cook undisturbed for 3 to 4 minutes, adjusting heat between medium and medium-high, as the chicken browns. Then, using a metal spatula, turn chicken over and pan-fry 3 to 4 minutes, or until chicken is browned on the other side, but not cooked through. Pour off any excess fat. Sprinkle on salt, rice wine mixture, browned lemon, and ginger slices. Cover and simmer on medium heat 3 to 4 minutes. Turn the chicken, reduce heat to low, and simmer 3 to 4 minutes, or until chicken is cooked through. Serve immediately.

Serves 4 to 6 as part of a multicourse meal.

Seafood Sandpot

This dish has very little in the way of seasonings. It relies heavily on the use of a good homemade chicken broth. The Napa cabbage and the seafood add a sweetness to the broth after all the ingredients are cooked. The purpose of the ginger is to take away any of the "fishiness" the seafood may have. There is no soy sauce added, as the scallops, tofu, and cellophane noodles should be as creamy white as possible, and there is only enough liquid added so that the sandpot has liquid in it, without being soupy.

Sandpots are ancient cooking vessels made in a variety of sizes, from two quarts to six quarts, and are used for braised dishes and soups, as they are said to be best for slow cooking and sealing in flavor. They are inexpensive and widely available in Chinatown, and well worth the investment, for the Chinese believe it is one of the healthiest ways to cook. The pots are cream colored with a sandy unglazed texture on the outside, and are dark brown and glazed on the inside. Some sandpots have a large wire mesh on the outside, but be sure to examine the interior of the pot for any cracks to avoid a pot that will leak. There are several schools of thought on whether a sandpot requires seasoning. I have simply washed the pot and cooked in it with no problems. But some cooks soak the pot in cold water for twenty-four hours, while there are others who rub the bottom and sides of the pot lightly with vegetable oil for several days until the pot can no longer absorb more oil. Both of these methods are said to prolong the life of a sandpot and prevent cracking. The pots are only treated the first time they are used. The sandpot should never be set directly on high heat; the cold pot with the ingredients must always start on low heat and be allowed to heat slowly. After cooking, never set the pot on a cold surface or change the temperature dramatically.

8 Chinese dried mushrooms

One 1.7-ounce package cellophane noodles

8 ounces sea scallops

In a medium bowl, soak the mushrooms in ½ cup cold water for 30 minutes, or until softened. Drain and squeeze dry, reserving soaking liquid. Cut off and discard stems and thinly slice caps.

In a medium bowl, cover the cellophane noodles in cold water and soak for 15 minutes, or until softened. Drain thoroughly.

- **2 squares firm tofu, about 6 ounces**
- **4 cups shredded Chinese Napa cabbage, washed**
- **4 slices ginger**
- **1½ cups Homemade Chicken Broth (page 234)**
- **8 ounces medium shrimp, shelled and deveined**
- **¼ cup canned sliced bamboo shoots, rinsed**
- **1 scallion, finely shredded**
- **2 teaspoons sesame oil**
- **½ teaspoon salt**
- **¼ teaspoon ground white pepper**
- **Cilantro sprigs**

Halve the sea scallops so that they are close in size to the shrimp and will cook for the same amount of time. Rinse the tofu and pat dry. Cut it into ½-inch cubes.

Place the cabbage and ginger slices in the bottom of a 2-quart sandpot. Add the chicken broth and reserved mushroom liquid. Imagine the bottom of the sandpot divided into quarters, and place the softened cellophane noodles in one quarter, the shrimp in another, then the scallops, and, finally, the tofu.

Sprinkle the surface with the bamboo shoots, scallion, reserved sliced mushrooms, sesame oil, salt, and pepper. Place cover on the sandpot.

Set the sandpot over low heat for 10 minutes. Gradually increase heat to medium; after 8 to 10 minutes, you should begin to hear the liquid simmering. Uncover and gently stir to make sure everything cooks evenly. Re-cover and cook an additional 2 to 3 minutes, or until seafood is just cooked through. Garnish with cilantro sprigs. Bring the pot to the table and serve immediately.

Serves 4 to 6 as part of a multicourse meal.

Sandpot Braised Lamb

This is an excellent dish for the winter when the Chinese believe that lamb, the most warming meat, paired with ginger (another warming food) invigorates the body and soul. Gingko nuts, also a winter food, are said to promote digestion. Lamb neck bones are meaty with almost no fat, and the bones give this braise a rich flavor. This recipe also requires a sandpot (see Seafood Sandpot, page 60, for sandpot information).

Stick dried bean curd (*foo jook*), also known as dehydrated bean curd or dried bean thread, comes in big plastic packages. The bean curd is ivory colored, about twelve inches long, and shaped like giant horseshoes. Choose bean curd that is slightly translucent.

4 Chinese dried mushrooms

⅔ cup unshelled gingko nuts (*bock guo*)

2 teaspoons vegetable oil

6 slices ginger

2 large cloves garlic, smashed and peeled

2 pounds lamb neck bones

2 sticks dried bean curd (*foo jook*)

2 fresh water chestnuts

3 tablespoons oyster flavored sauce

Cilantro sprigs

In a medium bowl, soak the mushrooms in ¼ cup cold water for 30 minutes, or until softened. Drain and squeeze dry, reserving soaking liquid. Cut off and discard the stems and quarter the caps.

Meanwhile, crack the gingko nuts lightly with a hammer, tapping on the opening and removing the shells. In a small saucepan, bring about 1 cup water to a boil over high heat. Blanch the shelled gingko nuts for about 1 minute. Drain, rinse under cold water, and remove skins.

Heat a 14-inch flat-bottomed wok or skillet over high heat until hot but not smoking. Add the oil, ginger, and garlic, and stir-fry 10 seconds. Add the lamb bones, spreading them in the wok. Cook, undisturbed, 1 to 2 minutes, letting the lamb begin to brown. Then, using a metal spatula, stir-fry 1 to 2 minutes, or until the lamb is browned on all sides but not cooked through. Remove the wok from the heat.

Place the lamb, ginger, and garlic in a 3½-quart sandpot with 2 cups cold water. Place the cover on the sandpot. Set the sandpot over low heat for 10 minutes, gradually increasing the heat to medium; after 8 to 10 minutes, you should begin to hear the liquid simmering. Uncover, and gently stir to make sure everything cooks evenly. Re-cover, reduce heat to medium-low, and simmer 40 minutes.

In a 1½-quart saucepan, bring 3 cups cold water to a boil over high heat. Break bean curd sticks into 2-inch pieces and add to boiling water. Cook, turning the pieces, 1 to 2 minutes, or until almost ivory-colored and softened. Drain and rinse under cold water.

Peel the water chestnuts with a paring knife and then cut them into ½-inch-thick slices.

After the lamb has simmered 40 minutes, uncover and stir. Skim any surface fat and discard. Add the blanched gingko nuts, mushrooms, reserved mushroom soaking liquid, drained bean curd, and water chestnuts, and return to a boil over medium heat. Cover, reduce heat to low, and simmer 40 more minutes, or until the lamb is tender. Stir in the oyster sauce. Garnish with cilantro sprigs. Bring the pot to the table and serve immediately.

Serves 4 to 6 as part of a multicourse meal.

Chestnuts and Mushrooms Braised with Chicken

This is a wonderful recipe to cook in the autumn when chestnuts are in season. The combination of chicken, chestnuts, and mushrooms is uniquely rich and savory. When the chestnut season ends (all too soon), I make this sumptuous dish with dried chestnuts, which are impressively delicious, unlike the canned or jarred chestnuts that so often are tasteless. However, since the fresh chestnut season is so short, I have written the recipe for dried chestnuts. If using fresh chestnuts, use ½ pound and follow the instructions for Mama's Rice Stuffing (page 186). Drain the chestnuts, reserving about ¾ cup of their cooking liquid. Then shell the chestnuts and remove the thin inner skin.

As with many chicken recipes, the traditional way of preparing the chicken is to chop it into bite-sized pieces with a meat cleaver. However, you can simply disjoint it into serving pieces and increase the cooking time until the chicken is just cooked through.

¾ cup dried chestnuts, about 4 ounces

8 Chinese dried mushrooms

2 pounds mixed chicken parts, on the bone

I tablespoon Shao Hsing rice cooking wine

I tablespoon vegetable oil

I tablespoon thin soy sauce

I tablespoon cornstarch

I teaspoon sesame oil

½ teaspoon dark brown sugar

½ teaspoon salt

¼ teaspoon ground white pepper

4 slices ginger

Cilantro sprigs

Rinse the chestnuts in several changes of cold water. Drain, completely cover in cold water, and soak for 3 hours, or until soft. Discard soaking water and, using a paring knife, remove any visible skin from the chestnuts. In a medium saucepan, bring 1 cup water to a boil over high heat. Add the chestnuts, cover, reduce heat to low, and simmer 40 to 50 minutes, or until the chestnuts are just tender. Set them aside in their cooking water.

In a medium bowl, soak the mushrooms in ½ cup cold water for 30 minutes, or until softened. Drain and squeeze dry, reserving the soaking liquid. Cut off and discard the stems and halve the caps.

Using a meat cleaver, chop the chicken through the bone into 2-inch bite-sized pieces (or disjoint the chicken). Rinse under cold water and pat dry with paper towels. Place the chicken in a shallow bowl. Add the rice wine, vegetable oil, soy sauce, cornstarch, sesame oil, brown sugar, salt, and pepper, and stir to combine.

Heat a 14-inch skillet over high heat until hot but not smoking. Add the ginger to the dry wok, and stir-fry 20 seconds. Using a slotted spoon, remove the chicken from the marinade, reserving the marinade (there will only be about 1 tablespoon).

Carefully add the chicken skin-side down, spreading it in the skillet. Cook, undisturbed, 3 to 4 minutes, letting it brown. Then, using a metal spatula, turn the chicken and pan-fry 3 to 4 minutes, or until browned on all sides but not cooked through. Remove the skillet from the heat and pour off any excess fat.

Return the skillet to high heat and add the mushrooms, reserved mushroom liquid, the chicken marinade, and the chestnuts and their cooking liquid. Bring to a boil over high heat. Cover, reduce heat to low, and simmer 15 minutes. Turn off the heat, and let the pot sit, covered, for 10 minutes without removing the lid. Garnish with cilantro sprigs. Serve immediately.

Serves 4 to 6 as part of a multicourse meal.

Sook Mai Gai Yong Tong

粟
米
鷄
蓉
湯

Chicken and Corn Soup

This recipe reflects a classic fusion of Eastern and Western ingredients. There was a time, in the 1950s and '60s, when American canned foods were exotic fare for the Chinese people in Hong Kong. This soup became popular, and among those who cook it best in my family is my Auntie Ivy.

4 ounces skinless, boneless chicken breast

2 teaspoons thin soy sauce

¼ teaspoon ground white pepper

3 teaspoons cornstarch

1 tablespoon vegetable oil

One 14¾-ounce can cream-style corn

½ teaspoon salt

1 large egg, beaten

Cut the chicken into ¼-inch dice. With a cleaver or chef's knife, chop until chicken is finely minced. In a small bowl, combine the chicken, soy sauce, pepper, and 1 teaspoon cornstarch.

Heat a 1½-quart saucepan over high heat until hot but not smoking. Add the vegetable oil and chicken, and cook, stirring, 10 seconds. Add the corn, 2 cups cold water, and salt, and bring to a boil over high heat.

In a small bowl, combine the remaining 2 teaspoons cornstarch and 2 tablespoons cold water. When soup comes to a boil, stir in the cornstarch mixture and cook, stirring, 1 minute, or until thickened. Remove from heat and quickly stir in beaten egg. Serve immediately.

Serves 4 to 6 as part of a multicourse meal.

Seafood Noodle Soup

Noodles and broth evoked so many memories of comfort food when I was growing up. When we were sick, Baba used to come home and make us a simple meal of broth and broad rice noodles similar to this. The following soup is my favorite quick meal to grab in a noodle shop in Chinatown when I'm in a rush, but it never compares to the homemade version. If the seafood is uncompromisingly fresh, the flavors will be pure and clear tasting. (See Beef Chow Fun, page 31, for broad rice noodle information.)

4 cups mung bean sprouts, about 8 ounces

1 small squid, about 1½ ounces

1 tablespoon vegetable oil

1 tablespoon finely minced garlic

1 pound fresh broad rice noodles (*haw fun*)

1 quart Homemade Chicken Broth (page 234)

8 ounces small shrimp, shelled and deveined

4 ounces sea scallops, halved

¼ cup cilantro sprigs

2 scallions, finely chopped

Wash the bean sprouts in several changes of cold water and drain thoroughly in a colander. Cut off and reserve the tentacles attached to the squid head. Remove the internal cartilage and head from squid body and discard. Peel off the purple membrane. Wash squid in several changes of cold water and thoroughly drain in a colander. Cut body in half lengthwise. Using a very sharp knife, lightly score the inside of the body in a crisscross pattern. Cut squid into 1-inch pieces.

Heat a small skillet over medium-high heat until hot but not smoking. Add oil and garlic and cook, stirring, about 1 minute, just until garlic is golden brown. Watch carefully to prevent the garlic from burning. Remove from heat.

Leaving the noodles as a slab, cut noodles crosswise into ¾-inch-wide strips. In a 3-quart saucepan, bring 1 quart water to a boil. Add the noodles, separating them, and cook 30 seconds to 1 minute, or until just softened and heated through. Drain well and divide noodles among 4 large soup bowls.

In a 1½-quart saucepan, bring broth to a boil over high heat. Add bean sprouts and return to a boil over high heat. Add the squid, shrimp, and scallops, and cook 1 to 2 minutes, or until seafood is just cooked through. Divide the broth, bean sprouts, and seafood among the soup bowls. Garnish with sautéed garlic, cilantro, and scallions. Serve immediately.

Serves 4 as a typical lunch meal.

Clear Soup Noodles

Growing up we often had this for lunch on weekends. Most Chinese families have rice vermicelli on hand as a staple pantry ingredient. These are the same dried noodles used for Singapore Rice Noodles (page 32), but because the noodles are cooked in liquid and not stir-fried, they do not need to be soaked first. Depending on my parents' mood we would have Soy Sauce Chicken (page 174), Salt Roasted Chicken (page 173), or White Cut Chicken (page 110) with the noodles. Napa cabbage and snow peas could also be used instead of the bok choy. The success of this soup depends on a good homemade broth.

8 ounces bok choy

8 ounces Soy Sauce Chicken, store-bought or homemade (page 174)

2 teaspoons sesame oil

8 teaspoons thin soy sauce

1 quart Homemade Chicken Broth (page 234)

8 ounces rice vermicelli (*mai fun*)

Cilantro sprigs

Separate the bok choy into stalks. Wash bok choy in several changes of cold water and allow to thoroughly drain in a colander. Trim ¼ inch from the bottom of each stalk and cut into 2-inch-long pieces.

With a meat cleaver, chop the chicken through the bone into bite-sized pieces. Pour ½ teaspoon sesame oil and 2 teaspoons soy sauce into each of 4 large soup bowls.

In a 2-quart saucepan, bring the chicken broth to a boil over high heat. Add the bok choy and noodles and return to a boil. Reduce heat to medium and cook 2 to 3 minutes, or until the noodles are tender and the bok choy is bright green and tender.

Divide the noodles and bok choy among the soup bowls and toss with the soy sauce and sesame oil. Top with the broth, chicken, and cilantro. Serve immediately.

Serves 4 as a typical lunch meal.

Fuzzy Melon Soup

This and the following four (pages 69 to 72) recipes are all typical weeknight soups that my parents would cook for us. We had a soup at every evening meal, but unlike many of the soups in the "Achieving Yin-Yang Harmony" section, which generally require three to four hours of simmering, not one of these requires more than fifteen minutes of cooking time. These simpler soups rely on the use of Homemade Chicken Broth (page 234) and although nourishing are not thought to be as balancing or cleansing as the soups in the yin-yang section. The pork is marinated in cornstarch and then rinsed before being tossed in oil. This is a typical home-style technique which is said to make the pork silky and tender. For information on fuzzy melon, see Braised Fuzzy Melon with Scallops (page 99).

4 Chinese dried mushrooms

2 ounces pork butt

1¼ teaspoons cornstarch

8 ounces fuzzy melon (zeet qwa)

3 cups Homemade Chicken Broth (page 234)

¼ teaspoon vegetable oil

¼ cup frozen peas, thawed

1 large egg, beaten

½ teaspoon sesame oil

½ teaspoon salt

In a medium bowl, soak the mushrooms in ¼ cup cold water for 30 minutes, or until softened. Drain and squeeze dry, reserving soaking liquid. Cut off and discard the stems and thinly slice the caps.

Julienne the pork and place in a small bowl. Sprinkle with cornstarch and 1 tablespoon cold water and stir to combine.

Peel the fuzzy melon and cut it into 1-inch-long pieces. Cut each piece into ¼-inch-thick by 1-inch-wide slices.

In a 1½-quart saucepan, bring the chicken broth to a boil. Rinse the pork in several changes of cold water. Drain and toss the pork in vegetable oil. Add the fuzzy melon, pork, mushrooms, and reserved mushroom liquid to the boiling broth and return to a boil. Cover, reduce to medium-low, and cook 5 minutes. Uncover, increase heat to high, add peas, and return to a boil. Stir in the beaten egg, sesame oil, and salt, and remove from heat. Serve immediately.

Serves 4 to 6 as part of a multicourse meal.

Cabbage Noodle Soup

When I first went to China, I was astounded by the piles and piles of Napa cabbage I saw in the food markets and along the roadsides, especially in Beijing. Cabbage is abundant and inexpensive in China and is used in dumplings, stir-fries, and in home-cooked soups. Unlike Western-style cabbage, Napa cabbage has a gentle, pleasing flavor.

8 Chinese dried mushrooms

One 1.7 ounce package cellophane noodles

6 large leaves Napa cabbage, about 12 ounces

2 squares firm tofu, about 6 ounces, rinsed

2 teaspoons vegetable oil

1 quart Homemade Chicken Broth (page 234)

½ teaspoon sesame oil

Salt to taste

1 scallion, finely minced

In a bowl, soak the mushrooms in ½ cup cold water for 30 minutes, or until softened. Drain and squeeze dry, reserving soaking liquid. Cut off and discard stems and slice the caps into fine shreds. In a medium bowl, cover the cellophane noodles in cold water and soak about 15 minutes, or until softened. Drain and set aside.

Wash the cabbage leaves in several changes of cold water and drain thoroughly in a colander until dry to the touch. Trim ¼ inch from stem end of cabbage leaves and discard. Stack 2 to 3 cabbage leaves at a time and cut crosswise into ¼-inch-wide shreds. Cut the tofu into ½-inch cubes.

Heat a 2-quart saucepan over high heat until hot but not smoking. Add the vegetable oil and cabbage, and stir-fry 2 minutes, or until cabbage is just limp. Add the chicken broth and bring to a boil over high heat. Reduce to low, cover, and simmer 10 minutes. Return the broth to a boil over high heat and add the mushrooms and their reserved liquid, drained cellophane noodles, and tofu. Reduce heat to low, cover, and simmer 5 minutes. Stir in sesame oil and season to taste with salt if necessary. Garnish with scallion. Serve immediately.

Serves 4 to 6 as part of a multicourse meal.

Family-Style Winter Melon Soup

Winter melon, *doong qwa,* is considered nutritious and extremely beneficial to the body—there are four versions of winter melon soup in this book. This one is the fastest cooking and is commonly prepared for weekday meals; the second is the elaborate Fancy Winter Melon Soup (page 143) reserved for special occasions; and the last two—Yen Yen's Winter Melon Soup (page 219) and Herbal Winter Melon Soup (page 220)—are the most cleansing and considered the purest in their therapeutic value. For those unaccustomed to winter melon, this soup is the most compatible version for Westerners.

Winter melon is similar in appearance to watermelon, but it is a vegetable, not a fruit. It is sold in Chinese produce markets whole or in wedges. The cut melon should have a clean, fresh smell. The best winter melons have a coating of white powder on the rind that must be scrubbed off and rinsed with water before cooking. For therapeutic recipes, the rind, seeds, and flesh can be cooked (Herbal Winter Melon Soup), but for this recipe only the flesh is used.

I small wedge winter melon, about I pound

2 fresh water chestnuts

I square firm tofu, rinsed

¼ cup canned whole bamboo shoots, rinsed

I quart Homemade Chicken Broth (page 234)

½ cup frozen peas, thawed

Wash the winter melon and scrub off the white powder with a vegetable brush. Using a cook's knife, remove the rind from the winter melon. Discard seeds and pulp. Cut into ½-inch cubes. Peel the water chestnuts with a paring knife and dice into ½-inch pieces. Cut the tofu into ½-inch cubes. Cut bamboo shoots into ½-inch cubes.

In a 2½-quart saucepan, bring the chicken broth to a boil over high heat. Add the winter melon and water chestnuts, and return to a boil. Cover, reduce heat to medium-low, and simmer 10 minutes, or until the winter melon is translucent and tender when pierced with a knife. Increase heat to high and return soup to a rolling boil. Add the tofu, peas, and bamboo shoots, and cook 1 to 2 minutes, or until heated through. Serve immediately.

Serves 4 to 6 as part of a multicourse meal.

酸
辣
湯

Hot-and-Sour Soup

Too often, the Hot-and-Sour Soup served in restaurants is made with canned chicken broth, bamboo shoots, and too much goopy cornstarch. This is a far cry from the flavors of a homemade soup, which should have a good balance of heat, sharpness, and sweetness. Made correctly, it is a perfect example of a soup that satisfies the principles of yin and yang, a marriage of opposite flavors and textures. If the soup is not hot enough for your taste, add more white pepper. Chinese cooks prefer white pepper to black pepper, as it has not only heat but fragrance.

¼ cup cloud ears (*wun yee*)

¼ cup lily buds (*gum tzum*)

I square firm tofu, rinsed

I quart Homemade Chicken Broth (page 234)

I ounce pork butt, slivered, about ¼ cup

⅓ cup canned shredded bamboo shoots, rinsed

2 tablespoons cornstarch

2 tablespoons cider vinegar

I large egg, beaten

¼ cup finely minced scallions

¾ teaspoon sugar

½ teaspoon ground white pepper

Place the cloud ears and lily buds in separate bowls. Pour about ½ cup cold water over each and soak for about 30 minutes to soften. When softened, drain each ingredients, discarding all water. Remove any hard spots from the cloud ears and cut in half. Remove the hard end from the lily buds and tie them into knots. Cut the tofu into ½-inch cubes.

In a 2-quart saucepan, bring chicken broth to a boil over high heat. Add the cloud ears, lily buds, tofu, pork, and bamboo shoots, and return to a boil. In a small bowl, combine cornstarch, vinegar, and 1 tablespoon water. When soup returns to a rolling boil, stir in cornstarch mixture, stirring constantly until thickened, 1 to 2 minutes. Remove from heat and stir in egg, scallions, sugar, and pepper. Serve immediately.

Serves 4 to 6 as part of a multicourse meal.

Seaweed Tofu Soup

The Chinese believe seaweed, or *zee choy* as it is called in Cantonese, is beneficial for regulating the thyroid. Seaweed is sold in many different forms, but for this recipe it is the Japanese seaweed, *nori,* which comes in sheets, that is best. *Nori* is also known as *purple seaweed* or *laver.* It can simply be rinsed in cold water without cleaning before it is cooked. Seaweed from China and Canada, on the other hand, often needs to be soaked in cold water for at least an hour and then rinsed in several changes of water; they each have lots of sand, and both are impossible to thoroughly clean.

Do not tear or break up the *nori* before adding it to the soup; as it cooks it will break apart naturally. One package of *nori* generally holds ten folded sheets. Unfortunately, most packages do not state the weight or how many sheets of seaweed you'll find in the package.

8 ounces silken tofu

1 quart Homemade Chicken Broth (page 234)

4 sheets Japanese seaweed (*nori*)

1 large egg, beaten

Cut the tofu into scant ½-inch cubes.

In a 2-quart saucepan, bring the chicken broth to a boil over high heat.

Rinse the seaweed in cold water. Add seaweed to boiling broth and return to a boil. Add the tofu and return to a boil. Remove from heat and stir in beaten egg. Serve immediately.

Serves 4 to 6 as part of a multicourse meal.

GOING TO MARKET WITH MAMA

Grandmother (Popo) Fung Tong Lai Lan, Mama, Uncle Sam, Auntie Katheryn, and Uncle Norman (with aviator glasses) in the park. Shanghai, China, circa 1938.

MAMA IS AN EXPERT IN THE ART OF selecting (*gan*). It embarrasses Mama when I say this because she doesn't perceive her expertise as anything special. One of my earliest memories involves going to market with Mama and watching her choose her produce. As with many Chinese housewives, every ingredient Mama has ever bought has been carefully chosen for beauty (*gan langde*). Whether it was several pounds of snow peas or a few delicate papayas, each item was individually examined for fragrance, ripeness, and blemishes. If I ever brought home produce chosen without careful examination, her dismay upon discovering something that was blemished would be palpable.

Partially from my parents' training and partially because I am a food stylist, I, too, am very particular when it comes to fresh produce. It baffles my husband, Michael, that I need to look at every fruit and vegetable stand along Canal and Mulberry Streets before I will make my selection. It upsets me to buy mangoes from one stand and then to see riper, more beautiful mangoes two stores down the block. My own perfectionism notwithstanding, it still astounds me how Mama will willingly walk to three or four markets until she finds bean sprouts that meet with her approval—plump, short, and never limp.

As finicky as I think I am, Mama has an altogether higher standard of excellence. She is totally energized by the adventure of shopping for produce. Despite the fact that I am nearly thirty years her junior, I often cannot keep pace with her as she whips in and out of markets on Stockton or Clement Streets, as if on a treasure hunt. In every store she seems to know who the owner is, greeting him, complimenting him on his outstanding produce, while often politely asking him to check his storeroom for specialty items. Every vegetable has criteria that must be met and an equally serious list of what to avoid. Regardless of my admiration of Mama's expertise, she, too, will occasionally buy produce that disappoints her. Perplexed, she will confer with friends, seeking tips and advice, ever ardent to master the art of produce shopping.

We have a family friend, Chen Mei, who was raised on a farm in China and who almost unconsciously will pinch and squeeze Chinese turnips and taro root until she finds the perfect vegetable. She is so proficient at choosing produce that Mama often instructs me to learn from Chen Mei. For example, in selecting Chinese broccoli, she advises that the bunch should never have open flowers. Buds are acceptable, although Chen Mei warns me that sometimes the buds have insects hidden inside, which explains why some people wash broccoli in salt water, hoping to force the insects out. Some Hong Kong food connoisseurs eat only the stalks to avoid this danger. (There is also a superstition that if you eat broccoli flowers, you will become deaf.) When choosing the best fuzzy melon (*zeet qwa*), Chen Mei insists it be bright green, stubby, fat, and have tiny hairs that lightly prick you. If the melon is hairless, it's too old and not worth cooking. On the other hand, the most coveted winter melon (*doong qwa*) must be as old as possible to be worthy of selection. The outside of the melon must be well covered with white powder, and the rind must be very hard, all good signs of proper maturity. My Auntie Katheryn reminisces that winter melon rind in China, even after hours of cooking, would seem as though it was as hard as tin. "Sadly, American winter melon rind is so soft," she says, but "at least choose the end pieces, which are preferable to the center portion." (Winter melon is sold in pieces, much like watermelon.)

Years ago Mama and Auntie Katheryn used to commiserate on how inferior American produce was compared to Chinese produce. "Everything is grown bigger but is less flavorful." When I was a child, they spoke of fruits and vegetables from China as though they were from a fairy tale. All fruits had a crispness (*choy hui*) that the Chinese prize—from plums and peaches to Asian pears which, unlike many American varieties, are soft and without fragrance. In China, most fruits and vegetables are picked before dawn and delivered to the markets early in the morning. Mama and Auntie Katheryn tasted that rare sweetness and crispness of just-harvested produce. Today, the quality of Asian produce available in America has improved tremendously because of the influx of Asian farmers. The variety and quality of produce is a far cry from what was available when we were growing up. In addition, the more exotic vegetables and fruits of China and Thailand, like lotus root, fresh lichees, and durian, are flown in when in season.

Sometimes as we race through the open-air markets, Mama will spot some farm-fresh produce, like bitter melons, that have just been brought out to be sold, and she will linger in front of the stand wanting to buy. I remind her we still have three in the refrigerator, which she is fully aware of, but flawless produce is hard for her to resist. Reluctantly she walks away explaining to me how perfect those bitter melons were—light colored, fat, yet tapered like the shape of a rat, with the proper thick ridges. "Not," she says, "like the flavorless, skinny, dark green, bitter melons." Still, as particular as she is, she will not shop for anything she feels inexperienced at choosing. Fish and meat are Baba's domain and she will not risk wasting her time buying them. There are also certain vegetables she is less familiar with, like taro root, which she is reluctant to purchase.

I remember in the sixties, when supermarkets first began to wrap produce in cellophane, Mama would examine the sealed packages, frustrated that she couldn't touch the fruit to see for herself if the vegetable was indeed fine. It would annoy and embarrass my brother and me to hear Mama ask the clerk if the oranges were sweet. We'd ask Mama if she really thought he'd say no. Then she would say, "If he says yes and they're not sweet, I won't trust him again."

Although my parents will shop in a supermarket, their preference is to go to Chinatown. There, the demand for high quality and fresh ingredients naturally creates a market with high turnover. I believe this high standard manifests itself in the more nutrient-rich foods the Chinese eat. Compare supermarket produce, which has often sat for days in a warehouse, with produce you see in Chinatown, where just-delivered boxes are sometimes eagerly emptied by customers on the street. Even at the butcher shop, Baba points out to me the difference in freshness between supermarket meat and the kind sold in a Chinese butcher shop. When we buy a piece of pork butt (*moy tui*), he has me touch the package and take note that the pork is not cold to the touch. "Just slaughtered," he says to me with a wink (*sung seen tong zaw*), and as we walk out of the shop I notice the truck parked in front delivering the slaughtered pigs.

Baba and Mama shop daily, which is possible for them to do because they are retired. However, even when they worked, they would never shop for produce only once a week or stock up on frozen or canned fruits or vegetables. Freshness is such an important requirement in Chinese cooking that the extra effort to shop more frequently is accepted willingly. They appreciate the difference you can taste when food is *sung seen* (fresh).

In America, it is considered the height of luxury to call in an order to a fine market for home delivery. However, for the Chinese, allowing someone else to put produce into your bag, to do your selecting, would be unthinkable. It is impossible to assume that a stranger would take the proper care in selecting your food. The freshness and ripeness of the food you eat is so critical that you must personally oversee it if you are to be responsible to yourself and for your family's well-being. Lin Yu Tang, the great Chinese philosopher, wrote in *The Importance of Living,* "For me, the philosophy of food seems to boil down to three things: freshness, flavor and texture. The best cook in the world cannot make a savory dish unless he has fresh things to cook with, and any cook can tell you that half the art of cooking lies in buying."★

To my mother *and* my father and, indeed, most Chinese people, selecting farm-fresh produce brings them pure delight and satisfaction. They literally glow, and beam, to bring home choice, blemish-free produce. And this glee lasts through every mouthful of the delectable dishes they prepare.

★Lin Yu Tang, *The Importance of Living* (New York: William Morrow and Co., 1937), p. 252.

Shrimp with Spinach and Tofu

San Francisco has an Indian summer for at least one week every year, when the temperatures can reach eighty or ninety degrees. It was then that Mama would make us Shrimp with Spinach and Tofu, a dish she remembers eating in Shanghai in the summer, when the weather was unbearably hot. We always ate it chilled, and the fragrance of the sesame oil suits the cooling and re-freshing taste of the spinach and tofu. Squeeze as much water as you can from the cooked spinach or the excess water will dilute the flavors.

2 squares firm tofu, about 6 ounces

1 ½ pounds spinach, preferably young

2 tablespoons small Chinese dried shrimp, rinsed

1 tablespoon sesame oil

½ teaspoon salt

In a 1½-quart saucepan, bring 2 cups water to a boil over high heat. Add the tofu and return to a boil. With a slotted spoon, remove the tofu and place on a rack to cool.

Remove all stems from the spinach. Wash spinach in several changes of cold water and drain thoroughly in a colander. Return water to a boil over high heat, and add the spinach. Cook until it is just limp, about 30 seconds. Drain and rinse under cold water.

Squeeze the spinach to remove excess water and form into a tight ball. Chop the spinach by cutting the ball into ¼-inch slices. Place the spinach in a large bowl.

Cut the tofu into ⅛-inch dice. Finely chop the shrimp. Add the sesame oil, salt, tofu, and shrimp to the spinach, and toss to combine. Chill, if desired, or serve at room temperature.

Serves 4 to 6 as part of a multicourse meal.

Braised Mushrooms

Chinese dried mushrooms, also called *black, winter mushrooms,* or *shiitake,* as they are known in Japan, can vary broadly in quality and price (see Glossary, page 249). For everyday cooking I generally use inexpensive ones, which have thin brown caps and a soaking time of only about thirty minutes. However, for this dish, since the mushrooms are the featured ingredient, ideally one should use high-quality mushrooms, such as *fa qwoo;* this name will not appear on the package in English. These can easily cost over fifty dollars a pound. The color of the caps is not as black as that of the less expensive variety, and they are much thicker in both appearance and texture. They require three to four hours to soak, and their flavor is meatier and more intense. People who know mushrooms can judge their quality just by looking at the caps. *Fa qwoo* caps have deep cracks and are said to resemble flowers. In presenting this dish, always place the caps on the platter stem-side down. Cooking *fa qwoo* is reserved for special occasions.

4 Chinese dried oysters

20 medium Chinese dried mushrooms, preferably *fa qwoo,* about 8 ounces

1/2 teaspoon sugar

1 tablespoon vegetable oil

2 slices ginger

2 tablespoons oyster flavored sauce

8 slices (2 by 1 by 1/4 inch) Smithfield ham

Cilantro sprigs, optional

Rinse the oysters in cold water. In a small bowl, soak the oysters in ½ cup cold water for 3 to 4 hours, or until soft. Drain and squeeze dry, reserving the soaking liquid.

In a medium bowl, soak the mushrooms in 1⅓ cups cold water and sugar for 3 to 4 hours, or until softened (less time if inexpensive mushrooms are used). Drain and squeeze dry, reserving the soaking liquid. Cut off and discard stems, leaving the caps whole.

Heat a 14-inch flat-bottomed wok or skillet over high heat until hot but not smoking. Add the oil, ginger, oysters, and mushrooms, and stir-fry 1 minute. Add the oyster sauce, reduce heat to medium, and cook 1 minute. Add the reserved mushroom and oyster liquids and ham slices, and bring to a boil over medium heat. Cover, reduce heat to low, and simmer 30 minutes. Check the saucepan occasionally to make sure there is just enough liquid to simmer the mushrooms. Add a little water if necessary. Cook until only about 2 tablespoons of liquid is left in the pan and the mushrooms are tender. Discard the oysters. Place the mushroom caps and sauce on a platter and garnish with cilantro sprigs if desired. Serve immediately.

Serves 4 as part of a multicourse meal.

Braised Cabbage and Mushrooms

Napa cabbage, *wong gna bock,* varies in its water content depending on how old it is. Younger cabbage has more water and, therefore, may not need the addition of any liquid as it cooks. Older cabbage is drier and is sweeter in flavor but will need the addition of broth to prevent it from sticking in the wok. Mama recalls that her family would buy ten to twelve heads of cabbage at a time in Shanghai and hang them in their kitchen to allow them to wilt and dry slightly over one to two weeks, to obtain this sweeter flavor. Their household had at least nine people to feed, so it was easy to use up that amount of cabbage in no time.

12 Chinese dried mushrooms

¼ teaspoon sugar

8 large leaves Napa cabbage, about 1 pound

1 teaspoon plus 1 tablespoon vegetable oil

2 slices ginger

¾ cup Homemade Chicken Broth (page 234)

2 tablespoons oyster flavored sauce

½ teaspoon salt

1 tablespoon thin soy sauce

2 teaspoons sesame oil

In a bowl, soak the dried mushrooms and sugar in ¾ cup cold water for 30 minutes, or until softened. Drain and squeeze dry, reserving soaking liquid. Cut off and discard stems and halve the caps.

Wash the cabbage leaves in several changes of cold water and drain thoroughly in a colander until dry to the touch. Trim ¼ inch from stem end of the cabbage leaves and discard. Stack 2 to 3 cabbage leaves at a time and cut crosswise into ¼-inch-wide shreds.

Heat a small saucepan over high heat until hot but not smoking. Add 1 teaspoon of oil and 1 slice of ginger, and stir-fry 30 seconds. Add reconstituted mushroom caps and stir-fry 1 minute. Add the reserved mushroom liquid and ½ cup chicken broth, and bring to a boil. Reduce heat to low, cover, and simmer 25 minutes. Check the saucepan occasionally to make sure there is just enough liquid for the mushrooms to simmer. Stir in oyster sauce.

Meanwhile, heat a 14-inch flat-bottomed wok or skillet over high heat until hot but not smoking. Add the remaining 1 tablespoon oil and ginger slice, and stir-fry 30 seconds. Add the cabbage and stir-fry 1 to 2 minutes, or until vegetable is slightly limp. Stir in the salt, remaining ¼ cup chicken broth, soy sauce, and sesame oil and reduce heat to medium-low, cover, and simmer 5 minutes.

Transfer the cabbage to a platter with pan juices. Pour the mushrooms over the center of the cabbage and serve immediately.

Serves 4 as part of a multicourse meal.

Sprouting Soybeans

Mung bean sprouts (*gna choy*) are available in most supermarkets and are what everyone thinks of when they think of bean sprouts. Soybean sprouts (*dai dul gna choy*) are less common and are an excellent source of protein. If you live near a Chinatown, you'll see them sitting next to the mung bean sprouts. Soybean sprout heads are much larger (about the size of a Great Northern bean), and are also delicious (try Grandfather's Stir-Fried Soybean Sprouts, page 82), as they have a nuttier flavor than mung bean sprouts. Mung beans and soybeans can be sprouted very easily at home. If you live near a Chinatown, it's hard to match the uniform quality of the commercial sprouts you'll find there, but if you don't have access to a Chinatown, or a farmers' market, home sprouts are a good alternative. Do not be tempted to eat the soybean sprouts raw, as they are toxic unless cooked.

The fresher the dried soybeans used for sprouting, the better the quality of your sprouts. Unfortunately, it is impossible to tell the freshness of the beans just by looking at them. Soybeans are available in Chinatowns and in health-food stores. It's best to cover the jar with the special sprouting lid available in most health-food stores. If you use cheesecloth instead, change it daily to keep the sprouts fresh. The moisture from the rinsing helps the beans to sprout and keeps them fresh. Sprouts do best in a dark and damp environment. If the room temperature is over seventy degrees, the sprouts will not do well, so it's difficult to sprout them in the summer.

This method can also be used to sprout mung beans: 1/4 cup of dried green mung beans will produce about 3 cups of sprouts.

1/4 cup dried soybeans

Wash the soybeans in several changes of cold water. Soak the soybeans in cold water to cover overnight. Drain the beans and place them in a clean, wide-mouthed 1-quart jar. Cover with a plastic lid with tiny holes (available in most health-food stores for the express purpose of sprouting), or cover with a double thickness of cheesecloth and secure with a rubber band.

Set the jar on its side and place in a dark cabinet where there is no direct or indirect light. Two times a day (in the morning and evening) for the next 4 to 5 days, unscrew the lid and rinse the beans in cold water and drain them. Place the lid back on, turn the jar upside down to drain well, and set the jar back on its side in the cabinet.

Within 24 hours, you'll see about ¼ inch of the sprouts emerging. In 2 days, they will be about 1½ inches long, and the hulls will start coming off. In 4 to 5 days, the sprouts will be 2 to 3 inches long and the hulls will have separated from the heads. Rinse the sprouts and discard the hulls that float up. The stringy tails of the soybean sprouts can be removed. Store the sprouts in the refrigerator and use within 1 day.

Makes about 4 cups of sprouts, about 10 ounces.

Grandfather's Stir-Fried Soybean Sprouts

This stir-fry is a favorite home-style Cantonese dish that my grandfather particularly relished. It is very labor-intensive to do all the chopping, and as you chop you'll also find that one of the challenges is to keep all of the chopped sprouts from bouncing every which way. The sprouts must be cooked until they release all their water and are so dry that they start to stick to the wok. They will release lots of water at first and some cooks, like my Uncle Herbert, will drain the sprouts to quicken the "drying" process. I would not advise substituting mung bean sprouts for the soybean sprouts; the soybean sprouts are more nutritious, and they're much crunchier and nuttier in flavor. Choose fat, creamy-colored soybean sprouts that are not limp or slimy. This is not a saucy dish, but it is delicious with steamed white rice. (See page 80 for information on soybean sprouts.)

1¼ pounds soybean sprouts, about 8 cups

4 ounces ground pork butt

1 tablespoon cornstarch

2 teaspoons thin soy sauce

1 teaspoon Shao Hsing rice cooking wine

1 teaspoon sesame oil

¾ teaspoon plus 2 tablespoons vegetable oil

½ teaspoon sugar

½ teaspoon salt

¼ teaspoon ground white pepper

1 tablespoon finely shredded ginger

2 tablespoons thinly sliced scallions

Wash the soybean sprouts early in the day in several changes of cold water and drain thoroughly in a colander until dry to the touch. Remove the stringy tails and chop the sprouts into scant ¼-inch pieces. Then set them aside.

Place the pork in a medium bowl. Add the cornstarch, soy sauce, rice wine, sesame oil, ¾ teaspoon vegetable oil, sugar, ¼ teaspoon salt, and pepper, and stir to combine.

Heat a 14-inch flat-bottomed wok or skillet over high heat until hot but not smoking. Add the soybean sprouts to the dry wok and stir-fry 10 to 15 minutes, or until the sprouts are very dry. At first, the sprouts will be simmering from the water they release, but this water must completely evaporate, until the sprouts are dry and begin to stick to the wok. Transfer the sprouts to a plate and clean the wok.

Add the remaining 2 tablespoons vegetable oil and ginger, and stir-fry 10 seconds, or until fragrant. Add the pork and stir-fry 1 to 2 minutes, breaking up the meat. Add the remaining ¼ teaspoon salt and the soybean sprouts, and cook 1 minute, or until the pork is cooked through. Add scallions and remove from heat. Serve immediately.

Serves 4 to 6 as part of a multicourse meal.

Stir-Fried Bean Sprouts and Yellow Chives

Yellow chives, *gul wong*, are sold in small bunches and look like regular chives except that they are flat and pale yellow in color. Often, Chinese grocers will keep them in the back storeroom and you must ask to have them brought out. This combination of bean sprouts and yellow chives is popular in Cantonese cooking because the matching of two pale-colored ingredients is considered pleasing to the eye and palate. To preserve the paleness and delicate taste, only a very small amount of soy sauce is added. In preparing bean sprouts, traditional cooks like to remove both the tail (the thin string at the root end) and head (the bean itself) from each bean sprout. The Cantonese call these trimmed sprouts *gnun gna choy*, or silver sprouts. For this recipe, I remove only the tails, to make it less time consuming for the cook. Wash the bean sprouts early in the day, so they have time to sufficiently drain. If too much water clings to the vegetable when it is stir-fried, the dish will be watery.

8 ounces mung bean sprouts, about 4 cups

4 ounces yellow chives (gul wong)

1 1/2 teaspoons thin soy sauce

1/2 teaspoon salt

1/4 teaspoon sugar

2 tablespoons vegetable oil

1 tablespoon finely shredded ginger

Cilantro sprigs

Early in the day, wash the bean sprouts and yellow chives in several changes of cold water and drain thoroughly in a colander until dry to the touch.

Remove the tail end from the bean sprouts. Cut the yellow chives into 2-inch lengths. In a small bowl, combine the soy sauce, salt, and sugar; set aside.

Heat a 14-inch flat-bottomed wok or skillet over high heat until hot but not smoking. Add the vegetable oil and ginger, and stir-fry 30 seconds. Add the bean sprouts and stir-fry another 30 seconds. Add the yellow chives and stir-fry 1 to 2 minutes, or until the chives are just limp. Swirl in the soy sauce mixture and cook 1 minute, or until the sprouts are cooked but still crisp. Do not overcook. Garnish with cilantro sprigs. Serve immediately.

Serves 4 as part of a multicourse meal.

Lotus Root Stir-Fry

In Buddhist culture, the lotus is a sacred symbol of purity. The root, which grows in mud, emerges clean and pure, unchanged by the mud. My Uncle Sam remembers eating raw, sliced lotus root at the August Moon Festival—a time of year when lotus is plentiful in China. Its crisp texture is delightful whether raw or cooked.

This is one of my Auntie Anna's favorite dishes. She likes it because the combination of crisp lotus root, snow peas, cloud ears, and pickled vegetable is so pleasing. It is especially good if Chinese bacon is available. Fresh lotus root is sold in three connected sections—the larger section is best for stir-fries, the two smaller sections are best for soups (Lotus Root Soup, page 231). Some produce markets precut the lotus root into sections and seal them in Cryovac. I prefer not to buy lotus root that has been wrapped, because it prevents me from checking to see if it has a clean, fresh smell.

Salted turnip is only available in Chinese supermarkets. There are many different kinds of salted turnip, which are not distinguished in English on the label. You'll have to ask for it by its Cantonese name, *teem choy poe*. *Teem choy poe* is available in 7-ounce packages; the slices are 3 to 5 inches long, ½ inch wide, and khaki colored.

¼ cup cloud ears (*wun yee*)

¼ cup lily buds (*gum tzum*)

7 pieces salted turnip (*teem choy poe*), about 2 ounces

1 large section lotus root, about 6 ounces

3 ounces Chinese Bacon, store-bought or homemade (page 182)

1½ teaspoons Shao Hsing rice cooking wine

1 teaspoon thin soy sauce

¾ teaspoon sesame oil

Place the cloud ears and lily buds in separate bowls. Pour about ½ cup cold water over each ingredient and soak for about 30 minutes to soften. When softened, drain and discard the water. Remove the hard spots from the cloud ears, and remove the hard end from the lily buds, tying each lily bud into a knot.

Meanwhile, soak the salted turnip in cold water to cover for 30 minutes. Drain. Cut each piece in half crosswise, then thinly cut lengthwise into fine shreds and set aside.

Using a vegetable peeler, peel the lotus root, removing the rootlike strands, and rinse under cold water. Cut the lotus root in half lengthwise and rinse again to remove any mud lodged in the root. Slice the lotus root into ¼-inch-thick half moons. Rinse again in case there is any mud, and set aside to drain well.

- ¾ teaspoon sugar
- ¼ teaspoon salt
- ¼ teaspoon ground white pepper
- 1 tablespoon vegetable oil
- 4 thin slices ginger
- 8 ounces snow peas, strings removed

Remove the hard rind from the Chinese bacon, and the thick piece of fat attached to the rind, and discard. Cut the bacon crosswise into very thin slices.

In a small bowl combine 3 tablespoons cold water, rice wine, soy sauce, sesame oil, sugar, salt, and pepper.

Heat a 14-inch flat-bottomed wok or skillet over high heat until hot but not smoking. Add the vegetable oil and ginger, and stir-fry 10 seconds. Add the Chinese bacon and stir-fry 45 seconds. Add the lotus root and stir-fry 1 minute. Add the snow peas, cloud ears, lily buds, and turnip, and stir-fry another minute. Swirl in the rice wine mixture and stir-fry 2 to 3 minutes, or until the lotus root is tender but still crisp, and the snow peas are bright green. Serve immediately.

Serves 4 to 6 as part of a multicourse meal.

Gul Choy Chow Dan

韭菜炒蛋

Stir-Fried Egg and Chinese Chives

There are three different kinds of Chinese chives: Chinese chives, yellow chives, and flowering garlic chives. This recipe uses Chinese chives (*gul choy*), which are green and look similar to Western chives, except that they are flat. They are said to *san hoot,* or remove old blood from your system.

- 1 large bunch Chinese chives, about 4 ounces
- 4 large egg whites, beaten
- 2 teaspoons thin soy sauce
- 1 teaspoon sesame oil
- ½ teaspoon salt
- ¼ teaspoon ground white pepper
- 3 tablespoons vegetable oil

Wash the Chinese chives in several changes of cold water and drain thoroughly in a colander until dry to the touch. Cut the chives into ½-inch pieces.

Place the chives in a medium bowl. Add the egg whites, soy sauce, sesame oil, salt, and pepper, and stir to combine.

Heat a 14-inch flat-bottomed wok or skillet over high heat until hot but not smoking. Add the vegetable oil and egg mixture, and stir-fry 1 minute. Reduce heat to medium and cook another 1 to 2 minutes, or until eggs are set but not dry. Serve immediately.

Serves 4 as part of a multicourse meal.

Stir-Fried Five Spice Tofu and Vegetables

Stir-fries can be time consuming—finely shredding vegetables, soaking special ingredients, and measuring all the seasonings. But, in a stir-fry such as this, all the work is worth it when you taste the results. The tremendous array of vegetables and seasonings creates a range of textures, tastes, fragrances, and colors.

Five spice tofu is found in the refrigerator case of most Asian grocery stores. It is much firmer than even extra-firm tofu, because all the excess water has been pressed out. The tofu is chocolate-colored and is sold in 2-inch squares or 2-by-3½-inch blocks that are ½ to 1 inch thick. The dark color is the result of cooking the tofu with five spice seasoning, which both flavors and colors the tofu. See Lotus Root Stir-Fry (page 84) for information on *teem choy poe*, or salted turnip.

4 Chinese dried mushrooms

2 ounces salted turnip (*teem choy poe*)

3 pieces five spice tofu (*nmm heung dul foo gawn*), about 4 ounces

1 carrot

1 celery stalk

3 fresh water chestnuts

1 red bell pepper

1 yellow bell pepper

1 tablespoon thin soy sauce

1½ teaspoons Shao Hsing rice cooking wine

1 teaspoon sesame oil

¼ teaspoon sugar

¼ teaspoon ground white pepper

¼ teaspoon salt

4 tablespoons vegetable oil

2 scallions, cut into 2-inch sections

Cilantro sprigs

In a medium bowl, soak the mushrooms in ¼ cup cold water for 30 minutes, or until softened. Drain and squeeze dry (reserve the soaking liquid for use in soups). Cut off and discard the stems and thinly slice the caps. In a small bowl, soak the salted turnip in 1 cup cold water for 30 minutes, or until vegetable is only mildly salty. Rinse the salted turnip and pat dry. Cut it into fine shreds to make about ½ cup. Discard the water.

Cut the tofu, carrot, and celery into julienne strips. Peel the water chestnuts with a paring knife and then thinly slice. Cut the red and yellow peppers into thin slivers. In a small bowl, combine the soy sauce, rice wine, sesame oil, sugar, white pepper, and ⅛ teaspoon salt. Set aside.

Heat a 14-inch flat-bottomed wok or skillet over high heat until hot but not smoking. Add 2 tablespoons vegetable oil and the tofu, spreading it in the wok. Sprinkle on the remaining ⅛ teaspoon salt, reduce the temperature to medium, and cook undisturbed 1 to 2 minutes, letting the tofu begin to brown. Then, using a metal spatula, carefully turn the tofu and continue cooking undisturbed 3 to 4 minutes, or until the tofu is lightly browned. Transfer to a plate and set aside.

Increase the heat to high and add 1 tablespoon vegetable oil and the julienned carrot to the wok; stir-fry 1 minute. Add the remaining 1 tablespoon oil, mushrooms, salted turnip, celery, water chestnuts, peppers, and scallions, and stir-fry 1 minute. Swirl in the reserved soy sauce mixture and tofu, and stir-fry 2 to 3 minutes, or until the vegetables are crisp and tender. Garnish with cilantro sprigs. Serve immediately.

Serves 4 to 6 as part of a multicourse meal.

炒芥蘭 *Chow Gai Lan*

Stir-Fried Chinese Broccoli

Chinese broccoli (*gai lan*) looks like a cross between basic supermarket broccoli and the Italian broccoli rabe. The vegetable tastes more like broccoli rabe, with its big green leaves and its pungent bite. Stir-frying is the best way to cook Chinese broccoli, as it brings out the natural flavor, accented here with a touch of sugar, ginger, and rice wine. It will need to be washed and drained several hours before stir-frying, and it must be stir-fried in small amounts (about twelve ounces) to achieve the best *wok hay* (see "The Breath of a Wok," page 20). It's better to cook two separate recipes than to try to fit too much in the wok.

Choose broccoli that has buds and no flowers. If there are flowers, the broccoli is too old. The stalks are never as thick as those of regular broccoli, but if they are thicker than ½ inch, they need to be halved lengthwise. The vegetable is better in the colder months, but is available year-round in Chinese produce markets.

10 stalks **Chinese broccoli**
  (*gai lan*), about 12 ounces
1 tablespoon **vegetable oil**
3 slices **ginger**
¾ teaspoon **sugar**
½ teaspoon **salt**
1 tablespoon **Shao Hsing rice
  cooking wine**

Wash the broccoli in several changes of cold water and drain thoroughly in a colander until dry to the touch. Trim ¼ inch from the bottom of each stalk. Stalks that are more than ½ inch in diameter should be peeled, then halved lengthwise. Cut the broccoli stalks and leaves into 2½-inch-long pieces, keeping the stalk ends separate from the leaves and buds.

Heat a 14-inch flat-bottomed wok or skillet over high heat until hot but not smoking. Add the oil and ginger, and stir-fry 30 seconds. Add only the broccoli stalks and stir-fry 1 to 1½ minutes until the stalks are bright green. Add the leaves, and continue cooking for 1 minute until the leaves are just limp.

Sprinkle on the sugar, salt, and rice wine. Stir-fry 2 to 3 minutes, or until the vegetables are just tender but still bright green. Serve immediately.

Serves 4 as part of a multicourse meal.

Stir-Fried Chinese Broccoli and Bacon

Chinese broccoli is especially good stir-fried with mellow-flavored Chinese Bacon, a touch of rice wine, sugar, and a hint of garlic. Chinese Bacon is available in Chinese meat markets (though you can make it yourself, page 182). To cut thin slices, use a sharp cleaver or a heavy-duty cook's knife, as it is hard and can be difficult to slice. (See Stir-Fried Chinese Broccoli, page 87, for information on broccoli.)

10 stalks Chinese broccoli (*gai lan*), about 12 ounces

3 ounces Chinese Bacon (*lop yok*), store-bought or homemade (page 182)

1 teaspoon thin soy sauce

1 teaspoon Shao Hsing rice cooking wine

½ teaspoon sugar

2 teaspoons vegetable oil

2 garlic cloves, smashed and peeled

Wash the Chinese broccoli in several changes of cold water and drain thoroughly in a colander until dry to the touch. Trim ¼ inch from the bottom of each stalk. Stalks that are more than ½ inch in diameter should be peeled with a paring knife, then halved lengthwise. Cut the broccoli stalks and leaves into 2 ½-inch-long pieces, keeping the stalk ends separate from the leaves and buds.

Remove and discard the hard rind and thick layer of fat attached to the rind from the Chinese bacon. Cut into very thin slices crosswise. In a small bowl, combine the soy sauce, rice wine, and sugar; set aside.

Heat a 14-inch flat-bottomed wok or skillet over high heat until hot but not smoking. Add the vegetable oil and garlic, and stir-fry 15 seconds. Add the Chinese bacon and stir-fry 30 seconds. Add only the broccoli stalks and stir-fry 1 to 1½ minutes, or until the stalks are bright green. Add the leaves and continue stir-frying 1 minute, or until the leaves are just limp. Swirl in the soy sauce mixture and continue stir-frying 2 to 3 minutes, or until the vegetables are just tender but still bright green. Serve immediately.

Serves 4 as part of a multicourse meal.

Braised Taro and Chinese Bacon

Taro root has the same starchy quality as a potato, but the flavor is more un-usual, sort of like a cross between a potato and a chestnut. It is a cylindrical root, about 6 to 10 inches long and about 3 to 4 inches wide. The skin is dark brown, hairy, and dusty. It is an earthy and humble ingredient and, when cooked with wet bean curd and Chinese bacon, the flavor becomes dense and rich. It is food for the soul, especially in cold weather. For some people, the outside of the taro root can be irritating to the skin, so it's always a good idea to wear rubber gloves when handling it. See Nom Yu Spareribs (page 56) for information on wet bean curd.

One ¾-pound taro root

4 ounces Chinese Bacon (*lop yok*), store-bought or homemade (page 182)

1 tablespoon vegetable oil

2 cubes red wet bean curd (*nom yu*)

1 scallion, cut into 2-inch lengths

½ teaspoon sugar

Wearing rubber gloves, peel the taro root with a cook's knife. Cut taro root lengthwise into quarters, then cut crosswise into scant ½-inch-thick slices. Remove and discard the hard rind and thick layer of fat attached to the rind from the Chinese bacon. Cut crosswise into scant ½-inch-thick slices.

Heat a 14-inch flat-bottomed wok or skillet over high heat until hot but not smoking. Add oil and bacon, and stir-fry 15 seconds. Add bean curd and taro, and stir-fry 2 minutes, breaking up curd with a spoon. Add 1 cup boiling water and bring to a boil over high heat. Cover and cook 3 minutes. Stir in the scallion, reduce heat to medium-high, cover, and cook 5 minutes. Reduce heat to medium, stir mixture again, cover, and cook until taro is just tender when pierced with a knife, about 5 minutes. Stir in sugar and serve immediately.

Serves 4 to 6 as part of a multicourse meal.

炒
豆
角
紅
椒

Stir-Fried Long Beans with Red Bell Peppers

For the Cantonese, Chinese long beans are the only vegetable a woman is permitted to eat the first month after childbirth. Vegetables in general are said to be too cooling (too yin), but long beans are neutral—neither too yin nor too yang. Long beans are only available in Chinese produce stores and can be either dark green or pale green. The dark green beans are preferred by my family, as the texture is crisper. The beans are about 18 to 30 inches long and should be unblemished.

8 ounces Chinese long beans
1 large red bell pepper
1 tablespoon vegetable oil
¼ teaspoon salt
¼ teaspoon sugar

Wash the beans in several changes of cold water and drain thoroughly in a colander until dry to the touch. Trim the ends and cut the beans into 2½-inch sections. Wash the red pepper, then stem, seed, and cut into slivers.

Heat a 14-inch flat-bottomed wok or skillet over high heat until hot but not smoking. Add the oil and beans, and stir-fry 1 minute. Add ¼ cup boiling water. Cover and cook on high heat 3 minutes. Add the red pepper, re-cover, and cook on high heat 1 minute. Add salt and sugar, and stir to combine. Serve immediately.

Serves 4 to 6 as part of a multicourse meal.

Long Bean Stir-Fry

Mama and all her siblings attended boarding school in China. Returning home for the weekend, they would complain of the horrible food at school. So on Sunday nights each child would be sent back to school with two big jars of this stir-fry, meant to supplement their meals for a few days. Instead, Mama's two jars would be completely finished by the end of Sunday night! This stir-fry has a wonderful balance of sweet, piquant, and spicy flavors and textures. See Stir-Fried Long Beans with Red Bell Peppers (page 90) for information on Chinese long beans (*dul gock*).

8 Chinese dried mushrooms

1 bunch Chinese long beans, about 12 ounces

2 ounces Sichuan preserved vegetable, about ¼ cup

½ Chinese sausage (*lop chong*)

2 ounces pork butt

½ teaspoon salt

2 teaspoons thin soy sauce

1½ teaspoons Shao Hsing rice cooking wine

1 teaspoon sesame oil

¼ teaspoon ground white pepper

¾ teaspoon sugar

4 tablespoons vegetable oil

¼ cup thinly sliced scallions

¼ cup cilantro sprigs

In a medium bowl, soak the mushrooms in ½ cup cold water for 30 minutes, or until softened. Drain and squeeze dry (reserve the soaking liquid for use in soups). Cut off and discard the stems and mince the caps.

Wash the long beans in several changes of cold water and drain thoroughly in a colander until dry to the touch. Cut into ¼-inch-long pieces to make about 3 cups.

Rinse the preserved vegetable in cold water until the red chili-paste coating is removed and pat dry. Finely chop to make about ⅓ cup. Chop the Chinese sausage into ¼-inch pieces. Dice the pork into ¼-inch pieces and sprinkle with ¼ teaspoon salt. Stir to combine and set aside. In a small bowl, combine the soy sauce, rice wine, sesame oil, pepper, ½ teaspoon sugar, and ⅛ teaspoon salt; set aside.

Heat a 14-inch flat-bottomed wok or skillet over high heat until hot but not smoking. Add 1 tablespoon vegetable oil, sausage, and pork, and stir-fry 1 minute. Transfer to a plate. Add the 1 tablespoon oil and mushrooms to the wok, and stir-fry 1 minute. Add the remaining ⅛ teaspoon salt and remaining ¼ teaspoon sugar, and stir-fry another minute. Remove the mushrooms from the wok and add to the sausage mixture. Add the remaining 2 tablespoons vegetable oil and the green beans to the wok, and stir-fry 1 minute. Cover for 20 seconds. Uncover, add 2 tablespoons water, and stir-fry 10 seconds. Cover and cook 30 seconds. Return the sausage mixture and the preserved vegetable to the wok along with the scallions, cilantro sprigs, and soy sauce mixture. Stir-fry 1 to 2 minutes, or until the vegetables are just tender. Serve immediately.

Serves 4 to 6 as part of a multicourse meal.

Stir-Fried Amaranth

Amaranth (*yeen choy*), with its green and red variegated leaves, looks like red Swiss chard. Choose young, small bunches; the older amaranth is tough and stringy. If it is past its prime, you'll see very small flowers hidden near the bottom of the stem. The Cantonese like amaranth for soups or for simple stir-fries and value it for its ability to lessen internal heat, especially in the summer. Amaranth is rich in iron and calcium. For this recipe, use the pale beige-colored wet bean curd (*fu yu*), not the red variety. See Nom Yu Spareribs (page 56) for information on purchasing wet bean curd. Like spinach, this will cook down to a small amount, but no more than 1 pound should be cooked at one time. It's better to cook this in two batches than to overcrowd the wok.

1 pound young amaranth

1 tablespoon vegetable oil

3 cloves garlic, smashed

1 cube wet bean curd (*fu yu*)

1 tablespoon liquid from wet bean curd jar

Wash the amaranth in several changes of cold water and drain thoroughly in a colander until dry to the touch. If the amaranth is young, the entire vegetable can be eaten. If it is old, remove and discard the bottom 6 inches of the stem, and use only the leaves.

Heat a 14-inch flat-bottomed wok or skillet over high heat until hot but not smoking. Add the oil, garlic, and amaranth, and stir-fry until the leaves are almost limp, 2 to 3 minutes. Add the bean curd and bean curd liquid. Stir-fry 2 more minutes, or until vegetable is just tender but bright green and bean curd is well distributed. Serve immediately.

Serves 4 as part of a multicourse meal.

Stir-Fried Water Spinach

Although called Chinese water spinach, this vegetable, also known as *toong sum choy* or *oong choy*, hardly resembles spinach. Two-thirds of it is a hollow reedlike stem. The vegetable is grown in marshy land, which increases the likelihood of little snails or insects living in the stems. I was taught that to kill any insects that might still be hidden in the water spinach stalks, you must always cook water spinach with garlic. One pound of washed water spinach equals about 20 cups of loosely packed spinach, but know that it will cook down to only about 3 cups. When I was a child, water spinach was very expensive because it was flown in to San Francisco from Hawaii, where it was grown. On the rare occasion that we had it, I remember the aromatic intensity of garlic and the wet bean curd, *fu yu,* drawing us to the kitchen. See Nom Yu Spareribs (page 56) for more information on wet bean curd. Today, water spinach is less expensive and is widely available in larger Chinatowns during the late spring and throughout the summer.

- 1 pound water spinach (*toong sum choy*)
- 2 tablespoons vegetable oil
- 3 cloves garlic, smashed and peeled
- 2 cubes wet bean curd (*fu yu*)
- ½ teaspoon sugar
- ¼ teaspoon salt

Break off about 2 inches from the bottom of each water spinach stalk and discard. Break each stem by hand into 4-inch pieces, rinse in several changes of cold water, and drain thoroughly in a colander until dry to the touch.

Heat a 14-inch flat-bottomed wok or skillet over high heat until hot but not smoking. Add vegetable oil and garlic, and stir-fry 30 seconds. Add all the water spinach and stir-fry 1 minute, or until leaves are just limp. Add bean curd, sugar, and salt, breaking up bean curd as you stir-fry 3 to 4 minutes more, or until vegetables are just tender but still bright green. Serve immediately.

Serves 4 as part of a multicourse meal.

Stir-Fried Cloud Ears and Luffa

Luffa, see *qwa*, can be as slim as an English cucumber, but has ridges, a pale green color, and is slightly curved on one end. It is widely available in the summer in Chinese produce markets. When it is young, the flesh and skin are tender and edible after cooking. As it ages, the skin becomes tough, leathery, and hard. (If left to dry in the fields, the vegetable becomes what we know as the luffa sponge, used for bathing.) Cloud ears are a dried fungus that expands after being soaked. They must be examined for hard spots, which need to be removed, before cooking with them. One time while doing this I found a small piece of bark, so it is important not to just soak and drain the cloud ears. This dish makes about three cups, the proper amount of vegetables for stir-frying without losing the *wok hay*.

¼ **cup cloud ears (*wun yee*), rinsed**

I young luffa (*see qwa*), about 8 ounces

2 teaspoons thin soy sauce

½ **teaspoon Shao Hsing rice cooking wine**

½ **teaspoon sesame oil**

¼ **teaspoon sugar**

¼ **teaspoon ground white pepper**

¼ **teaspoon salt**

3 tablespoons vegetable oil

I tablespoon sliced ginger

I tablespoon finely shredded scallion

In a small bowl, soak the cloud ears in ½ cup cold water for 30 minutes, or until softened and expanded. Drain and discard the water. Remove and discard any hard spots from the cloud ears. With a vegetable peeler, peel only the ridges on the luffa, leaving strips of green skin. If the skin appears to be tough, peel all the skin. Cut into 2-inch-long sections. Cut each section lengthwise into ¼-inch-thick rectangular slices.

In a small bowl, combine the soy sauce, rice wine, sesame oil, sugar, pepper, and salt; set aside.

Heat a 14-inch flat-bottomed wok or skillet over high heat until hot but not smoking. Add 1 tablespoon vegetable oil, ginger, and scallions, and stir-fry 10 seconds. Add the remaining 2 tablespoons vegetable oil, luffa, and stir-fry 30 seconds. Add the cloud ears and swirl in the soy sauce mixture, and continue stir-frying 1 to 2 minutes, or until luffa is just tender and still bright green. Serve immediately.

Serves 4 as part of a multicourse meal.

Eggplant in Garlic Sauce

Chili garlic sauce is a common ingredient in Chinese markets. It is the consistency of a thick puree and gives intense heat and flavor to any dish, especially when cooked with additional fresh garlic and ginger. The kitchen fills with a spicy fragrance as you cook the eggplant. This is delicious served at room temperature or chilled, and is a Sichuan-style dish—hot and spicy with sweetness from the pork. When I was growing up, spicy dishes like this were not a part of our Cantonese diet, but the flavors now appeal to me. Eggplant readily absorbs oil, so you could use more oil in this recipe, but I prefer the eggplant less rich. Chinese eggplant is more slender than a regular eggplant, and is said to be less bitter.

3 medium Chinese eggplants, about 1 pound

2 tablespoons chili garlic sauce

2 tablespoons thin soy sauce

2 tablespoons Chinese red rice vinegar

2 tablespoons Shao Hsing rice cooking wine

1 tablespoon sugar

7 tablespoons vegetable oil

¼ cup ground pork butt

2 tablespoons finely minced garlic

2 tablespoons finely minced ginger

½ cup chopped scallions

Remove the stem and trim the ends from the eggplants. Cut the unpeeled eggplants into scant ½-inch-thick by 2½-inch-long strips. In a small bowl, combine the chili garlic sauce, soy sauce, vinegar, rice wine, sugar, and ⅔ cup cold water.

Heat a 14-inch flat-bottomed wok or skillet over high heat until hot but not smoking. Add 3 tablespoons oil and half the eggplant, and stir-fry 2 minutes, or until some of the eggplant begins to brown and soften. Transfer the eggplant to a plate. Repeat with the remaining eggplant and 3 tablespoons of oil, transferring to the plate with first batch. Add the remaining 1 tablespoon oil, pork, garlic, and ginger, and stir-fry about 1 minute, or until golden and fragrant. Return the eggplant to the wok. Restir the chili sauce mixture, and swirl into the wok. Bring to a boil over high heat. Reduce heat to medium, cover, and cook 5 to 8 minutes or until the eggplant is just tender. Stir in scallions and serve immediately.

Serves 4 to 6 as part of a multicourse meal.

Stir-Fried Bitter Melon and Beef

I am not fond of bitter melon. My Auntie Lily says it's a taste that you acquire as you grow older. Bitterness has its place in the diet according to traditional Chinese principles of food. Mama likes the taste, which she describes as being bittersweet, cooling, and therefore refreshing to her mouth. Bitter melon is a summer vegetable that is considered to be extremely cooling. It can be light or dark green and should have skin with thick ridges; the light green is considered less bitter. Whether light or dark green, the pulp can be creamy white or bright orange. The melon is never cooked alone but is paired with strong-flavored ingredients like Chinese dried black beans to balance the bitterness.

2 medium bitter melons, about 1¼ pounds total

1 teaspoon salt

4 ounces flank steak, well trimmed

2 teaspoons plus 1 tablespoon finely shredded ginger

1 teaspoon Shao Hsing rice cooking wine

1 teaspoon thin soy sauce

1 teaspoon plus 5 tablespoons vegetable oil

1 teaspoon cornstarch

½ teaspoon sesame oil

½ teaspoon sugar

¼ teaspoon ground white pepper

1 tablespoon Chinese dried black beans

1 clove garlic, finely minced

Cut the bitter melons in half lengthwise, and remove the seeds. Place cut-side down on a cutting board and slice on the diagonal into ¼-inch-thick slices. The pieces will be quite big. In a 2-quart saucepan, bring 1 quart water to a boil over high heat with ½ teaspoon salt. Add the bitter melons and return to a boil. Drain, rinse under cold water, and set aside to drain thoroughly.

Halve the flank steak along the grain into two strips. Cut each strip across the grain into ¼-inch-thick slices. Place the flank steak in a shallow bowl and add 2 teaspoons shredded ginger, rice wine, soy sauce, 1 teaspoon vegetable oil, cornstarch, sesame oil, sugar, pepper, and ¼ teaspoon salt, and stir to combine. Set aside.

Rinse the black beans in several changes of cold water and drain. In a small bowl, mash the black beans and garlic with the back of a wooden spoon until it resembles a paste.

Heat a 14-inch flat-bottomed wok or skillet over high heat until hot but not smoking. Add 2 tablespoons oil and carefully spread the beef in the wok. Cook, undisturbed, 1 to 2 minutes, letting the beef begin to brown. Then, using a metal spatula, stir-fry 1 to 2 minutes, or until beef is browned on all sides but not cooked through. Remove from the wok to a plate and set aside.

Add the remaining 3 tablespoons oil, black bean paste, remaining 1 tablespoon shredded ginger, and drained bitter melon, and stir-fry 30 seconds. Return the beef and any accumulated juices to the wok, add the remaining ¼ teaspoon salt, and stir-fry 30 seconds, or until heated through. Serve immediately.

Serves 4 to 6 as part of a multicourse meal.

Vegetable Lo Mein

Vegetable Lo Mein is one of the easiest dishes for a beginner to make. The mastery comes in correctly slicing the vegetables and not overcooking the noodles. You will find a variety of fresh egg noodles in the refrigerator section of most Chinese food markets. The best noodles for *lo mein* are about ¼ inch thick, and come either uncooked or precooked. Either noodle can be used and will require one to three minutes of boiling; follow package directions. Do not use won ton noodles.

4 Chinese dried mushrooms

6 large leaves Napa cabbage, about 12 ounces

1-pound package Chinese fresh egg noodles

1 tablespoon sesame oil

2 tablespoons thin soy sauce

3 tablespoons vegetable oil

1 tablespoon finely minced ginger

1 cup julienne carrots

2 scallions, finely shredded

1 tablespoon oyster flavored sauce

In a medium bowl, soak the mushrooms in ¼ cup cold water for 30 minutes, or until softened. Drain and squeeze dry, reserving soaking liquid. Cut off and discard stems and thinly slice the caps.

Wash the cabbage leaves in several changes of cold water and allow to thoroughly drain in a colander until dry to the touch. Trim ¼ inch from the stem end of the cabbage leaves and discard. Stack 2 to 3 cabbage leaves at a time and cut crosswise into ¼-inch-wide shreds.

In a 4-quart saucepan, bring about 2 quarts water to a boil over high heat. Add noodles, return to a rolling boil, and boil 2 to 3 minutes. Rinse under cold water and drain the noodles thoroughly. Transfer to a medium bowl, add sesame oil and 1 tablespoon soy sauce, and mix well. Set aside.

Heat a 14-inch flat-bottomed wok or skillet over high heat until hot but not smoking. Add 1 tablespoon vegetable oil and ginger, and stir-fry 20 seconds. Add the carrots, scallions, and mushrooms, and stir-fry 1 minute, or until the vegetables are just limp. Transfer the vegetables to a plate.

Add the remaining 2 tablespoons vegetable oil and cabbage, and stir-fry 1 minute, or until cabbage begins to wilt. Add the cooked carrot mixture, noodles, and reserved mushroom soaking liquid, and stir-fry 2 to 3 minutes, or until noodles are heated through. Swirl in the remaining 1 tablespoon soy sauce and oyster sauce and toss to combine. Serve immediately.

Serves 4 to 6 as part of a multicourse meal.

Stuffed Fuzzy Melon

Fuzzy melon can be fat or slender, and has a mild flavor like zucchini. The Chinese feel that fuzzy melon is best when paired with richly flavored ingredients like the pork, shrimp, and mushroom stuffing used here. For making soups or stir-fries it doesn't really matter which size fuzzy melon you choose, but my Auntie Lily, who taught me this recipe, insists that when you stuff a fuzzy melon you want the slender melons, no more than 2¼ inches wide, for a more delicate presentation. Also, the skinny fuzzy melon has fewer seeds, which makes it easier to hollow out.

4 Chinese dried mushrooms

4 ounces medium shrimp, peeled and deveined

1½ teaspoons salt

8 ounces ground pork butt

¼ teaspoon sugar

1¼ teaspoons sesame oil

1 tablespoon oyster flavored sauce

¼ teaspoon ground white pepper

1½ teaspoons plus 2 tablespoons cornstarch, plus extra for dusting

6 small, skinny fuzzy melons (4½ to 5 inches long), about 3 pounds total

1 tablespoon vegetable oil

3⅓ cups Homemade Chicken Broth (page 234)

Cilantro sprigs

In a medium bowl, soak the mushrooms in ¼ cup cold water for 30 minutes, or until softened. Drain and squeeze dry, reserving the soaking liquid. Cut off and discard the stems and mince the caps.

In a small bowl, toss the shrimp with 1 teaspoon salt and set aside 2 to 3 minutes. Rinse them in cold water several times. Drain, place on a plate, loosely cover, and refrigerate for 30 minutes. Finely chop shrimp.

In a medium bowl, combine the pork, sugar, ¼ teaspoon sesame oil, and remaining ½ teaspoon salt. Stir in the reserved mushroom soaking liquid. Slowly stir in the shrimp and mushrooms, adding a little at a time. Add the oyster sauce, remaining 1 teaspoon sesame oil, pepper, and 1½ teaspoons cornstarch.

Peel the fuzzy melons. Cut each melon into 3 pieces (about 1½ inches long), making a total of 18 pieces. Using a teaspoon, scoop out the flesh from the center of each piece, leaving the bottom end intact. (This scooped-out melon can be reserved and used in soups.)

Dust the inside of each hollowed piece lightly with about ⅛ teaspoon cornstarch. Fill each piece with the pork-and-shrimp mixture, mounding it slightly.

Pour oil in a 14-inch skillet and place the stuffed fuzzy melon pieces in the skillet. Add 3 cups broth, cover, and bring to a boil over high heat. Reduce heat to medium, cover, and cook until tender when pierced with a knife and the meat is cooked through, 18 to 20 minutes. Transfer the pieces in the center of the skillet to a platter. Shift the outside pieces to the center of the skillet, re-cover, and continue cooking until cooked through, 2 to 4 minutes. Transfer to the platter.

Combine the remaining ⅓ cup cold broth and 2 tablespoons cornstarch. Bring the broth in the skillet to a boil over high heat. Add the cornstarch mixture and cook, stirring, until thickened, about 1 to 2 minutes. Pour the sauce over the melon. Garnish with cilantro sprigs if desired.

Serves 4 to 6 as part of a multicourse meal.

節瓜炆江瑤柱

Zeet Qwa Mun Gong Yu Chee

Braised Fuzzy Melon with Scallops

Fuzzy melon, *zeet qwa*, is oblong in shape, with a taste and texture somewhere between zucchini and winter melon. At its prime, in the summer, fuzzy melon should have short, fine, prickly hairs. As the melon ages, it loses the hairs. My family often served this typical, home-style, braised vegetable dish in which the melon takes on the deep flavors of the scallops, mushrooms, and rich chicken broth.

¼ cup Chinese dried scallops (*gawn yu chee*)

4 Chinese dried mushrooms

One 1.7-ounce package cellophane noodles

1 fuzzy melon, about 1¾ pounds

2 tablespoons vegetable oil

2 slices ginger

1 cup Homemade Chicken Broth (page 234)

¾ teaspoon salt

In a small bowl, soak the dried scallops in ½ cup cold water for 2 hours, or until softened. Drain the scallops, reserving the scallop liquid. Remove and discard the small hard knob from the side of the scallops. Finely shred the scallops. In a medium bowl, soak the mushrooms in ¼ cup cold water for 30 minutes, or until softened. Drain and squeeze dry, reserving soaking liquid. Cut off and discard stems and thinly slice the caps. In another bowl, soak the cellophane noodles in cold water to cover for 15 minutes, or until softened. Drain.

Peel the fuzzy melon and cut into 2-inch sections. Cut each section into julienne strips.

Heat a 14-inch flat-bottomed wok or skillet over high heat until hot but not smoking. Add 1 tablespoon oil and ginger, and stir-fry 20 seconds. Add the scallops and mushrooms, and stir-fry 30 seconds. Add the remaining 1 tablespoon oil and fuzzy melon, and stir-fry 1 minute. Add the reserved scallop and mushroom soaking liquids and chicken broth, and bring to a boil over high heat. Reduce heat to medium, cover, and simmer 2 to 3 minutes, or until the melon is just limp. Add the drained cellophane noodles and salt and stir until well combined. Cover and simmer on medium heat 2 to 3 minutes, or until the cellophane noodles are translucent and cooked through and the vegetables are tender. Serve immediately.

Serves 4 to 6 as part of a multicourse meal.

烹飪以養性

Pun Yum Yee Yeung Sim

COOKING AS A MEDITATION

Uncle Donald, Grandfather (Yeye) Young Suey Hay, and Baba. Kowloon, circa 1924.

FOR MY PARENTS, COOKING IS A meditation. Because they have informally studied and observed the process of cooking for over sixty years, they instinctually sense when an ingredient is properly prepared and cooked. In my family, we use no precise measurements. Nothing is timed or weighed. Rice flour is poured into a bowl, and water is added, not according to a recipe, but until it is the right consistency for a dough, neither too dry nor too sticky. Sesame seeds are toasted in a wok until the moment the crackling ceases. Glutinous rice is soaked in water until the grains of rice are no longer dry and powdery to the taste, but just soft. When my cousin Sylvia roasts poultry, she marinates the bird in a mixture of garlic, ginger, aromatic Chinese dried black beans, soy sauce, hoisin sauce, and ground bean sauce, adding enough of each ingredient until, as she says, it is fragrant and "smells right."

Trying to record a precise recipe by watching my parents cook is as difficult as catching an animal in the wild. Armed with a digital scale, timer, and dry and liquid measuring cups and spoons, I try to capture the recipe. I hand Baba a dry measuring spoon to see just how much cornstarch he uses to make his famous Steamed Tangerine Beef, and he swiftly plops a rounded spoonful into the bowl before I can apprehend a precise, level measure.

I was taught early in my life to appreciate the fragrance, texture, succulence, and taste of a well-composed dish. Baba and Mama pointed out to me how a chef achieves greatness only after years of practice. They called this honing of skills mastery, or *si fu*. I have since learned that it is also possible for nonchefs to master cooking without relying on elaborate techniques. When certain virtues are applied, an experienced cook can take the simplest ingredients and techniques to form a work of beauty. The most important virtue is alertness to the senses; knowing when an ingredient has the correct visual cues, smells, sounds, tastes, and texture is more valuable than mastering the intricacies of a complicated recipe.

In the modern home kitchen, the true art of cooking by instinct is diminishing, partially because of the emergence of so many appliances that replace the need to rely on one's own cooking judgment. Kitchen gadgets have replaced culinary expertise. Rice cookers alleviate the cultivation of judgment of when to slow the fire and when to simmer the rice to begin the steaming process. Deep-fat-fry thermometers indicate when oil has reached the right temperature for frying, and instant-read thermometers take the intuition out of knowing when meat is cooked. Food processors grind meat that once was hand-chopped with a cleaver, and shred vegetables in an instant rather than through hours of work. My parents maintain ardently that the patience to hand-chop or hand-shred produces a tangible difference in taste and texture.

There are indeed ways one cannot pretend to be a great chef; that can only be achieved from years of experience. For example, wrapping dumplings or Chinese tamales, *zoong*, requires mastery, and the same is true for making transparent and fine dough for dim sum. Slicing paper-thin ginger or chopping chicken through the bone is both dangerous and difficult. Yet, every attempt at those techniques brings reward. Baba or Mama never throw together a meal. When I cook with them, they will sometimes say, "Not so quickly; slowly, slowly arrive at your goal." Their philosophy is not to spend hours cooking a meal, but neither do they rush through the process.

My parents teach that when you cook you must be able to change directions, *chun bien*. You must use your powers of observation, regarding each situation as unique and adjusting accordingly. Dry ingredients like Chinese stick dried bean curd, *foo zook*, can soak in water for only fifteen minutes and be soft enough for cooking. But, sometimes, *foo zook* requires six hours or more of soaking, depending on the quality of the ingredient. The high heat on my parents' front burner is more powerful than the same setting on the back burner. This simple fact affects cooking time. Indeed, high heat varies not only from burner to burner but from range to range, especially from a gas stove to an electric range.

As in life, one must observe the subtleties of cooking and adjust, remembering not to be enslaved to a recipe's cooking times or measurements. It is mindfulness, attentiveness, and gaining self-confidence through experience that nourish success. And, finally, Baba and Mama remind me that cooking requires almost as much luck as skill. There is the Cantonese expression *chong choy,* meaning to bump into luck. My parents humbly attribute their success in the kitchen to *chong choy* and not experience.

PROBABLY NO CULTURE APPRECIATES celebratory opportunities to feast as much as the Chinese. We prize dishes that elevate food beyond the ordinary, and focus on the sublime pleasure of eating. The recipes in this section vary from the auspicious and meaning-laden specialties of the Chinese New Year to special delicacies that indulge and cater to the eater's every fancy. While some recipes require long and involved preparation, others are easy enough for a beginner.

The Art of Celebration

活魚報吉兆

THE GOOD OMEN OF A FIGHTING FISH

Great-Grandfather Young Ying Look. Canton, China, circa 1910.

POACHED FISH IS ONE OF THE CLASSIC dishes served on Chinese New Year's Eve. Interestingly, the importance of the fish derives from a play on words. The word for fish, *yu*, sounds like the word for wish. Thus, the Cantonese feel it is auspicious to eat fish to insure your wishes for the new year come true. It goes with the old Cantonese saying, *Yu yuen yee sheung*, or, "May your wishes be fulfilled."

Beyond fish and wish, the word *yu* also sounds like the word for extra or abundance. However, as Mama wisely points out, when you eat *yu* for its symbolic connection to abundance, you must be specific in your desire for abundance. It is dangerous to express a blanket wish for abundance because in truth, you don't really want extra of everything—like extra debt, humiliation, or problems. Rather, you want plenty of honor and wealth as you go into the New Year. The famous expression *Cheung mang foo quai*, associated with New Year's, is a wish for long life, wealth, and eminence.

The Cantonese insist on serving fish for New Year's Eve for many more reasons than simply the rich play on words. For one, fish commonly swim in pairs and are regarded as a symbol of marital bliss and fertility. The Chinese regard a marriage blessed with many children as the happiest union, and fish are known to produce many eggs. Fish are often depicted in Chinese art because their graceful movements convey a sense of freedom.

In cooking, Chinese people believe you must specially select a live fish, one that exhibits certain positive aspects of living, such as a fighting spirit and a strong will. My Baba is very particular about the fish he selects. When he buys fish, it must be what he calls a swimming fish, purchased from a fishmonger who keeps his fish in tanks. Baba studies the tank and always chooses the most active fish.

One New Year's Eve, Baba and I combed the markets of San Francisco's Chinatown searching for just the right swimming fish. As we approached each market, our sense of anticipation heightened. Would we find the perfect fish? Would he be vital and clear eyed? After the third or fourth market, our anticipation began turning to dread with the fear that we might not find the right fish, for we had come a little late and every market seemed to be sold out. My father would never even consider the fillets or steaks we saw sitting on ice, tantalizing as they might be to anyone else. When I shop in New York, I frequently cast my eyes over the grand fish-on-ice displays in fancy shops. I chuckle to myself picturing how absurd Baba would consider spending ten to twenty dollars per pound for fish that has been cut up into fillets, leaving the purchaser with no idea of when it was killed. He would consider it like throwing money out the window. On this particular New Year's Eve, I harbored the thought of how foolish it would be to suggest to Baba that he settle for a fillet.

Fortunately, we finally found a beautiful swimming steelhead, a sleek silver black fish. When we arrived home triumphant with the fish, Baba and Mama marveled at its liveliness as it thrashed about in its newspaper wrapping, despite the fact that it had already been killed, gutted, and scaled! My parents remarked on how valiantly the fish fought, right up until it was placed in the pan of boiling water for poaching. I have witnessed this scene countless times. Mama will slide the fish expertly into the pan of boiling water while Baba has the more difficult job of immediately placing the lid over the struggling fish. My father is barely able to keep the lid on for the first few seconds as the fish makes its final show of force. It is a war of wills for a moment, and then everyone relaxes and turns their thoughts to the delicious meal ahead.

It occurred to me that my American friends would find this scene inhumane and, I have to admit, because of the Western influences in my life, I sometimes have mixed feelings when we cook fish. But for the Chinese, a lively fish is a good omen. Its tenaciousness symbolizes the fish's immortality. Thus, to eat a fish that fights to the very end is to ingest the ultimate in long life and good fortune, especially on New Year's Eve.

The New Year's Eve meal is called *tuan neen,* or the uniting of family for thanksgiving. It is the most important meal of the two-week New Year's celebration and by custom the immediate family gathers for dinner at home. Every family's meal is slightly different but shares the tradition of being designed around meaning-laden foods. Traditionally, eight or nine courses are served because both are lucky numbers; eight sounds like the word for prosperity in Cantonese, and nine means long-lasting.

In China, a fish must be served with its head and tail intact to properly signify a favorable beginning and end for the New Year. From the Chinese perspective, to be a whole person one must have a good start and a happy ending in all aspects of life, and eating a whole fish is the epitome of this sentiment. A whole chicken also symbolizes a proper beginning and end to the year and the wholeness of life on earth. Clams or scallops, which have a shape similar to that of coins, represent wealth and prosperity. Roast pig signifies purification and peace, and oysters and lettuce represent good fortune and prosperity. Some families favor a sweet-and-sour pork dish because the Cantonese word for sour sounds like the word for grandchild. A fancy soup like shark's fin or bird's nest is said to be esteemed for its rarity and delicacy. Lobster represents the life and energy of the dragon. Luxury foods, such as squab, snow pea shoots, hearts of bok choy, shrimp, abalone, and crabs, have become a part of the tradition for some. And, of course, there must be steaming rice.

Finally, the fish should always be served as the last course. It is essential to prepare more than enough fish, so that some of it remains on the platter at the close of the New Year's Eve dinner. This symbolizes taking a reserve of food, or surplus, into the New Year, and is another play on the word *yu,* as it expresses fish, wish, and having enough to spare. By eating this extra fish the following day for the New Year's dinner, the family ensures that the year to come will be rich and plentiful, which, in turn, is the greatest wish of the Chinese people.

All of the following recipes would be appropriate to make for a Chinese New Year's Eve dinner. Each is delicious and, more important, has auspicious good meaning for a happy new year. The New Year's Eve dinner is the most sumptuous meal of the year, with the choicest delicacies.

Poached Steelhead Fish

My cousins Lin and Ben told me that when they were children, their father instructed them to eat a fish in the proper old-fashioned Chinese way. One side of the fish should be eaten, and then the bone lifted from the platter before finishing the underside. My Uncle Beyne was a very traditional man who believed, like many Chinese, that if a fish is flopped at the dinner table it portends the capsizing of a boat. In olden days when everyone traveled by boat, such a fate was a great fear.

Baba is partial to both steelhead, *soong yu,* and rock cod, *seck ban,* two varieties found in the Bay Area that he feels best replicate the fish he ate in China. Steelhead has a delicate flesh with very fine bones, and is well suited to being poached or steamed whole. In California, you will find it in Chinese fish markets swimming in tanks, but there it is known as *soong yu,* and the fishmonger is unlikely to know it by its other names: black trout, Sacramento blackfish, hardhead, and Chinese steelhead. If these varieties are not available in your area, rock cod, sea bass, or red snapper would be a suitable substitute. More important, choose a fish that is clear eyed and has a clean, fresh smell.

The Chinese technique of poaching fish is called *zum yu,* and is nearly foolproof for producing delicately cooked fish. The natural sweetness of the fish is enhanced by a light sauce of soy sauce, ginger, and scallions. If you do not have a fourteen-inch skillet, a fish poacher can be used.

One 1¼-pound steelhead, cleaned and gutted, with head and tail intact

1½ teaspoons salt

1 whole scallion

½-inch-thick slice ginger

2 tablespoons vegetable oil

2 tablespoons finely shredded ginger

2 tablespoons finely shredded scallions

3 tablespoons thin soy sauce

Thoroughly rinse the fish in cold water and drain. Gently rub the cavity and outside of the fish with salt and rinse again. Place the fish on a rack to drain.

Add 1½ inches cold water to a 14-inch skillet. Add the whole scallion and ginger and bring to a boil over high heat. When water is at a rolling boil, add the fish, cover, and return to a boil. Cook on high heat, covered, 1 minute. Reduce heat to low and continue simmering 5 minutes. Turn off heat and let stand, covered, 4 minutes, without removing lid. Test fish for doneness by poking the thickest part with a fork or chopstick; flesh should flake. If not, return water to a boil over high heat and cook 1 to 2 minutes more, or until fish just flakes.

Carefully pour off water from skillet. Gently slide the fish onto a warmed platter and pour off any water on the platter. Discard the scallion and ginger slice.

In a small skillet, heat the vegetable oil over high heat until hot but not smoking. Sprinkle shredded ginger and scallions and drizzle the soy sauce over the fish. Carefully pour hot oil over the fish. The oil will make a crackling sound as it hits the fish. Serve immediately.

Serves 4 to 6 as part of a multicourse meal.

炒白菜

Chow Bok Choy

Stir-Fried Bok Choy

Nearly every family stir-fries bok choy year-round, but it is also prized as a vegetable for such special occasions as New Year's. The mastery here is in choosing young, tender bok choy, no more than eight inches in length. Or, occasionally, you might be lucky enough to find hearts of bok choy, *bok choy sum,* in the produce market. Unlike the older bok choy, these vegetables are so tender that the stalks do not need to be peeled. Stir-fry the vegetables on high heat just until the greens are bright and the stalks are tender. A minute too much, and the vegetables lose their essence. Bok choy found in Western supermarkets is often old and past its prime, while the bok choy available in Asian markets is far superior in quality and much less expensive.

1 pound young bok choy

2 tablespoons Homemade Chicken Broth (page 234)

1 tablespoon oyster flavored sauce

1½ teaspoons thin soy sauce

1½ teaspoons cornstarch

½ teaspoon sugar

3 teaspoons vegetable oil

2 ginger slices

1 clove garlic, crushed and peeled

Separate the bok choy into stalks. Wash in several changes of cold water and drain thoroughly in a colander. Trim ¼ inch from the bottom of each stalk. Halve each stalk lengthwise and cut stalks and leaves into 2-inch-long pieces. In a bowl, combine the broth, oyster sauce, soy sauce, cornstarch, and sugar.

Heat a 14-inch flat-bottomed wok or skillet over high heat until hot but not smoking. Add 1½ teaspoons vegetable oil and ginger, and stir-fry 10 seconds, or until ginger is fragrant. Add the remaining 1½ teaspoons vegetable oil, bok choy, and garlic, and stir-fry 1 to 2 minutes, or until leaves are just limp and bok choy is bright green. Restir the broth mixture and swirl into wok. Stir-fry 1 to 2 minutes, or until the sauce has thickened slightly and lightly coats the vegetables. Serve immediately.

Serves 4 to 6 as part of a multicourse meal.

White Cut Chicken

Perfecting the cooking of White Cut Chicken is as important to the Cantonese home cook as learning to make rice. It is a classic dish for New Year's and for everyday fare at home. Every year for the Ching Ming Festival, Chinese families visit their family graves to pay their respects to their ancestors and to bring a plate of White Cut Chicken, roast pork, three bowls of rice, and three glasses of liquor as an offering. It is considered a pleasing dish for both heaven and earth.

My friend David Camacho, who has lived in Hong Kong for over ten years, gave me this outstanding recipe. Every Cantonese cook has a slightly different technique of poaching chicken, but most modern recipes include shocking the cooked chicken with ice water to prevent overcooking. The chicken should be juicy, flavorful, and never dry; it's best to use a broiler/fryer chicken. This recipe may seem simple and plain, but it takes skill to master this unique cooking method. A classic presentation is to serve the chicken with thinly sliced Smithfield ham on a bed of blanched Chinese broccoli.

One 4-pound broiler-fryer chicken

5½ teaspoons salt

1 thumb-sized piece of ginger, about 1 ounce

4 cloves garlic, peeled

4 quarts ice water

1 tablespoon sesame oil

3 tablespoons finely shredded green scallions

3 tablespoons finely shredded ginger

3 tablespoons vegetable oil

Remove any fat pockets from the chicken. Rub chicken with about 2 teaspoons of salt. Rinse the chicken under cold water and place on a rack to drain.

In a pot large enough to fit the chicken, bring about 3 quarts cold water, ginger, garlic, and 2 teaspoons salt to a boil over high heat, covered. Carefully add the chicken, breast-side up, adding more boiling water if necessary to completely cover the chicken. Return to a rolling boil and boil vigorously over high heat, uncovered, for 5 minutes, removing any scum that rises to the surface. Cover pot and let sit off heat for 20 minutes.

Uncover the pot and bring to a boil over high heat. When the broth returns to a rolling boil, boil vigorously, uncovered, 3 to 4 minutes. Remove from heat. Using two heavy spoons, carefully transfer the hot chicken to a colander in the sink. (The chicken should register 170 degrees when tested with a meat thermometer at the meatiest part of the thigh, but not touching the bone. If not, return to the pot and simmer several more minutes.) Slowly pour ice water over the chicken in the colander. Transfer the chicken to a cutting board. Rub the warm chicken with the sesame oil. Allow chicken to cool slightly before using a meat cleaver to chop through the bone into bite-sized pieces, reserving any chicken juices (or disjoint into serving pieces). (Reserve the chicken broth for making soups.)

Place the scallions, ginger, and remaining 1½ teaspoons salt in a small heatproof dish. In a small skillet, heat vegetable oil over high heat until hot but not smoking. Carefully pour hot oil over scallions and ginger. The oil will make a crackling sound as it hits the scallions and ginger. Serve chicken warm or at room temperature with scallion-ginger sauce.

Serves 4 to 6 as part of a multicourse meal.

Dul See Chow Heen

豆豉炒蜆

Stir-Fried Clams in Black Bean Sauce

Stir-fried plump and juicy clams cooked in smoky and aromatic black bean sauce are matchless. The sauce is as delicious in aroma as it is in flavor. Clams are served on New Year's because their shells resemble Chinese coins and, therefore, they symbolize prosperity. There is no need to add salt to this dish because clams are naturally salty, as are the Chinese dried black beans.

2 dozen littleneck or cherrystone clams

2 tablespoons Chinese dried black beans

3 tablespoons vegetable oil

2 tablespoons finely shredded ginger

1 tablespoon finely minced garlic

½ cup Homemade Chicken Broth (page 234)

2 tablespoons Shao Hsing rice cooking wine

1 scallion, finely shredded

Thoroughly wash the clams in several changes of cold water, discarding any open clams. Scrub the shells with a vegetable brush to remove grit and rinse well. Drain the clams in a colander. Rinse the black beans in several changes of cold water and drain. In a small bowl, coarsely mash the black beans with the back of a wooden spoon.

Heat a 14-inch flat-bottomed wok or skillet over high heat until hot but not smoking. Add 1 tablespoon vegetable oil, ginger, and garlic, and stir-fry 30 seconds, or until fragrant. Add the remaining 2 tablespoons vegetable oil, beans, and clams, and stir-fry 3 to 4 minutes, or until the shells just begin to open. Add the broth and rice wine and cover 2 to 3 minutes, or until some of the shells have opened. Transfer the opened clams to a platter and continue stirring, uncovered, on high heat until all the clams have opened and the broth is reduced slightly, about 3 to 4 minutes. Discard any unopened clams. Garnish with the scallion. Serve immediately.

Serves 4 to 6 as part of a multicourse meal.

Stir-Fried Snow Pea Shoots

Dau miu are the tender shoots of the snow pea plant. These vinelike shoots resemble young spinach in taste but are much more delicate. In China, Mama remembers, *dau miu* were cooked with chicken fat rather than oil, which must have been sinfully rich. Snow pea shoots are in season in the winter and in the early spring. As the weather begins to warm up, the stems of the shoots become thicker, tougher, and lose their delicacy. Snow pea shoots are one of the more expensive vegetables in Chinatown, but they are well worth the price. There are also hothouse-grown snow pea shoots, which I've occasionally seen in farmers' markets, some gourmet shops, and once in a while in Chinese produce markets. They look like small green sprouts, being uniform in size and much smaller than regular *dau miu*, but I much prefer farm-grown *dau miu*. Only a small amount of *dau miu* can be stir-fried at a time or you will lose the *wok hay*.

8 ounces young snow pea shoots, about 16 cups, loosely packed

2 tablespoons vegetable oil

2 cloves garlic, crushed and peeled

¼ teaspoon salt

Wash snow pea shoots in several changes of cold water and drain thoroughly in a colander until dry to the touch.

Heat a 14-inch flat-bottomed wok or skillet over high heat until hot but not smoking. Add 1 tablespoon vegetable oil and garlic, and stir-fry about 1 minute. Add the remaining tablespoon vegetable oil, salt, and snow pea shoots, and stir-fry 2 to 3 minutes, or until leaves begin to soften, shaking wok occasionally. Continue stir-frying until the vegetables are just tender but bright green, about 1 minute. Serve immediately.

Serves 4 as part of a multicourse meal.

Glazed Roast Squab

In my family, squab was a rare and expensive ingredient that was saved for special occasions. This soy sauce and rice wine marinade flavored with fresh cilantro, scallions, and ginger beautifully glazes the squab and leaves the meat succulent and fragrant. After oven-roasting, the squab are golden brown, and a touch of vinegar makes the skin crisper. Traditionally, the squab are chopped with a cleaver, but the bones of squab are so tender that I use poultry shears. Fresh squab are available in some specialty meat shops and in Chinese meat markets.

2 squab, about 12 ounces each

1 teaspoon salt

½ cup cilantro sprigs

2 scallions, finely shredded

2 tablespoons finely shredded ginger

2 tablespoons thin soy sauce

1 tablespoon black soy sauce

2 tablespoons Shao Hsing rice cooking wine

½ teaspoon sugar

½ teaspoon distilled white vinegar

Remove any fat pockets from the squab. Rub squab with salt. Rinse the squab under cold water and thoroughly pat dry the cavity and skin with paper towels. In a medium bowl, combine cilantro, scallions, ginger, thin soy sauce, black soy sauce, rice wine, and sugar, and stir to combine. Place half the cilantro, scallions, and ginger in each of the cavities and smear the soy sauce mixture in the cavities and on the outside of the squab. Marinate 30 minutes.

Preheat the oven to 350 degrees. Pour ¼ cup boiling water into an 8-inch glass baking dish and place the squab breast-side down in the dish, reserving the marinade. Roast 30 minutes and turn the squab breast side up, basting with reserved marinade. Roast 30 more minutes. Baste with marinade in pan and cook 15 minutes more, or until squab are golden brown and just cooked. Drizzle ¼ teaspoon of vinegar on each squab. Allow squab to rest 10 minutes before chopping into bite-sized pieces. Serve immediately.

Serves 4 to 6 as part of a multicourse meal.

Shark's Fin Soup

Shark's Fin Soup is one of China's great delicacies. Because it is so expensive and labor-intensive to make, it is a treat that I equate with banquets or special occasions at home. I was happy Mama could teach me to make Shark's Fin Soup because this, too, is becoming a lost art. Nothing compares to the taste of a bowl of Shark's Fin Soup that is well made. The strands have a rich gelatinous texture that is unique. It is extremely prized by the Cantonese, for it is considered to restore and replenish the body, especially if one is weak. And, of course, only a fine homemade chicken broth should be used to prepare the soup. Anything less would ruin the shark's fin.

Dried shark's fin can cost from sixty to well over three hundred dollars per pound, depending on its quality. In the dried form it can be sold as a whole fin, which is the most prized, or in a rectangular block that has been processed from the fin. It is also available frozen and canned, but the dried has the best quality. Ideally, each blond strand of shark's fin should be as thick as a fine toothpick, but a fin of this quality is outrageously expensive. Choose dried shark's fin in a block (which is the most common form). To prepare, you must first soak the shark's fin; sometimes, sand will come out. The soaking is to wash the shark's fin, and the first boiling with the ginger is to rid the shark's fin of its fishiness (*saang may*).

1 block of dried shark's fin, about 7 ounces

3 ounces Smithfield ham with bone

1 tablespoon light-brown sugar

3 slices (½ inch thick) ginger

1½ quarts Homemade Chicken Broth (page 234)

Cover the shark's fin in cold water and soak for 3 hours, or until softened. Drain the shark's fin, being careful not to lose even a strand of it.

Rinse the ham in cold water. In a small saucepan, bring 1 cup cold water to a boil over high heat. Add the ham and return to a boil. Reduce heat to medium-low, cover, and simmer for 20 minutes. Drain the ham and rinse under cold water. Pat dry with paper towels. Place the ham in a small heatproof dish and add brown sugar.

Bring water to a boil in a covered steamer over high heat. Carefully place the dish into the steamer, cover, reduce heat to medium, and steam 20 minutes, or just until ham is softened. Check the water level from time to time, and replenish if necessary with boiling water, keeping at a simmer. Carefully remove the dish from the steamer, and set the ham aside, discarding any juices that have accumulated in the dish.

In a 2½-quart saucepan, bring 1½ quarts of cold water to a boil over high heat with 1 slice of ginger. Add the shark's fin and return to a rolling boil. Turn off the heat and let stand, covered, 5 minutes. Drain in a colander and rinse under cold water again, being careful not to lose a strand of the shark's fin. Discard the ginger.

In a 2½-quart saucepan, bring the chicken broth to a boil over high heat with the remaining 2 ginger slices. Cut off about one-third of the ham and set aside. Add the larger piece, with the bone, to the broth. When the broth comes to a boil, add the shark's fin and return to a rolling boil. Cover, reduce heat to medium-low, and simmer for 3 hours, or until shark's fin is tender and separates into strands. Discard the ham.

Slice the reserved ham into paper-thin slices. Stack a few slices at a time and cut it into paper-fine shreds; then cut the shreds to make a superfine dust of ham.

When ready to serve, ladle the piping-hot soup into individual bowls and garnish with a sprinkling of ham dust. Serve immediately.

Serves 4 to 6 as part of a multicourse meal.

Oyster-Vegetable Lettuce Wraps

The Cantonese like the sound of the words for oyster, *hoe see,* which sound like the words for "good things," and for lettuce, *saang choy,* which sound like "growing fortune." So this dish is a must to eat for New Year's. Finely chopped oysters, mushrooms, fresh water chestnuts, Chinese sausage, carrots, celery, pine nuts, and pork make a sumptuous filling wrapped with lettuce leaves. Each mouthful of this decadent filling contrasts with the fresh, crisp texture of the lettuce wrap.

Choose lettuce leaves that are cuplike and small. The center to the middle of the lettuce head is best. Iceberg is the most typical lettuce used, but Boston lettuce has the right size leaves for making these small, tacolike packages. Many people like to eat this with a little hoisin sauce; Mama likes to eat it sauceless, for she likes the purity of flavor. To make ginger juice, grate a small amount of ginger and then squeeze it with your hands to extract the juice.

6 Chinese dried oysters

4 Chinese dried mushrooms

8 fresh water chestnuts

12 to 16 iceberg lettuce leaves

6 teaspoons vegetable oil

1 tablespoon Shao Hsing rice cooking wine

2 teaspoons ginger juice

1/2 Chinese sausage (*lop chong*), finely minced

1/4 cup pine nuts

1/2 cup finely minced carrot

1/2 cup finely minced celery

1/4 cup ground pork butt

1/2 cup cilantro sprigs

1 tablespoon thin soy sauce

Hoisin sauce

In a small bowl, rinse the oysters in cold water. Drain thoroughly, then add ⅔ cup cold water and soak the oysters 3 to 4 hours, or until soft. Drain and squeeze dry, reserving the soaking liquid. Finely mince and set aside.

In a medium bowl, soak the mushrooms in ¼ cup cold water for 30 minutes, or until softened. Drain and squeeze dry, reserving soaking liquid. Cut off and discard stems and mince the caps.

Peel the water chestnuts with a paring knife and then mince to make about ¾ cup. Wash the lettuce leaves in several changes of cold water and thoroughly drain in a colander.

Heat a 14-inch flat-bottomed wok or skillet over high heat until hot but not smoking. Add 2 teaspoons vegetable oil and oysters, and stir-fry 10 seconds. Add the rice wine, ginger juice, and 2 tablespoons of the reserved oyster liquid, and stir-fry 1 minute. Transfer to a bowl.

Add 2 teaspoons vegetable oil, mushrooms, and Chinese sausage to the wok, and stir-fry 10 seconds. Add 2 tablespoons of the oyster liquid, and stir-fry 1 minute. Transfer mixture to the bowl with the oysters.

Add the remaining 2 teaspoons vegetable oil, pine nuts, carrots, and celery to the wok, and stir-fry 1 minute. Transfer to the bowl with oysters, mushrooms, and sausage. Add ground pork to wok and stir-fry 10 seconds. Return all the stir-fried ingredients to the wok and toss to combine. Add the water chestnuts, cilantro, soy sauce, and 2 tablespoons of the reserved mushroom liquid and stir-fry 1 minute, or until pork is cooked through. Transfer to a platter and accompany with a platter of the iceberg leaves and a small condiment dish of hoisin sauce. Guests should fill lettuce leaves with about ¼ cup of the filling and 1 teaspoon of hoisin sauce, loosely wrapping the lettuce around the filling and eating it with their hands.

Serves 4 to 6 as part of a multicourse meal.

Shoon Chow Saang Choy

蒜炒生菜

Stir-Fried Garlic Lettuce

Cantonese people are extremely fond of iceberg lettuce. It's strange, because this lettuce can't even begin to measure up to the nutritional profile of most Chinese vegetables. In Hong Kong, stir-fried iceberg is extremely popular, and only the Cantonese could make iceberg so delicious. The iceberg attains sweetness from the soy sauce, sesame oil, and rice wine, and only takes three minutes to stir-fry. Bok choy is also delicious cooked in this manner.

1 medium head iceberg lettuce

1½ teaspoons thin soy sauce

1½ teaspoons sesame oil

1 teaspoon Shao Hsing rice cooking wine

¾ teaspoon sugar

¼ teaspoon ground white pepper

3 tablespoons vegetable oil

3 cloves garlic, smashed and peeled

¼ teaspoon salt

Core the iceberg and separate into leaves. Wash the lettuce in several changes of cold water, breaking the leaves in half. Drain thoroughly in a colander until dry to the touch.

In a small bowl, combine the soy sauce, sesame oil, rice wine, sugar, and pepper.

Heat a 14-inch flat-bottomed wok or skillet over high heat until hot but not smoking. Add vegetable oil and garlic, and stir-fry 10 seconds. Add the lettuce and stir-fry 1 minute. Add salt and stir-fry another minute, or until lettuce is just limp. Swirl in sauce and cook 1 more minute, or until lettuce is just tender and still bright green. Serve immediately.

Serves 4 to 6 as part of a multicourse meal.

Pepper and Salt Shrimp

The flavor and texture of this shrimp are fabulous. Once the shrimp are fried, the shells turn a rich shade of orange and are not only edible but crunchy and delicious. The shrimp meat also has a crispness that is unexpected while being juicy and flavorful.

It is very important that the shrimp be sufficiently dry before being marinated. If there is moisture on them, the oil will splatter when the shrimp are added. Be sure to prep all your ingredients before beginning to cook, and make sure the sharp spine has been removed from the tail!

1 pound medium shrimp, unshelled

3/4 teaspoon salt

1 1/2 teaspoons Shao Hsing rice cooking wine

3 tablespoons cornstarch

2 cups vegetable oil

1 teaspoon finely minced garlic

1 teaspoon finely minced ginger

1/4 teaspoon crushed red pepper flakes

1 scallion, finely minced

Using kitchen shears, cut through the shrimp shells two-thirds of the length down the back of the shrimp. Remove the legs and devein the shrimp, leaving the shells and tails on. Pull off the sharp spine that is about ½-inch long between the soft tail fins. Rinse the shrimp under cold water and set on several thicknesses of paper towels. With more paper towels, pat the shrimp dry. Because the shrimp are deep-fried, they must be bone-dry before cooking.

Place the shrimp in a medium bowl, sprinkle with ½ teaspoon salt and the rice wine, and toss to combine. Set aside for about 10 minutes. Do not allow the shrimp to sit for more than 10 minutes or the texture of the shrimp will be mushy. Sprinkle the shrimp with cornstarch and toss until well combined.

In a heavy 9-inch-wide, 4-inch-high pot, heat oil over medium-high heat to 375 degrees. Carefully add the shrimp and cook 45 seconds to 1 minute, or just until shrimp turn bright orange. Carefully remove shrimp with a slotted metal spoon to a platter lined with several thicknesses of paper towels. Remove oil from heat and set aside to cool.

Heat a 14-inch flat-bottomed wok or skillet over high heat until hot but not smoking. Carefully add 1 tablespoon of the reserved hot oil to the wok along with the garlic and ginger, and stir-fry 20 to 30 seconds, or just until mixture begins to brown. Add the shrimp, remaining ¼ teaspoon salt, and crushed red pepper flakes, and stir-fry 1 minute, or until combined and shrimp are just cooked through. Stir in the scallion and serve immediately.

Serves 4 to 6 as part of a multicourse meal.

Sweet and Sour Pork

Sweet and Sour Pork is an authentic Chinese dish, although most restaurants make it poorly. My grandfather, Gunggung, was very fond of it, as is my husband, Michael. Some Chinese families believe a sweet and sour dish of some sort must be eaten on New Year's Eve. The word for sour in Cantonese, *shoon*, sounds like the word for grandchild; thus, they believe by including sour in their meal they will have more grandchildren in the New Year.

I pound pork butt, well trimmed

2 tablespoons thin soy sauce

4 teaspoons Shao Hsing rice cooking wine

I teaspoon sesame oil

½ teaspoon plus 2 tablespoons sugar

¼ teaspoon salt

¼ teaspoon ground white pepper

½ cup plus I tablespoon cornstarch

½ cup all-purpose flour

One 20-ounce can pineapple chunks in juice

⅓ cup ketchup

⅓ cup distilled white vinegar

I cup plus I tablespoon vegetable oil

4 slices ginger

I large green bell pepper, cut into I-inch squares

Cut the pork into 1-inch cubes. In a medium bowl, combine the soy sauce, rice wine, sesame oil, ½ teaspoon sugar, salt, and pepper, and stir to mix thoroughly.

In a medium bowl, combine ½ cup cornstarch and flour. Drain the pork, reserving marinade. Lightly dredge the pork in the cornstarch mixture and set aside on a plate.

Drain the pineapple chunks, reserving ½ cup juice. In a medium bowl, combine pineapple juice, ketchup, vinegar, remaining 2 tablespoons sugar, 1 tablespoon cornstarch, and the reserved marinade, and stir to combine. Set the sweet and sour sauce aside.

In a 14-inch flat-bottomed wok or skillet, heat 1 cup vegetable oil over high heat until hot but not smoking. Carefully add half the pork, spreading it in the wok. Cook undisturbed 1 to 2 minutes, letting pork begin to brown. Then, using a slotted metal spoon, carefully turn pork until it is browned on all sides but not cooked through, 3 to 4 minutes. Transfer the pork to a plate lined with several thicknesses of paper towels, and repeat with remaining pork. Carefully pour the oil out of the wok and set aside to cool before discarding.

Wash the wok and dry thoroughly. Heat the wok over high heat until hot but not smoking. Add remaining 1 tablespoon vegetable oil and ginger, and stir-fry for 10 seconds. Add the green pepper and stir-fry 1 minute, or until pepper is bright green. Add reserved pineapple chunks and swirl the sweet and sour sauce into wok. Bring mixture to a boil over high heat, stirring constantly until just thickened, about 1 minute. Add the pork and cook, stirring, 2 to 3 minutes, or until the pork is just cooked through. Serve immediately.

Serves 4 to 6 as part of a multicourse meal.

Eight Precious Sweet Rice

Mama will occasionally make this for my cousin Fred, whose family is from Shanghai. The Chinese seldom eat desserts, but this is a favorite Shanghainese dessert that Mama loved when she lived there. In English, it is called Eight Precious Sweet Rice, in Cantonese, *Bot Bow Fan*. This dessert is not rich from cream, chocolate, or butter, but the combination of sweet rice, red bean paste, Chinese dried red dates, gingko nuts, walnuts, and lotus seeds is rich in its own way. The ingredients have auspicious meanings, and are all considered to have restorative attributes, so it is a dessert that is enjoyed for its taste, meaning, and nourishment. Dragon eye, also known as *longan*, is a fruit that is available fresh and dried. The fresh season is very brief, but the dried fruit is available year-round. The shell is about 1 inch round, brown, and very thin and brittle. The meat of the dried fruit is deep red to dark brown, about one-quarter inch thick, very sweet, and surrounds a one-half-inch dark pit; *longan* is also available shelled and pitted. Our family's dear friend Alice Woo taught me to include walnuts in the recipes.

¹⁄₃ cup whole blanched lotus seeds, rinsed

12 Chinese dried red dates

1¹⁄₂ cups sweet rice

2 teaspoons vegetable oil

³⁄₄ cup unshelled gingko nuts (bock guo)

1 ounce rock sugar, about 2 tablespoons

¹⁄₄ cup dried dragon eye, shelled and pitted (longan)

4 walnut halves

1 tablespoon dried red cherries

¹⁄₂ cup Sweetened Red Bean Paste, store-bought or homemade (page 139)

In a small bowl, soak the lotus seeds for 30 minutes in enough cold water to cover. Drain and remove the center stems. In a small bowl, soak the red dates in ½ cup cold water for 30 minutes, or until softened. When softened, drain, and remove and discard the pits.

Meanwhile, place the rice in a 1½-quart saucepan. Wash the rice in several changes of cold water until the water runs clear, and drain. Return the rice to the pan, add 1½ cups cold water and ½ teaspoon oil. Bring to a boil over high heat. When it comes to a rolling boil, stir the rice briefly, cover, reduce heat to medium, and cook 7 minutes. Reduce the heat to low and cook 20 minutes. Set aside to cool slightly.

Crack gingko nuts lightly with a hammer, tapping on the opening and removing the shells. In a medium saucepan, bring about 3 cups water to a boil over high heat. Blanch the shelled gingko nuts for about 1 minute. Drain, rinse under cold water, and remove the skins.

In a medium saucepan, combine rock sugar and ⅔ cup cold water. Bring to a boil over high heat. Add the gingko nuts, lotus seeds, and red dates, and return to a boil. Cover, reduce heat to low, and simmer 1 hour, or until lotus seeds are tender and about 2 tablespoons of the cooking liquid is left. Monitor the saucepan carefully to make sure the pan doesn't dry out.

Using a heatproof 4-cup round bowl, about 7 inches across and 6 inches deep, grease the entire interior of the bowl with 1 teaspoon oil. Decorate the bottom of the bowl with the dragon eye, walnuts, and cherries to form a 5-inch ring pattern. Pat all but ¾ cup of the cooked rice evenly in the bowl to within ½ inch of the edge. The rice should be about ¾ inch thick. Place the red bean paste in the center in a mound. Reserving the rock sugar cooking liquid, spoon the cooked gingko nut mixture around the bean paste. Spread the remaining ¾ cup cooked rice on top. Pour 2 tablespoons rock sugar cooking liquid over the rice. Cover the bowl with a heatproof plate.

Bring water to a boil over high heat in a covered steamer large enough to fit the bowl *without touching the sides of the steamer.* Carefully place the bowl in the steamer, cover, and steam on high heat 1½ hours. Check the water level from time to time and replenish if necessary with boiling water. Remove from heat and carefully remove the bowl from steamer. Uncover.

Rub the remaining ½ teaspoon oil on a flat rubber spatula. Gently run the spatula between the hot rice and the bowl to loosen the mixture. Place a 9-inch plate over the bowl and carefully flip the rice onto the plate. If the rice flattens after being unmolded, plump with your hands to make a round mound. Serve immediately.

Serves 6 to 8 as part of a multicourse meal.

帶
子
炒
荷
蘭
豆
青
椒

Stir-Fried Scallops with Snow Peas and Peppers

One of the secrets to stir-frying scallops successfully is to toss them in a little oil just prior to stir-frying. My Auntie Bernice remembers this was a tip her mother taught her, not only for scallops but for chicken and beef. The addition of oil is a technique Chinese home cooks use to prevent chicken, meat, or seafood from sticking to the wok or skillet. Here, golden brown scallops, sweet in flavor, are stir-fried with tender snow peas and crisp peppers, and scented with garlic, ginger, and scallions. This dish is pleasing to both the eye and palate.

4 ounces snow peas

I pound sea scallops

2 tablespoons plus 2 teaspoons cornstarch

I teaspoon plus I tablespoon thin soy sauce

2 teaspoons Shao Hsing rice cooking wine

I ½ teaspoons sesame oil

I ½ teaspoons sugar

⅓ cup Homemade Chicken Broth (page 234)

2 teaspoons oyster flavored sauce

¼ teaspoon salt

3 tablespoons vegetable oil

4 slices ginger

3 cloves garlic, smashed and peeled

I red bell pepper, cut into I-inch squares

2 scallions, cut into 2-inch sections

String the snow peas, rinse, and set them aside.

Wash the scallops in cold water, removing any visible bits of shell or grit. Drain well in a colander and pat dry with paper towels. If there are any large scallops, halve or cut into thirds to match the size of the other scallops. In a medium bowl, combine 2 tablespoons cornstarch, 1 teaspoon soy sauce, 1 teaspoon rice wine, ½ teaspoon sesame oil, ½ teaspoon sugar, and scallops and stir to combine; set aside.

In a small bowl, combine the chicken broth, oyster sauce, salt, and remaining 2 teaspoons cornstarch, 1 tablespoon soy sauce, 1 teaspoon rice wine, 1 teaspoon sesame oil, and 1 teaspoon sugar. Stir until the cornstarch is thoroughly dissolved. Set aside.

Stir 1 tablespoon vegetable oil into the scallop mixture and mix well. Heat a 14-inch flat-bottomed wok or skillet over high heat until hot but not smoking. Add 1 tablespoon vegetable oil and the scallops, spreading them in the wok. Cook undisturbed 1 to 2 minutes, letting scallops begin to brown. Then, using a metal spatula, stir-fry 1 to 2 minutes, or until scallops are firm and slightly brown. Remove scallops from the wok to a plate.

Wash and dry the wok and add the remaining 1 tablespoon vegetable oil, ginger, garlic, snow peas, red pepper, and scallions. Stir-fry 2 to 3 minutes, or until pepper begins to soften. Restir sauce mixture and swirl it into the wok. Return the scallops and any juices that have accumulated on the plate to the wok, and stir-fry 1 to 2 minutes, or until the sauce has thickened slightly and scallops are just cooked through. Serve immediately.

Serves 4 to 6 as part of a multicourse meal.

新年飲食與習俗

NEW YEAR'S FOODS AND TRADITIONS

Cousins Bing Shue and Yuen Wah, Uncle Sam, Mama, cousin Yuen Moy in chair, Auntie Katheryn, Uncle Norman, and Uncle Herbert. Hong Kong, circa 1940.

EVEN TODAY, WHEN I VISIT MY PARENTS at Chinese New Year's I awake on New Year's morning to find two tangerines, two oranges, and a pair of lucky money envelopes, *lysee,* by my pillow—all auspicious symbols of good luck. As a child, I could anticipate finding these as dependably as I could a gift from the tooth fairy when I lost a tooth. *Lysee* are beautiful small red envelopes with money tucked inside, given to children and family members by elders. The amount of money varies, depending on the generosity of the giver, but most Chinese place a dollar in each envelope. The envelopes are decorated with exquisite designs and symbols in gold that are ancient expressions of long life, gratitude, peace, and blessings. The color red is a symbol of happiness and good luck. *Lysee* are also traditionally given on birthdays and weddings.

Mama tells me that, when she was a child in China, they did not have decorated envelopes, so people made their own, wrapping the money in red paper. As a child I hoarded my lucky money like a chipmunk. My brother, however, would open his *lysee* and spend it immediately. Before the holiday, we, like most children, used to secretly anticipate who of our relatives and family friends we'd run into, and just how fat our stack of *lysee* would grow. Today, I still save my *lysee*. I tuck them into jacket pockets or deep inside my purse and count on them to rescue me long after I've forgotten they're there—in a moment when I think I've run out of money, on a bus or in a cab. Then, lo and behold, there is my lucky money. My husband, Michael, like my brother, Douglas, spends his immediately.

My parents' kitchen on New Year's Day is typically laid out with the ingredients for *Jai* (page 126), the Buddhist vegetarian dish: There are bowls of curious cloud ears, dried oysters, black moss, dried lily buds, dried bean curd sticks, cellophane noodles, and Chinese dried mushrooms—all soaking in cold water. Each ingredient for *Jai* has meaning and symbolism, from the wish for more children in the coming year, to blessings and wealth for the household. Mama rises early in the morning to begin the preparations. By late morning, the ingredients will be properly soaked and Mama begins the cooking. The family awaits expectantly, knowing that one of our favorite treats will soon be ready. Even though every family recipe for *Jai* varies slightly, they are all derived from ancient Chinese culture. In keeping with Buddhist traditions, no fish, chicken, or livestock is killed on the first day of the first moon of the lunar year. This is a time of purification and, in order to receive the proper celestial blessings, no blood should be shed for food.

In the evening of New Year's Day, my family follows the tradition of having dinner at home consisting of *Jai,* roast pork, chicken, and fish left over from the New Year's Eve dinner (see "The Good Omen of a Fighting Fish," page 105). These leftovers literally and symbolically carry abundance from the previous year into the New Year. Two or three stir-fried vegetable dishes are also prepared, along with fresh steamed rice and perhaps a fancy soup.

Our breakfast routine is also transformed by traditions during the two-week New Year's celebration. Every morning we have one or all of the following rich savory and sweet cakes: Turnip Cake, *Law Bock Gow* (page 128), Taro Root Cake, *Woo Tul Gow* (page 130), and New Year's Cake, *Neen Gow* (page 132). These, too, have special meanings: All the cakes symbolize rising fortunes, and their roundness is a reminder of family unity and continuity. The New Year's celebration lasts until the fifteenth day of the first moon, or the Lantern Festival, when the New Year's parade is held. Sometime during the two-week celebration my family meets our extended family for an elaborate banquet in a restaurant. This practice is common, for this officially opens the year, *hoy neen,* for the entire family.

My family's life is still dictated by thousands of years of Chinese history and culture. When Douglas and I were growing up, these ancient traditions were conducted within the routine of our typical American lives. Old-fashioned Chinese believe that on the twenty-third or twenty-fourth day of the twelfth month the Kitchen God ascends to heaven to report to the Jade Emperor on the state of every household. Alas, several days prior to the New Year every home is scrubbed and cleaned to renew the house. Our house was decorated with cherry blossoms and pictures of the Money God, and in the corner of the living room, bags of oranges and tangerines studded with *lysee* stood ready for our relatives' visits. Douglas's and my bedroom, nonetheless, was strewn with piles of comic books and rock-and-roll records. While Mama made *Jai,* Douglas was listening to the Rolling Stones. In between visits from our relatives, we would be immersed in an MGM musical on TV. I would move from a mesmerizing moment watching Fred Astaire dance to helping pour tea, *zum cha,* for my uncles, aunties, and cousins.

Popo, my grandmother, and Gunggung, my grandfather, prepared bags of tangerines, oranges, and *lysee* for their family. Boxes of New Year's Cake, *Neen Gow,* in pink cake boxes from the Eastern Bakery in Chinatown, sat, ready to be given to their children. Each of Popo and Gunggung's children, my uncles and aunties, would come with their spouses and children to pay their respects and to wish them a Happy New Year. They would be carrying their bags of oranges and *lysee* for Popo and Gunggung and they, in turn, would give them theirs. My grandparents would never go to visit them on the first day of the year. The Chinese have deep respect for age, and in turn, the younger uncles and aunts call on their elder brothers and sisters first. My parents' generation adheres to these traditions. In my generation, however, I know of no one who makes *Jai,* decorates their homes with cherry blossoms, and makes the traditional New Year's Cakes. None of my cousins have the time, expertise, or interest. However, we still exchange the oranges, tangerines, and *lysee,* along with a profusion of good wishes for the coming year.

My parents, meanwhile, still receive family and friends; eat the New Year's Cakes and Sesame Balls, *Zeen Doy* (page 138); and drink tea all day long, sampling the *Jai* of each home they visit during the two-week celebration. Every traditional Chinese household also has a *chuun hup,* a tray of togetherness, a teak or rosewood box with eight compartments filled with sweets that symbolize the sweetness of life. My parents fill their box with kumquats for golden luck; candied lotus seeds, symbolizing the wish for more sons; dragon eye for their sweetness and roundness; watermelon seeds for more children; chocolate gold coins for golden wealth; candied lotus root symbolizing endless friendship; candied winter melon representing a continuous line of descendants like the vines of the melon plant; and coconut for good relations between fathers and sons.

Throughout the celebration, family and friends repeatedly say to one another "*Gung Hay Fat Choy,*" "Happy New Year" or, literally, "Congratulations Prosperity." For the Chinese people, longevity, blessings to the household, prosperity, and endless friendship represent happiness in a New Year.

Jai

Buddha's Delight

I have heard *Jai* called Buddha's Delight in English, but my family has only known it as *Jai*. In keeping with Buddhist traditions to cleanse the body with only vegetables, no fish, chicken, or livestock is killed for food on the first day of the year, and *Jai* must be eaten on New Year's Day. This recipe is labor-intensive, for there are many ingredients that must be soaked. I have resisted learning to make it all these years, knowing that I am lucky enough to go home and enjoy Mama's delicious *Jai*. Even writing down the method was hard work, as Mama's recipe is quite traditional. Some families cook a more simplified *Jai*, while others use even more ingredients. Traditionally, there should be eighteen ingredients. In one form or another, the dish has been eaten for hundreds of years. Black moss, also known as seaweed hair, looks like fine black hair. The name of the ingredient in Cantonese, *fat choy*, is the same as the New Year's greeting, *Gung Hay Fat Choy*, so it has an auspicious meaning and symbolizes prosperity.

4 large leaves Napa cabbage, about 8 ounces

8 Chinese dried oysters

¼ cup cloud ears (*wun yee*)

¼ cup lily buds (*gum tzum*)

8 Chinese dried mushrooms

¼ cup packed black moss (*fat choy*)

1 teaspoon plus 3 table-spoons vegetable oil

One 3½ ounce package cellophane noodles

2 sticks dried bean curd (*foo jook*), about 1½ ounces

6 fried bean curd (*dul foo gock*), cut into 2 pieces

¼ cup unshelled gingko nuts (*bock guo*)

Rinse the Napa cabbage leaves in several changes of cold water and drain thoroughly in a colander until dry to the touch.

Wash the oysters in cold water. In a small bowl, soak the oysters in 1½ cups cold water for 3 to 4 hours, or until soft. Drain and squeeze dry, reserving the soaking liquid.

Place the cloud ears, lily buds, and mushrooms in separate bowls. Pour about ½ cup cold water over each ingredient and soak for about 30 minutes to soften. When softened, drain all the ingredients, discarding all the water except the mushroom liquid. Remove any hard spots from the cloud ears. Remove the hard end from the lily buds and tie each lily bud into a knot. Drain and squeeze dry the mushrooms. Cut off and discard the stems and halve the caps.

Place the black moss in a medium bowl, and cover with cold water. Add 1 teaspoon oil and soak for 15 minutes, or until softened. Drain and discard the water. In another bowl, soak the cellophane noodles in cold water to cover for 15 minutes, or until softened. Drain thoroughly.

Meanwhile, in a 2-quart saucepan, bring 3 cups cold water to a boil over high heat. Break up the bean curd sticks into 2-inch pieces and add to the boiling water. Cook, stirring the pieces, 1 to 2 minutes,

3 slices ginger

**3 cubes red wet bean curd
(*nom yu*)**

**3 tablespoons oyster flavored
sauce**

or until almost ivory colored and softened. Using a slotted spoon, remove to a colander, drain, and rinse under cold water. Add fried bean curd to boiling water and boil 1 to 2 minutes, or until puffed. Drain and rinse under cold water. Squeeze fried bean curd with hands to remove any excess water. Set aside.

Crack gingko nuts lightly with a hammer, tapping on the opening and removing the shells. In a small saucepan, bring about 1 cup water to a boil over high heat. Blanch the shelled gingko nuts for about 1 minute. Drain, rinse under cold water, and remove the skins.

Trim ¼ inch from stem end of cabbage leaves and discard. Stack 2 to 3 cabbage leaves at a time and cut crosswise into ¼-inch-wide shreds.

Heat a 14-inch flat-bottomed wok or skillet over high heat until hot but not smoking. Add 2 tablespoons vegetable oil and ginger, and stir-fry 30 seconds. Add the cabbage and stir-fry 2 to 3 minutes, or until cabbage is just limp. Transfer to a plate.

Add the remaining 1 tablespoon vegetable oil to the wok along with the oysters, red wet bean curd, and mushrooms, and stir-fry 30 seconds. Add the softened bean curd sticks, blanched fried bean curd, gingko nuts, and black moss, and cook, stirring to break up the red bean curd.

Add the reserved mushroom and oyster soaking liquids, and bring to a boil over medium-high heat. Cover, reduce heat to low, and simmer 20 minutes. Check the wok from time to time, adding up to 1 cup more cold water if the wok appears dry. Add the cellophane noodles, cloud ears, lily buds, cabbage, and oyster sauce (and any juices that have accumulated), and return to a boil over high heat. Cover, reduce heat to medium, and cook until cellophane noodles are translucent and cooked through and vegetables are tender, about 5 minutes. Serve immediately.

Serves 6 to 8 as part of a multicourse meal.

Turnip Cake

This is the delicious savory cake served in dim sum houses throughout the year and, most auspiciously, on New Year's Day as a symbol of prosperity and rising fortunes. Turnip cake is made with Chinese turnip, *law bock,* which is a type of daikon radish. There is also a daikon radish called Japanese daikon radish, which is similar to the Chinese turnip in appearance. To make matters more confusing, *law bock,* translated into English, means *turnip.* Some produce vendors do not realize there is a distinction, but the Chinese turnip is more blemished looking than the Japanese daikon, which has a creamier white color. Although Chinese turnip is best for this recipe, whichever one you use, choose a firm, heavy vegetable. The turnip should ideally be 8 to 12 inches long and about 4 inches wide.

Some people remove only the rind of the Chinese bacon and finely chop the whole piece, using all the fat. But I find this too rich, so I discard the thick layer of fat under the rind. In recipes that call for Chinese bacon to be sliced, all that is required is a sturdy cook's knife or cleaver. However, when the bacon needs to be finely chopped, as in this recipe, the bacon should be steamed first to make it easier. Make sure to use rice flour and not glutinous rice flour!

I've never met anyone who served an entire cake at once. During the first ten days of the New Year's celebration a few slices of all the different New Year's cakes are fried every morning for breakfast or when friends or family stop by. The cake will keep nicely in the refrigerator for ten days if wrapped in plastic wrap.

**6 ounces Chinese Bacon
(*lop yok*), store-bought or
homemade (page 182)**

**1 large Chinese white turnip,
about 2 pounds**

8 Chinese dried mushrooms

**⅓ cup Chinese dried shrimp,
about 1¼ ounces**

**2 teaspoons Shao Hsing rice
cooking wine**

1 teaspoon sugar

2 cups rice flour

Cut the bacon into 3 equal pieces and place in a 9-inch shallow heatproof bowl. Bring water to a boil over high heat in a covered steamer large enough to fit the bowl *without touching the sides of the steamer.* Carefully place the bowl into steamer, cover, reduce heat to medium, and steam 15 to 20 minutes, or just until the bacon is softened and there are juices in the dish. Check the water level from time to time and replenish, if necessary, with boiling water. Carefully remove the dish from the steamer and set aside to cool.

Peel the turnip and grate to make about 4½ cups. In a 3-quart saucepan, combine grated turnip and about 1 quart cold water, and bring to a boil over high heat. Reduce heat to low, cover, and simmer 30 minutes, or until very tender. Drain, reserving the cooking liquid.

Meanwhile, in a medium bowl, soak the mushrooms in ½ cup cold water 30 minutes, or until softened. Drain and squeeze dry, reserv-

1 ¼ teaspoons salt

Vegetable oil, for pan-frying

Oyster flavored sauce

ing the soaking liquid. Cut off and discard stems and mince the caps. In a small bowl, soak the dried shrimp in ½ cup cold water for 30 minutes, or until softened. Drain, reserving soaking liquid. Finely chop shrimp and set aside.

Remove the bacon from its dish and reserve the juices. Cut off and discard the rind and the thick layer of fat. Cut the remaining meat into paper-thin slices and then finely chop. In a 14-inch flat-bottomed wok or skillet, stir-fry the chopped bacon over medium heat for 2 to 3 minutes, or until meat releases fat and just begins to brown. Add the minced mushrooms and shrimp, and stir-fry 2 to 3 minutes. Add the rice wine, sugar, and pan juices from the bacon, and stir to combine. Remove from heat.

Return the cooked, drained turnip to the saucepan, add the bacon and mushroom mixture, and stir to combine. In a large bowl, combine the rice flour and the reserved mushroom and shrimp soaking liquids, stirring until smooth. Stir in 1 cup of the hot turnip broth. Pour this batter into the saucepan, add the salt, and stir until combined. The consistency will resemble that of rice pudding. Pour mixture into a heatproof 8-inch round, 3- to 4-inch-deep, straight-sided bowl, such as a soufflé dish.

Bring water to a boil over high heat in a covered steamer large enough to fit the dish *without touching the sides of the steamer*. Carefully place the dish in the steamer, cover, reduce heat to medium-low, and steam 1 hour, or just until cake is set and is firm to the touch. Check the water level and replenish, if necessary, with boiling water. Carefully remove the bowl from the steamer and allow to cool on a rack for about 1 hour. Cover and refrigerate at least 3 to 4 hours.

Run a knife along the edge of the cake to loosen sides. Place a cake rack over the bowl and invert to unmold. Flip the cake right-side up onto a cutting board. Wrap the cake in plastic wrap and refrigerate until ready to use.

When ready to eat, cut cake into quarters. Cut each quarter crosswise, not into wedges, but into two 2-inch-wide strips. Cut each strip crosswise into scant ½-inch-thick slices. This is the typical way of slicing a cake Chinese style.

Heat a 14-inch flat-bottomed wok or skillet over medium heat until hot but not smoking. Add just enough oil to barely coat the wok. Add the turnip cake slices in batches and cook 2 to 3 minutes per side, until golden brown. Serve immediately, with oyster sauce.

Makes one 8-inch cake, about 48 slices.

Taro Root Cake

Homemade taro root cake is unsurpassed if the home cook doesn't skimp on the ingredients. Thick slices of taro cake, richly flavored with scallops, mushrooms, shrimp, Chinese bacon, and creamy taro, are pan-fried until golden brown and fragrant. My Auntie Ivy's mother, Che Chung Ng, makes such a recipe and is famous in the family for both her Turnip Cake and Taro Root Cake. Every New Year, she cooks several cakes and gives them away as gifts to close family members. Nothing is measured exactly, and it is impressive to see her produce cake after cake, especially because she is over eighty years old. Spry and agile, she cooks with full energy and total intuition, never missing a beat. She kindly taught me this recipe and the preceding one for Turnip Cake.

Wear rubber gloves when handling taro, as some people can have an allergic reaction to touching it. See Glossary (page 264) for information on purchasing taro. Also, use rice flour and not glutinous rice flour!

See the introduction to Turnip Cake (page 128) for how to serve and store this New Year's cake.

¼ cup **Chinese dried scallops** (*gawn yu chee*) about I ounce

8 **Chinese dried mushrooms**

¼ cup **Chinese dried shrimp,** about I ounce

6 ounces **Chinese Bacon** (*lop yok*), store-bought or homemade (page 182)

I large **taro root,** about 2¼ pounds

1½ teaspoons **salt**

2 cups **rice flour**

Vegetable oil, for pan-frying

Oyster flavored sauce

In a small bowl, soak the scallops in ⅓ cup cold water for about 2 hours, or until softened. Drain, reserving the soaking liquid. Remove and discard the small hard knob from the side of the scallops. Finely shred the scallops

Meanwhile, in a medium bowl, soak the mushrooms in ½ cup cold water for 30 minutes, or until softened. Drain and squeeze dry, reserving the soaking liquid. Cut off and discard the stems and mince the caps. In a small bowl, soak the dried shrimp in ⅓ cup cold water for 30 minutes, or until softened. Drain, reserving the soaking liquid. Finely chop shrimp and set aside.

Cut the bacon into 3 equal pieces and place in a 9-inch shallow heatproof dish. Bring water to a boil over high heat in a covered steamer large enough to fit the dish *without touching the sides of the steamer.* Carefully place the dish in the steamer, cover, reduce heat to medium, and steam 15 to 20 minutes, or just until bacon is softened and there are juices in the dish. Check the water level from time to time and replenish, if necessary, with boiling water. Carefully remove the dish from the steamer and set aside to cool.

Meanwhile, wearing rubber gloves, peel taro root and cut into ½-inch cubes to make about 7 cups. In a 4-quart saucepan, combine the taro root, 1 teaspoon salt, and about 1½ quarts cold water, and bring to a boil over high heat. Reduce heat to low, cover, and simmer 15 to 20 minutes, or until taro has turned a pale lavender color and is just tender when pierced with a knife.

Remove the bacon from its dish and reserve the juices in the dish. Cut off and discard the rind and thick layer of fat underneath. Cut the remaining meat into paper-thin slices and then finely chop. In a 14-inch flat-bottomed wok or skillet, stir-fry the chopped bacon over medium heat 2 to 3 minutes, or until meat releases fat and just begins to brown. Add the minced mushrooms, scallops, and shrimp, and stir-fry 2 to 3 minutes. Stir in pan juices from the bacon and remove from heat.

Drain the taro in a colander, reserving the cooking liquid. Return the taro to the saucepan, add the bacon and mushroom mixture, and stir to combine. In a large bowl, combine the rice flour and the reserved mushroom, scallop, and shrimp soaking liquids, stirring until smooth. Stir in 1 cup of the reserved hot taro broth. Pour this batter over the taro mixture in the saucepan. Add the remaining ½ teaspoon salt and stir until combined. Consistency will resemble that of thick rice pudding. Pour mixture into a heatproof 8-inch round, 3- to 4-inch-deep, straight-sided bowl, such as a soufflé dish.

Bring water to a boil over high heat in a covered steamer large enough to fit the dish *without touching the sides of the steamer.* Carefully place the dish into the steamer, cover, reduce heat to medium-low, and steam 1 hour, or just until cake is set and is firm to the touch. Check the water level and replenish, if necessary, with boiling water. Carefully remove the bowl from the steamer and cool on a rack about 1 hour. Cover and refrigerate at least 3 to 4 hours.

Run a knife along the edge of the cake to loosen the sides. Place a cake rack over the bowl and invert to unmold. Flip the cake right-side up onto a cutting board. Wrap the cake in plastic wrap and refrigerate until ready to use.

When ready to eat, cut the cake into quarters. Cut each quarter crosswise, not into wedges, but into two 2-inch-wide strips. Cut each strip crosswise into scant ½-inch-thick slices. This is the typical way of slicing a cake Chinese style.

Heat a 14-inch flat-bottomed wok or skillet over medium heat until hot but not smoking. Add just enough vegetable oil to barely coat the wok. Add the taro cake slices in batches and cook for 2 to 3 minutes per side, until golden brown. Serve immediately with oyster sauce.

Makes one 8-inch cake, about 48 slices.

年糕 *Neen Gow*

New Year's Cake

Neen Gow, New Year's Cake, is the most important cake eaten on New Year's—the main ingredient, glutinous rice flour, is a symbol of cohesiveness. The egg-dipped, pan-fried slices have a mellow sweetness and are slightly chewy from the glutinous rice flour. Mama remembers watching her grandmother's servants scraping the slab brown candy, *peen tong*, for this cake, which is the traditional technique. Brown candy is a kind of sugar that is sold by the slab in 1-pound packages and is also available loose in bins in some Chinese markets. The slabs are about 5 inches long, 1¼ inches wide, and a scant ½ inch thick. The scraping of the sugar is extremely labor-intensive, so some cooks dissolve the slabs of sugar in water, which is less authentic but much easier to prepare. Be sure to use glutinous rice flour here, not regular rice flour!

See the introduction to Turnip Cake (page 128) for how to serve and store this New Year's Cake.

3 Chinese dried red dates

5 slabs brown candy (*peen tong*), about 11 ounces

3 teaspoons vegetable oil

7 cups glutinous rice flour

1 tablespoon white sesame seeds

1 large egg

Vegetable oil, for pan-frying

In a small bowl, soak the red dates in ¼ cup cold water for 30 minutes, or until softened. When softened, remove and discard the pits.

Cut each brown candy slab into 8 pieces. Place sugar in a heatproof bowl, pour 2 cups boiling water over the sugar, and set aside until dissolved and completely cooled.

Grease a heatproof 8-inch round, 3- to 4-inch-deep, straight-sided bowl, such as a soufflé dish, with 2 teaspoons vegetable oil.

In a large bowl, place rice flour. Make a well and stir in cold sugar water. Knead dough in the bowl, adding an additional ⅓ cup cold water until dough is smooth, slightly moist, and shiny, 5 to 10 minutes.

Place the dough in the prepared dish and pat until it fills the dish evenly.

Cut the red dates into halves and place cut-side down in a ring around the outside of the dough, leaving a few to decorate the center.

Sprinkle the top with sesame seeds. Coat with the remaining 1 teaspoon oil, using your fingers and lightly pressing down on the dates and sesame seeds.

Bring water to a boil over high heat in a covered steamer large enough to fit the dish *without touching the sides of the steamer.* Carefully place the dish into the steamer, cover, and steam 35 to 40 minutes on high heat. Check the water level and replenish, if necessary, with boiling water. The cake is done when it begins to pull away from the sides of the pan. Carefully remove the dish from the steamer and pour off any excess liquid on the surface. Place on a rack to cool. Loosely cover and set at room temperature in a cool room until the next day, when it will be ready to eat.

Run a knife along the edge of the cake to loosen sides. Place a cake rack over the bowl and invert to unmold. Flip the cake right-side up onto a cutting board. Wrap the cake in plastic and refrigerate until ready to use.

When ready to eat, cut the cake into quarters. Cut each quarter crosswise, not into wedges, but into two 2-inch-wide strips. Cut each strip crosswise into scant ¼-inch-thick slices. This is the typical way of slicing a cake Chinese style. Beat an egg in a small bowl, until frothy. Dip the slices in egg.

Heat a 14-inch flat-bottomed wok or skillet, over medium heat until hot but not smoking. Add just enough vegetable oil to barely coat the wok, add the egg-dipped slices in batches and cook 2 to 3 minutes per side, until golden brown. Serve immediately.

Makes one 8-inch cake, about 72 slices.

馬蹄糕

Ma Tai Gow

Water Chestnut Cake

Water Chestnut Cake is often served in dim sum houses and is popular around New Year's when water chestnuts are in season. Few home cooks know how to make this cake, but my Auntie Lily taught me this recipe. It is a dessert for Chinese tastes and does not resemble a Western cake at all, for it has a gelatinlike texture with finely chopped pieces of sweet and crisp water chestnuts, and it is cooked on the stove top.

Auntie Lily says it can be a little tricky to find good water chestnut flour for this cake. The flour should be as white as possible, not black. If it is black, it means the water chestnuts were not completely peeled before being made into flour; it can be saved for coating foods to be fried, but not used for Water Chestnut Cake. Not every Chinese grocery store carries water chestnut flour, and the quality will vary, but Pan Tang brand is generally very good.

As with the Taro Root and the Turnip Cakes, no one serves an entire cake at once. The cake will keep nicely in the refrigerator for ten days, if properly wrapped in plastic wrap.

16 fresh water chestnuts, about 12 ounces

2 teaspoons vegetable oil

One 1-pound package rock sugar

One 8⁴/₅-ounce package pure water chestnut flour

Vegetable oil, for frying

Peel the water chestnuts with a paring knife and finely chop them to make about 2 cups. The water chestnuts can also be quartered, placed in a food processor, and finely chopped. Coat the bottom and sides of an 8-inch-wide, 4-inch-deep pot with the vegetable oil.

In a 2-quart saucepan, combine 3½ cups cold water and the rock sugar. Cover and cook over medium heat until the sugar dissolves, about 10 minutes. Pour all but about 2 tablespoons into the prepared pot (the last bit of sugar water will often contain dirty residue from the rock sugar).

In a medium bowl, combine the water chestnut flour with 1 cup warm, not hot, water. Stir with a wooden spoon until smooth, adding ½ cup more warm water, until it looks like milk. Pour liquid through a fine-mesh strainer into a large bowl. Return the residue to the medium bowl and combine with ½ cup cold water. Pour the liquid through the strainer into the large bowl and stir to combine, discarding any remaining residue.

Add the water chestnuts to the sugar water and bring to a boil over high heat. Reduce the heat to medium and add the bowl of water chestnut milk, stirring constantly. Reduce heat to medium-low and cook, stirring constantly, until the mixture is very thick, 5 to 7 minutes. The mixture will become difficult to stir and will turn darker. Continue stirring vigorously for 2 to 3 minutes, on medium-low heat, until it is almost unstirrable. Remove it from the heat.

Smooth the mixture on top until it is spread evenly in the pot. Set aside to cool, uncovered, for 5 hours in a cool and breezy room.

When cool, run a knife along the edge of the cake to loosen the sides. Place a cake rack over the pot and invert it to unmold. Flip the cake right-side up onto a cutting board. Wrap the cake in plastic wrap and refrigerate until ready to use.

When ready to eat, cut the cake into quarters. Cut each quarter crosswise, not into wedges, but into two 2-inch-wide strips, then cut each strip crosswise into scant ½-inch-thick slices. This is the typical way of slicing a cake Chinese style.

Heat a 14-inch flat-bottomed wok or skillet over medium heat until hot but not smoking, and add just enough vegetable oil to barely coat the wok. Add the water chestnut slices in batches and fry each side 2 to 3 minutes, until golden brown. Serve immediately.

Makes one 8-inch cake, about 48 slices.

Nom Yu Peanuts

In China, peanuts are a popular snack item. Mama tells me vendors would walk the streets selling roasted peanuts late into the night. My Uncle Norman would buy a huge bag of peanuts, which the brothers and sisters would devour in one sitting. Peanuts are plentiful in China and are considered a food of longevity. There are numerous recipes for roasting them; Mama taught me this recipe years ago. Slowly oven-roasted, these peanuts are crisp and have an excellent mahogany color and a sweet, earthy taste. If you can, buy the one-pound bags of shelled peanuts in Chinese food markets for this recipe; otherwise use regular shelled peanuts. See Nom Yu Spareribs (page 56) for information on purchasing wet bean curd.

½ cup sugar

2 tablespoons salt

1 cube red wet bean curd (*nom yu*)

1 pound shelled peanuts with skins

In a small saucepan, bring 1½ cups cold water, sugar, salt, and bean curd to a boil over high heat, stirring to dissolve. Remove from heat and let bean curd water cool to room temperature, about 1 hour.

Place peanuts in a large, shallow bowl and pour the cooled mixture over the peanuts, stirring to combine. Marinate the peanuts about 4 hours, stirring occasionally.

Drain the peanuts in a colander, shaking out excess liquid. Discard the marinade. Line a 11-by-17-inch pan with aluminum foil.

Preheat oven to 250 degrees. Spread the peanuts on the prepared pan and bake 3½ hours, stirring occasionally, until peanuts are dry, crisp, and mahogany colored. Cool pan on a rack. Store peanuts in an airtight jar.

Makes about 4 cups.

Candied Walnuts

My Auntie Lulu made these nuts for me over thirty years ago. When I brought them home, Mama explained to me this was a famous treat from Beijing. It made her smile to taste them, for she hadn't had them since her days in China. The walnuts had a lovely nutty aroma and were covered by a thin sugar coating that was crisp and unlike anything I'd ever tasted before. Auntie Lulu shared the recipe with me and, for many years afterwards, my parents and I would make this together. You must work quickly and carefully, so it is much easier to do it with three sets of hands than to do it alone.

1 pound shelled walnut
   halves, about 4 cups

1 cup sugar

6 cups vegetable oil

Check through the walnuts to make sure only walnut halves are used, removing any small walnut pieces and reserving them for another use. Line the counter with about 2½ feet of aluminum foil.

In a 2½-quart saucepan, bring 1 quart cold water to a boil over high heat. Add the walnuts and return to a boil. Drain the walnuts in a colander and immediately place them in a large bowl.

Pour the sugar over the walnuts, and continually stir with a rubber spatula until the sugar is completely dissolved by the heat of the hot walnuts and no sugar is visible. Be careful not to break the walnuts as you stir. The walnuts should be shiny and coated in liquid sugar.

Heat a 14-inch skillet with the vegetable oil over medium-high heat until the oil registers 375 degrees on a deep-fat thermometer. Carefully add the walnuts, spreading them in the skillet. Cook undisturbed 2 minutes, letting the walnuts begin to brown. Then, using a metal slotted spoon, carefully stir the walnuts in the skillet to make sure they brown evenly. Fry an additional 1 to 3 minutes, or until golden brown.

When the nuts are golden, immediately turn off the heat. Carefully and quickly begin removing them with the slotted spoon to the foil, leaving as much space between the walnuts as possible. Do not place the walnuts on the foil in clusters, as they will harden that way.

To avoid severe burns, do not touch or taste the nuts until they have cooled. Carefully transfer them to a cookie sheet lined with several thicknesses of paper towel. Towel-dry the nuts to remove as much oil as possible. When they have cooled completely, transfer to an airtight jar. Let the hot oil cool before discarding.

Makes about 4 cups.

Sesame Balls

When we were children, we adored *zeen doy* (sesame balls). The dough is fried until golden brown so it is both crisp and chewy from the glutinous rice flour. It is eaten year-round, but especially for New Year's and for birthday celebrations. As the dough fries, it expands, so the Chinese believe if you eat Sesame Balls your fortunes will expand similarly. The Sweetened Red Bean Paste (page 139) for the filling can be purchased in a can or homemade. Sesame Balls must be eaten the day they are made. The following day, they can be heated in a 300-degree oven but, like so many foods, they are not nearly as good as when they are fresh. Remember to use glutinous rice flour and not rice flour! My Auntie Lil, who taught me this recipe, says the secret is to never knead the dough and to use cold sugar water. See the technique photos on page 17 for how to form and fill the balls.

2½ slabs brown candy (*peen tong*), chopped

3 cups glutinous rice flour

1 cup Sweetened Red Bean Paste, store-bought or homemade (page 139)

⅓ cup white sesame seeds

2 quarts vegetable oil

Dissolve the brown candy in 1 cup of boiling water and set aside to cool overnight.

Place the rice flour in a large bowl. Make a well and add candy water all at once. Stir until the water is incorporated; the dough will be smooth but slightly sticky.

Dust hands lightly with rice flour and roll dough into a thick rope. Cut the rope into 24 equal pieces, roll each piece into a ball, and flatten to make a 2½-inch round.

Using the thumbs and index fingers from both hands, pleat the edges of the dough to form a cup. Place one index finger into the cup and gently press the dough into the opposite palm on all sides of the cup to create a smooth, even surface and to make the dough even thinner.

Add a scant 1 teaspoon of the red bean paste mixture. Gently pack the filling down. Gather the edges of the dough over the filling and, again, pleat until the hole is about ½ inch in diameter. Squeeze together the dough, pressing to seal the dough securely. Roll between palms to form a ball. Continue filling the remainder of the dough. Place a sheet of waxed paper on the counter and sprinkle with the sesame seeds. Roll and press the outside of each ball in the sesame seeds.

In an 8-inch wide, 5-inch deep pot, heat vegetable oil over medium-high heat until hot but not smoking, about 330 degrees on a deep-fat thermometer. Carefully add 6 sesame balls at a time, and cook over medium heat until golden, 6 to 7 minutes. As the balls float to the surface, begin to press them gently with the back of a metal spatula against the sides of the pot. The balls will expand as they are gently rotated and pressed. Increase heat to medium-high and fry until golden brown, about 2 minutes. Place on a plate lined with several thicknesses of paper towels. Repeat with remaining sesame balls. Set aside oil to cool before discarding. Serve immediately.

Makes 24 sesame balls.

Dul Sah

豆沙

Sweetened Red Bean Paste

Canned red bean paste is an acceptable product, but the homemade kind is obviously much tastier. In Chinese markets, you'll find small, plump dried red beans called *hoong dul,* not to be confused with adzuki beans, *zeck siu dul,* also small red beans that are oblong in shape. This recipe makes about 1½ cups of red bean paste, just enough filling for Sesame Balls (page 138). If using it for Eight Precious Sweet Rice (page 120), make about one-half the recipe. Use regular brown sugar for this recipe.

**6 ounces small red beans
(hoong dul), about 1 cup**

**½ cup packed dark brown
sugar**

1½ teaspoons vegetable oil

Wash the red beans, cover with cold water, and soak overnight. Drain beans and discard water. Place beans in a 1½-quart saucepan, add 3 cups cold water, and bring to a boil over high heat. Cover, reduce heat to medium-low, and simmer 1 hour, or until very soft. Monitor the pan to make sure water doesn't dry up. Drain and discard the water.

Place the beans in a food processor and process until smooth. Add brown sugar and process until just combined. In a medium saucepan, heat the vegetable oil over medium heat until hot but not smoking. Add the bean paste and cook, stirring, 2 to 3 minutes, or until the mixture is dry. Remove from heat. Store in a covered container in the refrigerator until ready to use; it will keep for 1 week.

Makes 1½ cups.

新歲如在祖國

Sun Suey Yu Tchoy Tzoe Kwok

A DAY LIVED AS IF IN CHINA

Great-Grandfather Tong Kung Foon. Hong Kong, circa 1928.

ONE CHINESE NEW YEAR'S MORNING, Popo suddenly announced that she simply had to go to the market. Popo, my mother's eighty-nine-year-old mother, resided with my parents at the time. Although Popo has lived in America for nearly twenty years, she can still only say "yes," "no," "hello," "good-bye," and "thank you" in English. (We have a theory that she understands more, but that's another story.) In any case, Popo has fashioned her American life after her life in the Far East as much as she possibly can.

On this, the most special day in Chinese culture, she insisted that Baba drive her immediately to a nearby Chinese produce store to buy oranges and lettuce (*saang choy*). We already had about forty pounds of oranges in the house, but since oranges are the great symbol of good luck in the New Year and *saang choy* sounds like the Cantonese expression for "growing or producing fortune," Popo wanted to buy even more symbolic luck and fortune for herself and her family.

When we arrived at the market, I helped Popo out of the car, and she walked briskly into the store, intent on choosing the oranges and *saang choy* herself. After careful inspection, she deliberately selected eight oranges and the *saang choy*. (The number eight is yet another symbol of luck; in Cantonese, *bot*, eight, sounds like the word for fat, to rise—all expressions of prosperity.) As I watched Popo, I thought that, even as frail as she was, she forced herself out to do this to enhance her family's fortunes for the coming year.

As we drove home, Baba explained to me that there is a saying in Cantonese that sometimes in life it is wise to walk a full circle for good luck. Thus, our little drive to the market enabled Popo to do three things that would bring her good fortune: buy the symbolic oranges and *saang choy,* do something involving the number eight, and make a small circle home. I was left with the impression that Popo had begun the year with time-honored traditions, but later my Uncle Sam and Mama explained that, in China, stores were traditionally closed on New Year's Day. So Popo, as old-fashioned as she seems to me, had "Americanized" her customs to suit her Western life. It was a day lived as if in China, but with a small adjustment.

The following recipes in this chapter are extremely time consuming. My family will occasionally make them, but they reflect the kinds of dishes that were commonly made in Popo's life in China, where servants did all the cooking. Today most of these dishes, such as Fancy Winter Melon Soup (page 143) and West Lake Duck (page 146), are eaten in restaurants, and the Pork Dumplings (page 156), Won Ton (page 158), Pot Stickers (page 160), Shrimp Dumplings (page 162), Stuffed Noodle Rolls (page 164), Spring Rolls (page 166), and Scallion Cakes (page 168), specifically, are typical dim sum dumplings and pastries. In addition, Turnip Cake (page 128), Taro Root Cake (page 130), Water Chestnut Cake (page 134), Chicken Porridge (page 13), and Sesame Balls (page 138) are also customarily served in dim sum teahouses.

Dim sum literally means "a dot on the heart," or the eating of little things to touch the heart. It is the Cantonese teahouse tradition of sampling steamed and fried dumplings along with a wondrous variety of bite-sized wrapped foods and pastries while drinking tea and chatting leisurely in the morning to early afternoon. The Cantonese also call this *yum cha,* or drinking tea.

Many years ago a friend and I were visiting Hong Kong when we heard about one of the last traditional dim sum teahouses. There the sun-drenched teahouse opened at six in the morning and was mainly frequented by men who brought their tiny birds in exquisite cages and hung them on a long bamboo pole along the wall. The men sampled the dim sum leisurely, drank fine tea, admired one another's birds, and philosophized about life over the course of many hours—a slow-paced enjoyment of life's pleasures as occurs in a French café. I have always appreciated this glimpse I was given of old-world China. Today in Asia and America dim sum houses are often five- to twenty-thousand-square-foot multilevel restaurants with chandeliers and gold-trimmed decor. They are meeting places for Chinese families to gather, especially on weekends, when the wait to get in can be long. The restaurants are a whirl of activity and commotion, with hostesses working the floors with microphones, shouting out table availability. Waitresses wheel stainless-steel carts with a grand variety of dim sum items, and people rarely linger leisurely.

Few Chinese families know how to make any of the countless dumplings or classic dim sum items. Our lives are too busy to take time to learn to make these labor-intensive delicacies. My family always considered dim sum to be far too complicated to make at home. For me, I wanted to learn to make some of the classic items to preserve this great Cantonese tradition and the beautiful memory of the teahouse I saw many years ago.

Fancy Winter Melon Soup

One of the great Cantonese delicacies is winter melon soup served in the melon. The Cantonese prize foods that are nourishing to the body, and winter melon double-steamed in the melon is the most esteemed presentation. Winter melon is said to cleanse the body, the lotus seeds invigorate the kidneys, and the lily bulbs lubricate the organs. What's more, it is delicious when made with fine Homemade Chicken Broth (page 234), flavorful Chinese mushrooms, bamboo shoots, and Roast Duck (page 180), and served with a fine dusting of Smithfield ham.

Traditionally, a 10-pound winter melon is cooked for banquets, but there is no way most home cooks could find a pot big enough to fit such a melon. I can remember my parents making this soup a half dozen times on special occasions when I was a child. Baba would artistically carve two meaningful Chinese characters on the outside of the melon; restaurants often carve dragons, fish, or cherry blossoms. Guests were always stunned by the dramatic presentation when he brought the melon to the table, and also because this soup is seldom attempted by the home cook.

To decorate a winter melon, use the sharp tip of a bamboo skewer like an etching tool to incise a pattern on the outside of the melon. The idea is to scratch away the dark-colored rind to expose the lighter-colored flesh beneath. The contrast between the dark rind and the light flesh is what makes the pattern visible. Just be careful not to pierce the winter melon skin too deeply, as it will collapse when it is steamed. The depth of your etching should be no deeper than a scant 1/4 inch.

Although the larger winter melons are dramatic, the more practical size—and the one most commonly cooked in home kitchens—is no more than 5 pounds. The melon must be small enough to fit in a heatproof bowl like a 2-quart large soufflé dish or a round Pyrex casserole. The melon and bowl must then fit on a rack in a large canning or lobster pot without touching either the sides or lid of the pot. The roast duck can be purchased in a Chinese deli, or use the recipe from page 180; only a small portion is needed.

(continued on next page)

3 ounces **Smithfield ham,
preferably Chinese-style
with bone**

I tablespoon **light brown
sugar**

8 **Chinese dried mushrooms**

¼ cup **whole, blanched lotus
seeds**

I½ **quarts Homemade
Chicken Broth (page 234)**

¼ cup **lily bulbs** (*bock hup*),
rinsed

⅓ cup **diced canned bamboo
shoots, rinsed**

One 5-pound, **evenly shaped,
whole winter melon**

⅓ cup **diced Roast Duck,
store-bought or
homemade (page 180)**

Rinse the ham in cold water. In a small saucepan, bring 1 cup cold water to a boil over high heat. Add the ham and return to a boil. Reduce heat to medium-low, cover, and simmer 20 minutes. Drain the ham and rinse under cold water. Pat it dry with paper towels. Place the ham in a small heatproof dish and add the brown sugar.

Bring water to a boil over high heat in a covered steamer. Carefully place the dish into the steamer, cover, lower heat to medium, and steam 20 minutes, or just until the ham is softened. Check the water level and replenish, if necessary, with boiling water. Carefully remove the dish from the steamer and set the ham aside, discarding any juices that have accumulated in the dish.

Meanwhile, in a medium bowl, soak the mushrooms in ½ cup cold water for 30 minutes, or until softened. Drain and squeeze dry, reserving the soaking liquid. Cut off and discard the stems and dice the caps.

Rinse the lotus seeds and cover with cold water for 30 minutes. Drain and remove the tiny green sprout in the center of each seed.

In a 2½-quart saucepan, bring the chicken broth to a boil over high heat. Cut off about one-third of the ham and add the larger piece with the bone to the broth. Slice the remaining ham into paper-thin slices. Stack a few slices at a time and cut into paper-fine shreds; then cut the shreds to make a superfine dust of ham. Wrap with plastic wrap and set aside.

When the broth comes to a boil, add the mushrooms and their soaking liquid, lotus seeds, lily bulbs, and bamboo shoots, and return to a rolling boil. Cover, reduce heat to medium-low, and simmer 45 minutes to 1 hour, or until the lotus seeds and lily bulbs are tender. Remove the ham and discard it.

Meanwhile, prepare the winter melon. Wash the melon under cold water with a hard bristle brush to remove the white powder coating on the outside. Cut a paper-thin slice from the bottom of the melon so the melon can sit upright. Place the melon in a 2-quart soufflé dish or Pyrex bowl. The melon should fit snugly; if the melon is a little too small, simply place a piece of ginger between the melon and the bowl to wedge the melon firmly in place (it should not be able to move).

Cut off the top of the melon, as you would a pumpkin, using a sharp knife to make V-cuts about 3 inches from the top of the melon. Remove the lid, seeds, and string pulp.

Place about 2 inches cold water in a pot large enough to fit the winter melon in the heatproof bowl on a rack *without touching the sides of the pot* (for example, a canning kettle or a lobster pot). Carefully ladle the hot soup into the winter melon, leaving 1½ inches of space from the top. Place a round cake rack on the bottom of the pot, and carefully place the bowl with the winter melon on the rack. Cover the pot and bring to a boil over medium-high heat. Steam on medium-high heat 2½ hours, checking the water level, and never letting the depth of the water fall below 1½ inches; replenish with boiling water as necessary.

After 2½ hours, remove the cover and turn off the heat. Check to see if the melon is tender by piercing it with a small, sharp knife. If it is nearly tender, add the roast duck and all but 1 tablespoon of the minced ham. Cover and return the water to a boil (check the water level and replenish with boiling water if necessary). Reduce heat to low and simmer an additional 10 to 15 minutes, or until the winter melon is tender. *Check the melon every 5 to 10 minutes, because the melon can cook quickly and the sides can collapse if overcooked!*

Remove from heat and, using thick potholders, carefully remove the bowl from the pot. Sprinkle the remaining ham on the serrated edge and bring the bowl to the table. To serve, run a sharp knife between the melon rind and flesh, about ¼ inch in from the rind and 2 inches down the side of the melon. The cooked melon flesh will collapse inward and fall into the soup. Ladle the piping-hot soup, with some of the melon flesh, into individual bowls. Trim off the top piece of melon rind and discard. Continue cutting melon from the rind in the same fashion before ladling the hot soup. Serve immediately.

Serves 6 to 8 as part of a multicourse meal.

West Lake Duck

I learned to make West Lake Duck from our family friend Chen Mei. Patiently, she browned the duck by cleverly holding it by its neck and repeatedly turning it over until every nook and cranny was a rich golden brown color. Ducks are sold in Chinatown with head and feet and, if you buy it this way, the total weight should be about four pounds rather than three pounds.

West Lake Duck is a winter specialty. The stuffing of lotus seeds, chestnuts, mushrooms, barley, and gingko nuts soaks up the sublime cooking juices from the browned duck and marinade. The kitchen is enveloped with lovely aromas that tease the senses until the duck is finally cooked. If it weren't so time-consuming to make, I would eat this all the time.

According to Chen Mei, older ducks require longer cooking. You cannot tell the age of a duck when it is raw. A cook must use his or her judgment to decide the age of a duck as it cooks.

One 3-pound duck

4 teaspoons salt

12 dried chestnuts, about 1 1/2 ounces

1/2 cup whole, blanched lotus seeds

1/3 cup barley

8 Chinese mushrooms

3 tablespoons Shao Hsing rice cooking wine

2 tablespoons thin soy sauce

1 tablespoon light brown sugar

2 teaspoons sesame oil

1 1/2 teaspoons black soy sauce

1 teaspoon ground white pepper

1 cup unshelled gingko nuts

1 pound Napa cabbage

Cilantro sprigs

Remove any fat pockets from the duck. Rub the duck all over with 2 teaspoons salt. Rinse under cold water and place it on a rack. Pat the duck dry inside and out with paper towels.

Rinse the chestnuts in several changes of cold water. Completely cover the chestnuts in cold water and soak for 3 hours, or until soft. Drain and, using a paring knife, remove any visible skin from the chestnuts.

Meanwhile, rinse the lotus seeds and cover with cold water for 30 minutes. Drain and remove the tiny green sprout in the center of each seed. Rinse the barley in several changes of cold water and drain.

In a medium saucepan, bring 1 cup water to a boil over high heat. Add the chestnuts, cover, reduce heat to low, and simmer 15 minutes. Add the lotus seeds and barley, and return to a boil over high heat. Turn off the heat and let stand, covered, 45 minutes, or until the chestnuts, lotus seeds, and barley are just tender. Drain, transfer to a medium bowl, and set aside.

Meanwhile, in a medium bowl, soak the mushrooms in 1/2 cup cold water for 30 minutes, or until softened. Drain and squeeze dry, reserving the soaking liquid. Cut off and discard stems and slice the caps.

In a large roasting pan, combine the rice wine, thin soy sauce, brown sugar, sesame oil, remaining 2 teaspoons salt, black soy sauce, and pepper, and stir to combine. Add the duck and rub the mixture all over the skin and in the cavity. Marinate the duck for 45 minutes.

Crack the gingko nuts lightly with a hammer, tapping on the opening and removing the shells. In a small saucepan, bring about 1 cup water to a boil over high heat. Blanch the shelled gingko nuts for about 1 minute. Drain, rinse under cold water, and remove the skins.

Separate the Napa cabbage into leaves. Wash the leaves in several changes of cold water and drain thoroughly in a colander until dry to the touch.

Remove the duck from the marinade, reserving the marinade.

In a 14-inch skillet, add the duck breast-side up and cook undisturbed for 5 minutes on medium to medium-high heat, until light golden brown. Carefully turn the duck over and cook 4 to 5 minutes. Pour off any excess fat or blot it away with paper towels. Keep turning the duck, adjusting the heat between medium to medium-high heat until the duck is a deep golden brown on all sides, 10 to 15 minutes.

Carefully transfer the duck to a platter lined with several thicknesses of paper towels. Carefully pour the fat from the skillet and set aside to cool before discarding.

Add the gingko nuts, mushrooms, and the reserved duck marinade to the bowl of barley chestnut mixture and stir to combine. Stuff this into the duck's cavity. Return the duck to the skillet breast-side up. Add ½ cup boiling water and the reserved mushroom liquid, and bring to a boil over high heat. Cover, reduce the heat to medium, and simmer for 30 minutes. Carefully turn the duck over and continue cooking for 30 minutes. Skim any surface fat.

Trim ¼ inch from the stem end of the cabbage leaves and discard. Stack 2 to 3 cabbage leaves at a time and cut them crosswise into ¼-inch-wide shreds.

Return the liquid to a boil over high heat. Add the cabbage to the skillet and return to a boil. Reduce the heat to medium-high and cook, uncovered, stirring frequently, until the duck is just tender, about 10 minutes. Carefully transfer the duck to a platter and place the cabbage and sauce around the duck; garnish with cilantro. Serve immediately.

Serves 4 to 6 as part of a multicourse meal.

Braised Nom Yu and Taro Duck

Nom Yu and Taro Duck is traditionally eaten on August 15 on the Lunar calendar, which is roughly in September or October on the Roman calendar. It
signifies the changing of the seasons and a time to begin eating heartier, warming foods, in contrast to the cooler foods suitable for the summer. After the
duck and taro have been braised in wet bean curd, soy sauce, brown sugar,
sesame oil, and rice wine, they become sinfully rich. It is best when cooked the
day before, so that the flavors can penetrate the duck and taro.

In Chinatown, duck will be sold with head and feet, and should weigh
about four pounds. Otherwise, it should be about three pounds. The duck is
best when marinated overnight, but it is still delicious even after just 1½
hours of marinating. See Nom Yu Spareribs (page 56) for information on
purchasing wet bean curd.

One 3-pound duck

3 teaspoons salt

**4 cubes red wet bean curd
(*nom yu*)**

3 tablespoons thin soy sauce

**2 tablespoons Shao Hsing
rice cooking wine**

1 tablespoon black soy sauce

**1 tablespoon light brown
sugar**

4 teaspoons sesame oil

**½ teaspoon ground white
pepper**

1 taro root, about 3 pounds

1 teaspoon sugar

Cilantro sprigs

Remove any fat pockets from the duck and rub it all over with 2 teaspoons salt. Rinse the duck under cold water and place on a rack.
Pat the duck dry inside and out with paper towels.

In a large roasting pan, combine the 3 cubes wet bean curd, 2 tablespoons thin soy sauce, rice wine, black soy sauce, brown sugar,
2 teaspoons sesame oil, ½ teaspoon salt, and pepper, and stir to combine, mashing the wet bean curd. Add the duck and rub the mixture all over the skin and in the cavity. Marinate at least 1½ hours
in a cool and breezy room.

Wearing rubber gloves (raw taro can be irritating to the skin), peel
the taro root with a cleaver or cook's knife and quarter it lengthwise. Cut each quarter crosswise into scant ½-inch-thick slices.
Place the taro in a large bowl and add the remaining 1 tablespoon
thin soy sauce, 2 teaspoons sesame oil, sugar, ½ teaspoon salt, and
remaining 1 cube bean curd, and stir to combine.

Remove the duck from its marinade, reserving the marinade.

In a 14-inch skillet, add the duck breast-side up and cook, undisturbed, 5 minutes on medium to medium-high heat until light
golden brown. Carefully turn the duck and cook 4 to 5 minutes.
Pour off any excess fat or blot with paper towels. Keep turning the
duck, adjusting the heat between medium and medium-high until
the duck is a deep golden brown on all sides, 10 to 15 minutes.

Carefully transfer the duck to a platter lined with several thicknesses of paper towels. (Carefully pour off any fat from skillet and set aside to cool before discarding.) Add 1½ cups water and the reserved marinade to the skillet. Add the duck breast-side up and bring to a boil over high heat. Cover, reduce the heat to medium, and cook 30 minutes. Turn the duck over and cook 30 minutes. Add the taro root and return to a boil over high heat. Cover, reduce heat to low, and cook another 30 to 45 minutes, or until the duck and taro root are cooked through. The cooked taro will have the texture of potato. Garnish with cilantro. Serve immediately.

Serves 4 to 6 as part of a multicourse meal.

Stuffed Chicken Wings

When my parents used to entertain, I remember Mama cooking this for special occasions. I would watch her painstakingly debone the wings and, with equal dexterity, stuff each one. I fondly recall how amazing it was to taste slivers of mushroom, chicken, ham, and bamboo all in one bite. This summer, when I requested that Mama show me how to make it, it had been thirty years since I last tasted this dish. It was as delicious as I remember, but I gained a renewed appreciation for the culinary expertise it demands. For the Chinese, chicken wings are a great delicacy; they are said to bless one with the ability to soar a thousand miles.

4 Chinese dried mushrooms

2 ounces Smithfield ham

**2 teaspoons light brown
  sugar**

**10 chicken wings, about
  2¼ pounds**

**¾ cup canned whole bamboo
  shoots, rinsed**

1 teaspoon cornstarch

Cilantro sprigs

In a medium bowl, soak the mushrooms in ¼ cup cold water for 30 minutes, or until softened. Drain and squeeze dry, reserving the soaking liquid. Cut off and discard the stems and thinly slice the caps.

Meanwhile, rinse the ham in cold water. In a small saucepan, bring 1 cup cold water to a boil over high heat. Add the ham and return to a boil. Reduce the heat to medium-low, cover, and simmer for 20 minutes. Drain the ham and rinse under cold water. Pat it dry with paper towels. Place the ham in a small heatproof dish and add brown sugar.

Bring water to a boil over high heat in a covered steamer. Carefully place the dish into steamer, cover, reduce heat to medium, and steam 20 minutes, or just until ham is softened. Check the water level and replenish, if necessary, with boiling water. Carefully remove the dish from the steamer, set the ham aside, reserving any juices that have accumulated in the dish. When cool enough to handle, slice the ham into paper-thin slices. Stack a few slices at a time and cut into paper-fine shreds.

Meanwhile, rinse the chicken wings under cold water and place on a rack. On a cutting board, cut the wings at the joint above the drumette (the section with a single bone that looks like a mini drumstick). Reserve the drumettes for another use (they're excellent for chicken stock). Using a paring knife, starting at the end where the wing was attached to the drumette, carefully scrape the meat off the 2 wing bones toward the wing tip, without tearing the skin or removing the wing tip. Twist both wing bones, rotating them until they can be easily pulled out. Discard the bones.

Slice the bamboo shoots into 2-inch long, scant ¼-inch-thick slices. Stack the slices and cut into fine shreds.

Stuff each chicken wing with a few mushroom, ham, and bamboo shreds. Place the stuffed wings in one layer in a 9-inch shallow heat-proof bowl.

Bring water to a boil over high heat in a covered steamer large enough to fit the dish *without touching the sides of the steamer.* Carefully place the dish into the steamer, cover, and steam on high heat, 8 minutes. Check the water level and replenish, if necessary, with boiling water. Turn off the heat. Let stand, covered, 7 minutes. Test the chicken for doneness by poking it with a knife; juices should run clear. If not, resteam 1 to 2 minutes, or until chicken is just cooked.

Remove from heat, carefully remove the bowl from steamer, and pour off any liquid into a small saucepan. Add the reserved mushroom and ham juices. In a small bowl, combine cornstarch and 2 tablespoons cold water. Bring the mixture in the saucepan to a boil over high heat. Add the cornstarch mixture and cook, stirring, 1 minute, or until thickened. Pour sauce over chicken wings. Garnish, with cilantro. Serve immediately.

Serves 4 to 6 as part of a multicourse meal.

Savory Rice Tamales

One of the most traditional recipes in the Cantonese repertoire is *zoong,* or rice tamales. They are made for the Dragon Festival on the fifth day of the fifth month of the lunar calendar to commemorate the summer solstice. My family never made *zoong,* but sometimes Mama's friends would do so and offer them as gifts. It was such a treat to get homemade *zoong,* for they are far superior to the ones sold in Chinatown. Each *zoong* is a meal in itself: It typically has sweet rice, pork, sausage, dried shrimp, mung beans, and duck eggs. The filling ingredients for the savory tamales are up to the cook. In addition to the ingredients called for below, you can put in Chinese mushrooms, dried scallops, chestnuts, lotus seeds, or peanuts.

The process of making *zoong* is difficult and very time consuming, but the results are so heavenly that I wanted to learn to make them. The number of people who know how to do this is diminishing quickly, so to help preserve this art I have included the two styles of *zoong:* savory (*hom zoong*), below, and sweet (*gan soy zoong),* which follows. The sweet tamales are much easier to make, though, to my taste, the savory are better. No one ever makes two or three *zoong,* because the process is so involved. A recipe generally makes about thirty, but by the time you have given a few away to privileged friends, and your family has eaten a few, they seem to disappear far too quickly. The bamboo leaves that wrap the *zoong* are called *zook yeep* in Cantonese.

1 package bamboo leaves

1 pound pork butt, well trimmed

¼ cup plus 5¼ teaspoons salt

5 pounds sweet rice

⅔ cup vegetable oil

2 packages (14 ounces each) yellow mung beans

12 salted duck eggs (*hom dan*)

3 Chinese sausages (*lop chong*)

½ cup Chinese dried shrimp

Find the stem end of the bamboo leaf. Cut ½ inch from this end on each leaf (photo 1). Place leaves in a large canning pot, cover in hot, but not boiling, water, and soak overnight.

Cut the pork into 2- by ½-inch pieces. Toss with ¾ teaspoon salt. Cover and refrigerate overnight.

Rinse the bamboo leaves in cold water. Place the leaves, ¼ cup salt, and enough cold water to cover in a large canning pot. Bring to a boil over high heat. Cover, and boil on high heat, 30 minutes. Turn off the heat and leave pot covered until the water cools to room temperature. Drain and scrub the leaves, one at a time, under cold water and drape in a colander so that the water can drip off. It's important to wash the leaves carefully to prevent the finished tamales from molding.

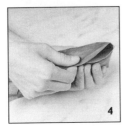

Rinse the rice in several changes of cold water and soak in enough cold water to cover for 1 hour, or until rice is soft to the bite. Transfer rice to a colander and drain well. Place the rice in a large bowl and mix in remaining 4½ teaspoons salt and oil, and stir until combined.

Rinse the yellow mung beans in several changes of cold water and drain well. Crack open the duck eggs, discarding egg whites, which are watery and cloudy. Cut egg yolks, which are very sticky, in half and set aside. Cut each Chinese sausage into 2-inch-long pieces, then quarter each piece lengthwise. Rinse the dried shrimp in several changes of cold water and drain well.

Using only untorn bamboo leaves, take two moist leaves, with the hard rib–side down, and place them on top of each other lengthwise, overlapping all but 1 inch along the bottom length. With the 1-inch overlap facing you, fold the leaves in half crosswise, with the bottom edges together (the top edges stay open). Fold the 1-inch overlap to close the bottom and to form a pocket (photo 2). Hold the pocket in one palm with the ends of the leaves facing you. Place about ½ cup rice into the pocket. Make a well and add 1 tablespoon of the yellow mung beans, ½ egg yolk, 2 pieces of Chinese sausage, 4 to 5 dried shrimp, and 1 piece of pork. Sprinkle on 1 tablespoon of the yellow mung beans and 2 to 3 tablespoons of the rice so that the filling is almost covered. Wrap a third leaf around the two leaves to extend the depth of the pocket by ½ inch (photo 3). Pinch the two top edges together and fold the top edge tightly over the filling to seal (photo 4). Stand the tamale with the open end up and lightly tap to help the filling settle. The filling should be as compact as possible. Turn the tamale so one of the folded edges is facing you, and fold the open ends tightly over the filling toward you to seal (photo 5). This will force the tamale to form a tight pyramid.

Using about 3 feet of string for each tamale, place the center of the string in the center of the tamale and wind 7 or 8 times across the width and then 2 or 3 times lengthwise. Secure tightly with a knot. Repeat with the remaining ingredients to make about 30 tamales.

In a large canning pot, bring water to a rolling boil over high heat. Add as many tamales as can fit into the pot and still be totally covered in water. You may need to use 2 or 3 pots to cook all the tamales, depending on the size of your pots. Return to a boil, cover, and cook at a rolling boil on high heat 5 hours, replenishing with boiling water frequently, so that the tamales are always totally covered in boiling water. Carefully monitor the pots as the tamales cook.

(continued on next page)

Halfway through cooking, rotate the tamales so that the ones on top are shifted to the bottom. Drain. To serve, string and carefully unwrap, discarding the bamboo leaves. Place any remaining, wrapped tamales in the refrigerator where they will keep for about 10 days. To reheat refrigerated tamales, cook on high heat in enough boiling water to cover 30 minutes, or until heated through. Tamales can be frozen, wrapped securely in plastic bags, and will keep for about 4 months. Reheat in boiling water for about 45 minutes.

Makes about 30 tamales.

Gan Soy Zoong

梘水粽

Sweet Rice Tamales

The name Sweet Rice Tamales is deceptive, for they are not in the least bit sweet. I believe they are so named because the main ingredient is sweet rice. The preparation of the Sweet Tamales differs slightly from that of the Savory Tamales. Only two leaves are used instead of three for wrapping and the method of wrapping is simpler for the novice to master. The final shape is not a pyramid but a flat rectangular package, and it's wrapped slightly more loosely than the savory tamale, which makes the rice fluffier.

Potassium carbonate solution, or *gan soy,* is available in bottles in most Chinese grocery stores.

½ package bamboo leaves

1/4 cup salt

2 pounds sweet rice

2 tablespoons potassium carbonate solution

1 tablespoon vegetable oil

Find the stem end of the bamboo leaf. Cut off ½ inch from this end on each leaf (photo 1, page 153). Place the leaves in a large canning pot, cover in hot, but not boiling, water, and soak overnight.

Rinse the bamboo leaves in cold water. Place the leaves, ¼ cup salt, and enough cold water to cover in a large canning pot. Bring to a boil over high heat. Cover, and boil on high heat 30 minutes. Turn off heat and leave covered until water cools to room temperature. Drain and scrub the leaves, one at a time, under cold water and drape in a colander so that the water can drip off. It's important to wash the leaves carefully to prevent the finished tamales from molding.

Rinse the rice in several changes of cold water and soak in enough cold water to cover for 30 minutes (do not soak the rice for more than 30 minutes or it will absorb too much potassium carbonate and become bitter). Transfer rice to a colander and drain well. Place the drained rice in a large bowl and add potassium carbonate, which will immediately turn the rice a pale yellow color. Mix with hands until well combined. Add oil, and stir until combined.

Using only untorn bamboo leaves, take two moist leaves, with the hard rib–side down, and place them on top of each other lengthwise, overlapping all but ¾ inch along the bottom length. With the ¾-inch overlap facing you, fold the leaves in half crosswise, with the bottom edges together (the top edges stay open). Fold the ¾-inch overlap to close the bottom and to form a pocket (photo 2, page 153). Hold the pocket in one palm with the ends of the leaves facing you. Place ½ to ⅔ cup rice into the pocket and spread it (photo 3, page 153). Pinch the two top edges together and fold the top edge over the filling to seal (photo 4, page 153). Cut off excess leaves at the open ends and fold the ends over the filling to form a compact rectangle (photo at left).

Using about 2½ feet of string for each tamale, place the center of the string in the center of the tamale and wind 7 or 8 times across the width and then 2 or 3 times lengthwise. Secure tightly with a knot. Do not wrap too tightly; allow room for the rice to expand. Repeat with remaining ingredients to make about 10 tamales.

In a large pot, bring water to a rolling boil over high heat. Add as many tamales as will fit into the pot and still be totally covered in water. You may need to use 2 pots to cook all the tamales, depending on the size of your pots. Return to a boil and cook, covered, at a rolling boil on high heat 5 hours, replenishing with boiling water frequently, so that the tamales are always totally covered in boiling water. Carefully monitor the pots as the tamales cook. Halfway through cooking, rotate the tamales so that the ones on top are shifted to the bottom.

Drain and allow to cool to room temperature. (If eaten immediately, the tamales will cause hiccups.) To serve, cut the string, unwrap, discarding the bamboo leaves. Place any remaining, wrapped tamales in the refrigerator where they will keep for about 10 days. To reheat refrigerated tamales, cook on high heat in enough boiling water to cover 20 minutes, or until heated through. Tamales can be frozen, wrapped securely in plastic bags, and will keep for 4 months. Reheat in boiling water for about 30 minutes.

Makes about 10 tamales.

Pork Dumplings

There are many different kinds of pork dumplings, and *siu mai* are one of the most popular, typically served in dim sum restaurants. When homemade, the dumplings are unsurpassed, if they are made with an equal amount of fresh water chestnuts to ground pork, Chinese mushrooms, cilantro, and scallions.

Siu mai are distinctly different from other dumplings, because they are made with round won ton skins, not the typical square-shaped skins. Each brand has a different thickness of dough, but the thinner the better; the dumplings will be more delicate. If round won ton skins are not available, I cut square wrappers into 3-inch-wide circles. This recipe makes about 3½ dozen *siu mai*. Steam as many as you need, or cover in plastic wrap, refrigerate, and steam within two to three hours.

8 Chinese dried mushrooms

14 fresh water chestnuts, about 12 ounces

8 ounces ground pork butt

2 tablespoons finely chopped cilantro

1 cup minced scallions

1 tablespoon plus 1 teaspoon Shao Hsing rice cooking wine

1 tablespoon thin soy sauce

1½ teaspoons sesame oil

2 teaspoons sugar

¼ teaspoon salt

¼ teaspoon ground white pepper

½ cup cornstarch

2 large egg whites, beaten

½ package fresh round won ton skins, about 8 ounces

8 large flat Napa cabbage leaves

In a medium bowl, soak the mushrooms in ½ cup cold water for 30 minutes, or until softened. Drain and squeeze dry (reserve soaking liquid for use in soups). Cut off and discard stems and mince the caps.

Peel water chestnuts with a paring knife and finely mince to make about 2 cups. In a medium bowl, combine the pork, mushrooms, water chestnuts, cilantro, and scallions. Add the rice wine, soy sauce, sesame oil, sugar, salt, and pepper, and stir to combine. Add cornstarch and combine by hand. Add the egg whites and continue to combine by hand. You should have about 3 cups.

Place won ton skins on work surface and lightly cover with a damp towel. If you are right-handed, touch the tip of your left index finger to the tip of your thumb to form a small circle. Place one won ton skin over the hole and place about 2 teaspoons of filling in the center of the won ton skin (photo 1). Gently let the won ton filling drop halfway through the hole, and gently squeeze in with your left hand. Then, carefully pleat excess skin, pressing down filling (photo 2). Stand filled dumpling on the work surface and continue filling the rest of the won ton skins.

Line a bamboo or metal steamer basket or cake rack with 2 cabbage leaves. Place the dumplings on the leaves in a single layer, ½ inch apart. The size of your steamer rack will determine how many dumplings can be cooked at one time.

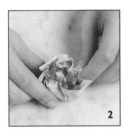

Bring water to a boil in a covered steamer over high heat. Carefully place the steamer basket or rack (if using a rack, the water level cannot touch the cabbage leaves) into steamer, cover, and steam 5 to 7 minutes on high heat until the pork is just cooked through. Carefully remove dumplings from the steamer and continue steaming remaining dumplings using fresh cabbage leaves and replenishing steamer with more boiling water, if necessary. Serve immediately.

Makes about 42 dumplings. Serves 6 to 8 as part of a multicourse lunch.

Won Ton

The translation of won ton is "cloud swallow." If made correctly, won tons should be heavenly morsels, sweet from the shrimp and mushrooms, and crisp with fresh water chestnuts. Although we rarely made these at home, I have fond memories of watching waiters wrap won tons, and of wishing I could imitate their graceful movements. Around three or four in the afternoon, when most Chinese restaurants quiet down, waiters in many Cantonese restaurants sit around a big round table and make won tons. With a flick of the wrist, they seem to wrap them effortlessly, as if by magic.

4 Chinese dried mushrooms

6 ounces medium shrimp, shelled and deveined

4 ounces ground pork butt

3 tablespoons minced scallions

2 tablespoons minced fresh water chestnuts

2 tablespoons finely chopped cilantro

1 tablespoon plus 4 teaspoons thin soy sauce

1 ½ teaspoons Shao Hsing rice cooking wine

5 teaspoons sesame oil

¼ teaspoon ground white pepper

¼ teaspoon sugar

½ package fresh square won ton skins, about 8 ounces

1 quart Homemade Chicken Broth (page 234)

Cilantro sprigs

In a medium bowl, soak the mushrooms in ¼ cup cold water for 30 minutes, or until softened. Drain and squeeze dry, reserving the soaking liquid. Cut off and discard the stems and mince the caps.

Finely chop the shrimp. In a medium bowl, combine the shrimp, pork, 2 tablespoons scallions, water chestnuts, cilantro, 1 tablespoon soy sauce, rice wine, 1 teaspoon sesame oil, pepper, sugar, and mushrooms, and stir to combine.

Remove the won ton skins from their package and cover loosely with a dampened cloth. With one corner of a won ton skin facing you, place a rounded teaspoon of filling on the bottom corner (photo 1). Starting at the bottom, roll the wrapper up ¾ of the way, covering the filling. Press the wrapper on both sides of the filling to seal (photo 2). Lightly brush a little water on one of the two side corners. Bring the side corners together and overlap them. Press to seal (photo 3). Place the won tons on a plate and lightly cover with a dampened towel until all the won tons have been wrapped. Makes about 48 won tons.

In a 4-quart pot, bring 3 quarts of water to a boil, covered, over high heat.

Meanwhile, in a separate 1½-quart pot, combine the chicken broth and reserved mushroom soaking liquid. Cover and bring to a boil over high heat. Reduce heat to low, cover, and simmer until serving time. Divide the remaining 4 teaspoons soy sauce, sesame oil, and 1 tablespoon of minced scallions among 4 large, deep soup bowls.

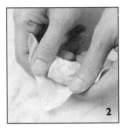

Once the water comes to a boil, add half the won tons, and return to a boil over high heat. Add 1 cup cold water and return to a boil. When the won tons float to the surface, they are done, 3 to 4 minutes. Remove the won tons with a slotted spoon, placing about 12 won tons in each of two soup bowls. Gently toss the won tons in the sauce mixture. Ladle in half of the hot chicken broth and garnish with fresh cilantro. Repeat with remaining won tons. Serve immediately.

Makes about 48 won tons. Serves 4 for a typical Chinese lunch.

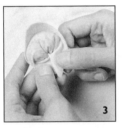

鍋貼 *Kuo Tiep*

Pot Stickers

I discovered Pot Stickers at about the same time I was introduced to Scallion Cakes (page 168). Pan-fried on only one side, the dough for these dumplings is at once crisp and chewy. When I was about eleven years old, I could sometimes devour a dozen of these fried dumplings in one sitting. It was such a sweet pleasure to eat as much as you wanted and still be a skinny child. Filled with pork, cabbage, and a rich broth, every bite was heavenly.

The secret of these pot stickers is to reduce the Homemade Chicken Broth (page 234) until it is concentrated enough to jell when refrigerated. The broth should then be roughly chopped and stirred into the filling mixture right before the dumplings are formed. The Pot Stickers are pan-fried only on one side a few minutes until golden. A little water is added, the lid is placed on the pan, and then, as the dumplings steam-cook, the broth melts. To eat, place a pot sticker in a deep spoon (traditionally, a Chinese porcelain spoon) and sprinkle with a few ginger shreds and a little red rice vinegar. Gently bite into the dumpling and the delicious broth that has now melded with the flavors of the pork filling will burst forth.

The technique for making this dough has some similarities to the preparation of Savory Rice Dumplings (page 16). Read the introduction for more information on handling a hot water dough safely.

1 cup Homemade Chicken Broth (page 234)

2 cups all-purpose flour, plus additional for kneading

4 large leaves Napa cabbage, about 8 ounces

1 tablespoon salt

4 ounces ground pork butt

¼ cup finely minced scallions

1 tablespoon finely minced ginger, plus ¼ cup finely shredded ginger

1 tablespoon thin soy sauce

In a small saucepan, bring the broth to a boil over high heat. Boil on high heat, uncovered, 5 to 10 minutes, or until the broth is reduced to about ¼ cup. Pour the broth into a small bowl and refrigerate until firm.

Measure ¾ cup boiling water into a glass measuring cup and cool for 10 minutes. Place 2 cups flour in a medium bowl. Add the hot water and stir until the mixture begins to pull away from the sides of the bowl. Lightly dust your hands with flour and work the mixture for a few seconds at a time, as the mixture will be very hot, to form a dough. Turn onto a work surface that has been lightly dusted with about 1 tablespoon flour, and knead briefly for 5 minutes with lightly floured hands, adding more flour if necessary, until smooth. Cover with a slightly damp cloth and allow to rest for 1 hour.

Trim ¼ inch from the stem end of each cabbage leaf and discard. Stack 2 to 3 cabbage leaves at a time and cut crosswise into ¼-inch-

1 ½ teaspoons sesame oil

2 teaspoons plus 4 table-spoons vegetable oil

1 teaspoon Shao Hsing rice cooking wine

½ teaspoon sugar

⅓ cup Chinese red rice vinegar

wide shreds to make about 8 cups. Add salt and toss to combine. Transfer the cabbage to a colander and drain. About 1 cup of liquid will be released, especially if you squeeze the cabbage from time to time.

In a medium bowl, combine the pork, scallions, 1 tablespoon minced ginger, soy sauce, sesame oil, 2 teaspoons vegetable oil, rice wine, and sugar. Set aside.

After the dough has rested, continue kneading 5 more minutes on a lightly floured surface. The dough should be elastic, smooth, and not sticky. Roll the dough into an even rope about 15 inches long. Cut the rope into ½-inch pieces to form about 30 pieces. Roll each piece into a ball. Flatten each ball with a rolling pin that has been lightly dusted with flour into 3-inch rounds, rolling from the center to the edges, making the center slightly thicker and the edges thinner. Cover all unused dough with a slightly damp cloth.

The chicken broth should be firm by now. Roughly chop the broth into bite-sized pieces. Refrigerate until ready to use.

Squeeze any excess moisture from the cabbage. The cabbage should have the appearance of having been cooked. Add the cabbage and chopped chicken broth to the pork mixture. Place about 2 teaspoons of pork in the center of each round of dough. Fold in half to form a half-moon, and pinch one end of the half-moon together. Using your thumb and index finger, make 4 or 5 small pleats in the front piece of dough, then pinch together the other end of the dough to seal the dumpling (photo at left). If necessary, brush a little water to help the dough stick together. Dust each dumpling lightly with flour. Stand each dumpling so the rounded edge is upright.

Heat a 14-inch flat-bottomed wok or skillet over medium-high heat until hot but not smoking. Add 1 tablespoon oil, and carefully add 8 dumplings, rounded-side up, about ½ inch apart. Pan-fry 1 to 2 minutes, or until golden brown, gently using a metal spatula to make sure the dumplings are not sticking to the wok. Add ⅓ cup cold water, immediately cover the wok, and cook 3 minutes. Uncover the wok, and fry 2 more minutes on medium heat, or until almost all the water has evaporated. The dumplings should be served immediately. Place the vinegar and the remaining shredded ginger in little condiment dishes and serve with the dumplings. Using 1 tablespoon oil for each batch, continue frying the remaining dumplings, 8 at a time.

Makes about 30 pot stickers. Serves 6 to 8 as part of a multicourse lunch.

Shrimp Dumplings

When we were children, shrimp dumplings were our favorite dim sum dish. The classic filling is shrimp and bamboo shoots. The dough is not difficult to make, but it is very important that the water be boiling hot. If it is not hot enough, the wheat starch will not cook and the dough will not work. Handling this dough is similar to the technique for making Savory Rice Dumplings (page 16). Read the introduction for information on handling dough safely. Wheat starch (*dung fun*) is only available in Chinatown; regular white flour is not a substitute.

The tortilla press used here is excellent for making the dough into thin, uniform rounds, but you can also make the dumplings by hand: Roll the dough into scant 1-inch balls. Place one ball between your lightly floured hands and press to form a circle. Press the dough evenly with your fingertips to make it as thin as possible, about 3 inches in diameter and a scant ⅛-inch thick.

8 ounces medium shrimp, shelled and deveined

3½ teaspoons plus ¼ cup cornstarch

½ teaspoon salt

½ large egg white, beaten

1 teaspoon thin soy sauce

1 teaspoon Shao Hsing rice cooking wine

¾ teaspoon sesame oil

¼ teaspoon sugar

¼ teaspoon ground white pepper

½ cup canned shredded bamboo shoots, rinsed and finely chopped

1 tablespoon finely minced bacon fat

In a medium bowl, combine the shrimp and 2 teaspoons cornstarch. Let stand for 10 minutes. Rinse in several changes of cold water and drain well. Finely chop the shrimp and place in a medium bowl. Add the salt, egg white, soy sauce, rice wine, sesame oil, sugar, pepper, and 1½ teaspoons cornstarch. Stir in the bamboo shoots and minced bacon fat. Loosely wrap with plastic wrap and set aside.

In a large bowl, combine the wheat starch and remaining ¼ cup cornstarch, and stir to combine. Make a well and add 1 cup boiling water, immediately stirring with a rubber spatula as you add the water (the mixture will have a faint fragrance of wheat starch). Stir in the vegetable oil. Carefully begin working the mixture for a few seconds at a time by hand, as the mixture will be very hot. Add an additional 1 to 2 tablespoons boiling water if dough is dry, and knead an additional 2 to 3 minutes, or until smooth and still hot to the touch.

Divide the dough into 4 equal pieces. Roll each piece into a cylinder about 8 inches long. Place 3 rolls in a plastic bag so they will not get dry. Cut the remaining roll into 10 pieces. Place each piece of dough between 2 sheets of lightly oiled foil, place the foil in a tor-

**1½ cups wheat starch
(*dung fun*)**

1 tablespoon vegetable oil

**8 large, flat Napa cabbage
leaves, about 1 pound**

tilla press, and press into a thin round (photo 1). Peel off the round of dough; it should be about 3 inches in diameter and a scant ⅛ inch thick.

Place about 1½ teaspoons of the filling in the center of a dough round. Fold in half to form a half-moon and pinch one end of the half-moon together. Using your thumb and index finger, make 4 or 5 small pleats in the front piece of dough, then pinch together the remaining end of the dough to seal the dumpling (photo 2). Place the dumpling on a plate. Continue making dumplings.

Line a bamboo steamer, metal tier, or rack with 2 cabbage leaves. Place the dumplings on the leaves ¼ inch apart. The dumplings should be cooked in batches; the size of your steamer rack will determine how many dumplings can be cooked at one time.

Bring water to a boil over high heat in a covered steamer. If using a rack, the water level must not touch the cabbage leaves. Carefully place the bamboo steamer, metal tier, or rack into the steamer, cover, and steam 5 minutes on high heat, or until the shrimp is orange and visible through the translucent dough, and is just cooked. Check the water level and replenish, if necessary, with boiling water. Carefully remove dumplings from the steamer. Dumplings should be served immediately. Continue steaming the remaining dumplings using fresh cabbage leaves and replenishing the steamer with more boiling water.

Makes about 40 dumplings. Serves 6 to 8 as part of a multicourse lunch.

Stuffed Noodle Rolls

My cousin Kathy makes *guen fun* a treat that we loved as children. She and her sister Sylvia used to make this with my Auntie Bertha for special occasions; today Kathy makes this recipe with her children, Mark and Sarah.

The noodle is the same broad rice noodle used to make Beef Chow Fun (see page 31 for instructions on how to buy the noodle). It is sold as a long sheet that has been steamed, lightly oiled, and then folded to roughly the size of a kitchen towel.

On the day you plan on making the rolls, leave the broad rice noodle at room temperature until you're ready to use it. Never refrigerate the noodle, because the refrigeration will harden it into a stiff block. If refrigerated, the noodle can still be used for stir-fries like Beef Chow Fun, because it will soften as it cooks, but it can never be used for noodle rolls. Once made, the rolls should be eaten immediately. Any leftovers can be refrigerated, then pan-fried as a way of softening the noodles, but reheated rolls do not compare to the fresh rolls.

6 cups mung bean sprouts, about 12 ounces

6 ounces Chinese Barbecued Pork, store-bought or homemade (page 176)

4 teaspoons vegetable oil

2 large eggs, beaten

¼ teaspoon salt

3 scallions, slivered

⅓ cup chopped cilantro

1 tablespoon thin soy sauce

¼ teaspoon sugar

1 fresh broad rice noodle (*haw fun*), 1 pound

Oyster flavored sauce

Wash the bean sprouts in several changes of cold water, and drain thoroughly in a colander until dry to the touch. Cut the barbecued pork into fine julienne pieces.

Heat a 14-inch flat-bottomed wok or skillet over medium heat until hot but not smoking. Add 1 teaspoon vegetable oil and half the beaten eggs and cook 2 to 3 minutes, tilting the wok so that the eggs cover the wok bottom to form a thin egg pancake. When the bottom begins to brown and the eggs are set, turn the pancake over and cook 30 seconds. Remove from wok and transfer to a cutting board to cool. Add another 1 teaspoon vegetable oil to the wok and cook the remaining eggs in the same manner. Cut egg pancakes into ¼- by 2-inch shreds.

Heat a 14-inch flat-bottomed wok or skillet over high heat until hot but not smoking. Add the remaining 2 teaspoons vegetable oil and bean sprouts, and stir-fry 1 minute. Add salt and stir-fry 1 to 2 minutes, or just until bean sprouts are barely limp. Remove from heat. Add the egg, barbecued pork, scallions, cilantro, soy sauce, and sugar, and stir until just combined. Set aside to cool slightly.

Unroll the broad rice noodle onto a large cutting board. Don't be alarmed if there are little tears in the noodle. Once the noodle is filled and rolled up, you won't see the tears.

Cut the noodle into 4 equal rectangles, about 9 by 10 inches. Place ¼ of the filling on lower half of each rectangle, spreading it into an 8½-by-2-inch rectangle. Roll up jelly-roll style, as tightly as possible. Rolls can be cut into 1-inch sections with a sharp knife or cut in half. Serve immediately with oyster sauce.

Makes 32 1-inch rolls. Serves 4 to 6 as part of a multicourse lunch.

Spring Rolls

Nearly everyone has tasted a Spring Roll, as they are served in dim sum houses and Chinese restaurants all over America. But a homemade Spring Roll is a rare treat. The roll should have a crackling crisp skin with a filling of fine shreds of mushroom, barbecued pork, celery, cabbage, and just a touch of bean sprouts. Most restaurant spring rolls are full of bamboo shoots, celery, and bean sprouts; have a chewy or soggy wrapper; and are seldom fried in fresh oil.

The wrapping dough is available in most Chinese markets, sold as spring roll wrappers, and should be as thin as possible. There are about ten wrappers per package, although most packages do not indicate how many they contain. Keep the dough covered with a slightly damp cloth as you work with it, to prevent it from drying out.

4 Chinese dried mushrooms

8 ounces Chinese Barbecued Pork, store-bought or homemade (page 176)

1 tablespoon vegetable oil

1 cup finely shredded Napa cabbage

1 cup mung bean sprouts

½ cup finely shredded celery

1 scallion, finely shredded

½ cup canned shredded bamboo shoots, rinsed and drained

1½ teaspoons thin soy sauce

¼ teaspoon ground white pepper

1 package (4 ounces) spring roll wrappers

1 tablespoon all-purpose flour

1 quart vegetable oil

In a medium bowl, soak the mushrooms in ¼ cup cold water for 30 minutes, or until softened. Drain and squeeze dry (reserving the soaking liquid for use in soups). Cut off and discard stems and thinly slice the caps.

Cut the barbecued pork into fine julienne pieces. Set aside.

Heat a 14-inch flat-bottomed wok or skillet over high heat until hot but not smoking. Add vegetable oil, barbecued pork, cabbage, bean sprouts, celery, scallion, bamboo shoots, and mushrooms, and stir-fry 2 to 3 minutes, or until the cabbage and celery are just limp. Add soy sauce and pepper, remove from heat, and allow to cool.

When mixture has cooled, place spring roll wrappers on work surface and loosely cover with a dampened cloth. In a small bowl, combine the flour and 4 teaspoons cold water. Place 1 wrapper on the cutting board with a corner facing you. Spread about ¼ cup of the mixture near the bottom corner into a ¾-by-2-inch rectangle. Fold the corner nearest you over the mixture. Roll the wrapper up once, then fold in the sides. Continue rolling the wrapper up tightly but, before you reach the end, lightly paint the far corner with the flour-water mixture. Continue rolling to seal the roll into a tight cylinder. Set aside seam-side down, and cover with a dampened cloth. Repeat with remaining wrappers.

In a 3-quart saucepan, heat vegetable oil over high heat until oil temperature reaches 375 degrees. Carefully add 3 to 4 spring rolls at a time, and fry until golden brown, turning rolls, about 2 minutes. Remove with a slotted spoon and place on a plate lined with several thicknesses of paper towels. Carefully cut in half or in thirds. Repeat with remaining spring rolls. Set oil aside to cool before discarding. Serve immediately.

Makes about 10 spring rolls. Serves 6 to 8 as part of a multicourse lunch.

Scallion Cakes

I first tasted scallion cakes at Henry Chung's Hunan Restaurant on Kearny Street in San Francisco. I think I was about eleven years old as I sat on a stool at the counter and watched these curious rounds of dough being fried until golden brown and fragrant with scallion flavor. As I devoured the delicious, crisp cakes, Mama looked on, pleased that I loved them, for she had grown up eating them as a favorite street snack in China. This was the first Hunan restaurant I'd ever eaten in and, until then, our diet had been strictly Cantonese food.

Be careful when frying these cakes, as the oil will splatter, especially when you press a cake in its center. Any uncooked dough can be placed in a plastic container, refrigerated, and cooked the following day. If you do make them ahead, redust the dough lightly with flour to absorb any moisture from refrigeration, and allow the dough to sit at room temperature briefly so that it is not ice-cold when fried.

2 cups all-purpose flour, plus additional flour for kneading

¾ teaspoon sugar

2 teaspoons sesame oil

1¼ plus ½ teaspoon salt

⅓ cup finely minced scallions

⅔ cup vegetable oil

In a medium bowl, combine flour and sugar. Stir in ⅔ cup boiling water, mixing flour and water just until flour absorbs all the water. Gradually stir in enough cold water (¼ to ⅓ cup) so that a dough is formed and pulls away from the sides of the bowl. The dough should not be sticky.

Remove dough from the bowl and knead on a lightly dusted board with floured hands 3 to 5 minutes, or until the dough is smooth and elastic, adding more flour if necessary. Lightly cover with a dampened cloth and allow to rest for 1 hour.

Redust surface and hands with flour, and knead again for a few minutes or until smooth. Divide the dough into 4 equal pieces. As you work, always cover any unused dough with a lightly damp cloth. Using a floured rolling pin, roll each section into a 7-inch round. Lightly brush each round with sesame oil. Evenly sprinkle 1¼ teaspoons salt and scallions on each round, and then tightly roll each round into a fat rope. Tightly coil each rope, pinching the end of the rope into the dough to seal. Cover with a lightly damp cloth and allow to rest 15 to 20 minutes. Redust surface with flour, and using a floured rolling pin, roll each coiled bun into 7-inch rounds.

In a 14-inch flat-bottomed wok or skillet, heat vegetable oil over medium-high heat until oil is hot but not smoking. Carefully add one scallion round and fry 1 to 2 minutes, until golden. Carefully turn cake over and fry 30 seconds to 1 minute, or until golden brown. As the cake fries, lightly press the center with a metal spatula to make sure center is cooked. Transfer each cake to a plate lined with several thicknesses of paper towels. Continue frying the remaining scallion rounds one at a time. Sprinkle with remaining ½ teaspoon salt. Set oil aside to cool before discarding. Cut cakes into 6 to 8 wedges and serve immediately.

Makes 4 scallion cakes. Serves 6 to 8 as part of a multicourse lunch.

DUTIFUL DAUGHTER RETURNS HOME

Great-Grandmother Fung Leung Shee. Hong Kong, circa 1912.

THE CANTONESE HAVE A NAME FOR Chinese born in America—*toe zhu,* or native product. The term has a slightly negative connotation. Though my brother Douglas and I were raised in America, we were instructed to think in the Chinese way. Even so, my parents still commiserate with our uncles and aunties about how Douglas and I, and our cousins, have been so assimilated that we talk, think, and act like Americans.

Chinese New Year, celebrated roughly from January 21 to February 19 (depending on the lunar calendar), is the most important holiday of the Chinese calendar. No other occasion means as much to my family—or would cause as great a disappointment to them if I didn't come home. For the Chinese, it is a time to honor the sacredness of family and to reaffirm family ties. In China, no matter how great the distance, you must return home to pay respects to your elders and ancestors. It is a time for reunion and renewal.

Every year, when I leave behind my life in New York City to return home to San Francisco for the holidays, I resume my role as a Chinese daughter. Last January, as I sat on the plane, I reflected on my family's customs and traditions, for at New Year's, more than any other time of the year, it would be important for me to think like a dutiful daughter.

According to ancient Chinese custom, every thought and deed at this time determines the outcome of the entire year. Optimism and a positive mood and demeanor insure blessings, while anger and negativity obstruct the possibility of noteworthy aspirations. Spending so much time in an American world completely different from the Chinese one I was raised in, I felt it important to bring these thoughts to mind, so that I would not inadvertently bring bad luck upon myself or my family. After all, by traditional standards I am not a dutiful daughter. I live too far away from my family, and my self-sufficient behavior and thinking are much too American. More important, a dutiful daughter would be married to a Chinese husband and would return to her husband's family's home for the New Year's celebrations. However, I *am* the definition of dutiful as it has been rewritten for daughters born in America.

But living up to the duties of a Chinese daughter, even as rewritten, can be especially trying at New Year's, a holiday steeped not only in tradition but in superstition. For example, you must not cut or wash your hair on New Year's Day, or you will wash away your fortunes. Similarly, you must not sweep the floors. In fact, you must keep the broom out of sight—in our family, the vacuum cleaner stays safely in the closet. Sharp objects like scissors or knives are not used, for they symbolize the severing or cutting of relationships. Doctors, herbalists, and pharmacists are avoided, as it is feared that they portend sickness in the year ahead. Douglas and I often find it hard to follow these superstitions without questioning or challenging them. On New Year's Day it is easy for us to forget that we shouldn't shampoo our hair or pay a bill (the Chinese prefer to pay up all debts at the end of the year and not to spend money on the first day). With our inevitable transgression, Mama or Baba will turn to us and say, "You have *fang quai pay hay,*" the behavior of a Westerner. Sighing within, I vow to myself that I will try to be a more dutiful daughter.

This year, I arrived home a few days early. I had been working hard on a book that had been recently published and was carrying a copy for Baba. Eager for his admiration, I proudly presented it to him. "You know, it's really not a good omen to give a book as a gift at this time," he said, dismissing me. Fortunately, we were still a few days shy of the official New Year's Day, but Baba explained that the word for book in Cantonese is *shu,* which sounds like the word "to lose." In other words, to give a book as a New Year's gift is to suggest that the receiver will be a "loser" in the coming year. My father's response to my well-intended gift was twisted by ancient superstition and left me deeply disappointed. I was hardly able to contain my *fang quai pay hay* and felt lost between two cultures. Clearly, this was one superstition with which I was unfamiliar. I later asked my Uncle Herbert about Baba's comments, and he explained that in China bookcases would be completely covered during New Year's to prevent anyone from seeing books or even thinking of loss. Bookstores would stop selling books, and instead sell New Year's posters for the two weeks of celebrations. My Uncle Sam tells me it was taboo to even read a book in my grandparents' home during New Year's.

Every year I seem to trip over some new superstition. Despite my love for this holiday, I still anticipate it with some anxiety. . . . Maybe someone will break a dish, get sick, say the wrong words, not be able to buy a traditional food, or burn the rice! I have been known to absentmindedly walk into a pharmacy or wander into a used bookstore on New Year's Day. Recently I learned to make three of the traditional New Year's cakes (which are always given as gifts to friends and relatives), but I'm not sure if I have the courage to attempt them. What if, somehow, they failed to rise, or, worse yet, one of the cakes didn't taste right! My older relatives would feel uneasy about the inauspiciousness implied by the gift. Imagine the anxiety of feeling responsible—that the outcome of your relative's New Year relates to your ability to make a perfect cake? Even if the family joked and dismissed my failure as unimportant, they still would be fearful of challenging the old ways.

I remain haunted by the memory of one New Year's Eve dinner when we had clams, a traditional dish symbolizing prosperity. As the family savored the meal, Douglas bit into a bit of sand that had inadvertently been left in a clam and chipped a tooth. A terrible silence fell over the table. I don't remember whether any of us had a good or bad year, but the ominous sign of a year of financial problems cast a pall over the dinner and implanted fear in each of us.

I am a soul born into two worlds. Some Chinese traditions do not come naturally to me, and sometimes it seems my American feelings get lost in ancient Chinese ritual. My American world is without the superstitions or customs that stifle me from being my own person. At the same time, my American life, being void of ritual and ancient custom, offers less richness and meaning. I respect and appreciate the symbolism and beauty of Chinese traditions, but I find it difficult to master them with my partially American soul.

If you ask my parents and elder relatives how they feel about New Year's, they will describe it in the most glowing terms—for them, it is truly the most joyous of holidays. They do not fear saying the wrong words or doing the wrong thing. They were born and raised with these customs and traditions as part of their every breath. I take a breath from both worlds, feeling I can draw an American breath without thinking, but a Chinese breath requires my full consciousness.

Many of the following recipes are typically found in Chinese delis and are not made at home. It is an homage to my Chinese heritage that, as a "dutiful daughter," I have tried to learn to make these specialties. Also included are a few recipes that reflect the fusion of Chinese and American traditions.

Salt-Roasted Chicken

The traditional recipe for this chicken was made by heating rock salt in a wok, then burying the chicken in the hot salt and cooking on the stove, as most homes in China did not have ovens. The modern convenience of having an oven makes it much easier to control the cooking temperature. Oven-roasting produces a skin that is crisp, golden brown, and mellow in flavor, with exceptionally juicy and flavorful meat. *Mei Kuei Lu Chiew* tastes a little like grappa. It's hard to believe 2 tablespoons makes much of a difference, but the liquor contributes fragrance and sweetness to the chicken. If unavailable, grappa and vodka are adequate substitutes.

One 4-pound broiler-fryer chicken

2 teaspoons plus 1 tablespoon salt

2 tablespoons *Mei Kuei Lu Chiew* liquor

¼ cup finely minced shallots

2 tablespoons finely minced ginger

1 tablespoon thin soy sauce

1½ teaspoons honey

1 teaspoon sesame oil

Remove any fat pockets from the chicken and rub the chicken all over with 2 teaspoons salt. Rinse the chicken under cold water and place on a rack. Pat the cavity and skin dry with paper towels. Air-dry at least 1 hour in a cool and breezy room. When dry, rub the skin of the chicken with liquor and allow to sit for 15 minutes.

Preheat the oven to 425 degrees. In a small bowl, combine the shallots, ginger, remaining 1 tablespoon salt, soy sauce, honey, and sesame oil. Stir until the honey is dissolved and the mixture is well combined. Smear about 3 tablespoons of the mixture into the cavity and the remainder all over the chicken skin.

Place the chicken breast-side up on a rack set in a roasting pan lined with heavy-duty aluminum foil and filled with water to a depth of ¼ inch. Roast 30 minutes, or until chicken is just beginning to turn golden. Using several thicknesses of paper towels to grip the chicken, carefully turn the chicken breast-side down, and roast an additional 20 minutes. Again using paper towels, turn the chicken breast-side up. Roast a final 5 to 10 minutes, or until a meat thermometer registers 170 degrees when inserted at the meatiest point of the thigh but not touching the bone, and the skin is a rich golden brown color. Allow the chicken to rest for 15 minutes. With a meat cleaver, chop the chicken through the bone, into bite-sized pieces (or disjoint into serving pieces), reserving any chicken juices. Serve immediately or at room temperature with any pan juices.

Serves 4 to 6 as part of a multicourse meal.

鼓
油
鷄

Soy Sauce Chicken

Soy Sauce Chicken is often seen hanging in restaurant windows in China-town, and is a staple of the Cantonese diet. The mixture the chicken cooks in is considered a master sauce. It is a blend of very special seasonings: soy sauce, rice wine, sugar, Sichuan peppercorns, star anise, Chinese cinnamon, dried ginger, and Chinese licorice. The Chinese cinnamon is said to promote circulation, the dried ginger (like fresh) aids in digestion and warms the sys-tem, while the licorice is thought to harmonize all the other herbs and spices that are used. The recipe works perfectly well without using the special spices, but their addition gives the sauce its depth and richness. If rock sugar is unavailable, use a total of 1 cup packed "American" light brown sugar. The sauce can be reused; it will develop even more flavor as it ages. To store the sauce after using it to cook the chicken, bring it to a full boil and cool com-pletely. Place in a plastic container, then cover and store in the freezer.

One 4-pound broiler-fryer chicken

2 teaspoons salt

1 1/2 cups thin soy sauce

1/3 cup black soy sauce

1/3 cup Shao Hsing rice cooking wine

6 ounces rock sugar, about 3/4 cup

1/2 cup packed light brown sugar

1 teaspoon Sichuan peppercorns (fa ziu)

4 star anise (bot guok)

One 6-inch piece Chinese cinnamon (yok quai zee), broken in half

5 pieces dried ginger (sa geung)

4 pieces Chinese licorice (gum cho)

Remove any fat pockets from the chicken and rub it all over with salt. Rinse the chicken under cold water, place on a rack, and pat dry with paper towels. Air-dry at least 1 hour in a cool and breezy room.

In a 14-inch flat-bottomed wok or skillet, combine the thin soy sauce, black soy sauce, rice wine, rock sugar, and brown sugar. Bring to a boil over medium-high heat.

Meanwhile, in a small skillet cook the Sichuan peppercorns over medium heat, stirring, 3 to 5 minutes, or until fragrant. Place the toasted peppercorns, star anise, cinnamon, dried ginger, and licorice in a 6-inch square of cheesecloth and tie securely with kitchen string to form a bundle. Add the spices to the wok and cook, stirring, over medium heat until rock sugar has completely dissolved, 10 to 15 minutes.

Bring the sauce to a boil over medium-high heat. Add the chicken breast-side down, and return the sauce to a boil over medium-high heat. Immediately reduce heat to a gentle simmer. Cover and cook, 40 to 45 minutes. As the chicken cooks, carefully turn it 2 to 3 times, being careful not to pierce the skin, and baste it so that the color is even. Adjust the heat, if necessary, to keep the sauce at a gentle simmer. Turn off heat and allow chicken to sit, covered, 20 to 30 minutes, or until a meat thermometer registers 170 degrees when inserted at the meatiest point of the thigh but not touching the bone.

Using 2 heavy spoons, carefully transfer the hot chicken to a cutting board. Cool 10 to 15 minutes. With a meat cleaver, chop the chicken through the bone into bite-sized pieces (or disjoint into serving pieces), reserving any chicken juices. If desired, remove about ½ cup sauce from the wok, skim the fat, add ¼ cup water (or enough water until the flavors seem balanced; the flavors of the sauce are very concentrated and need to be diluted) and serve this diluted sauce with the chicken. Serve warm or at room temperature.

Serves 4 to 6 as part of a multicourse meal.

义
烧

Cha Siu

Chinese Barbecued Pork

Chinese Barbecued Pork should be tender and juicy with a caramelized, almost burnt, crust. Seldom made at home in China, because most households did not have ovens, it was, and is, typically bought in the same Chinese delis where you can buy Soy Sauce Chicken (page 174), Salt-Roasted Chicken (page 173), and Roast Duck (page 180). As a child I often watched the butcher deftly chop the pork into thick chunks. On the way home, it smelled so good that sometimes Mama would let us have a taste while it was still warm and juicy.

It is not difficult to make your own Barbecued Pork, and there are many dishes that require it: Spring Rolls (page 166), Fried Rice (page 9), Stir-Fried Eggs with Barbecued Pork (page 27), and Flavored Sweet Rice (page 8), to name but a few.

2 pounds pork butt, well trimmed

4 tablespoons sugar

2 tablespoons thin soy sauce

2 tablespoons hoisin sauce

2 tablespoons black soy sauce

2 tablespoons Shao Hsing rice cooking wine

2 tablespoons ground bean sauce

2 teaspoons sesame oil

¼ teaspoon ground white pepper

2 tablespoons honey

Quarter the pork butt lengthwise. Rub with 2 tablespoons sugar, place it in a large bowl, and set aside for 15 minutes. Pour off any excess liquid.

In a small bowl, combine the remaining 2 tablespoons sugar, thin soy sauce, hoisin sauce, black soy sauce, rice wine, ground bean sauce, sesame oil, and pepper, and stir to combine. Pour mixture over the pork, making sure the pork is well coated. Loosely cover with plastic wrap, and refrigerate overnight, turning the pork from time to time.

When ready to roast, let the pork come to room temperature, allowing it to sit for at least 30 minutes. Preheat the broiler. Place a rack in a roasting pan and add enough water so that it reaches a depth of ¼ inch in the pan. Remove the pork from the marinade, reserving the marinade. Using your hands spread honey on the pork evenly. Place the pork on the rack, leaving about 1 inch of space between the pieces.

Carefully place the pan under the broiler (the pork should be about 4 inches from the broiler element), and broil until the meat is just beginning to char slightly, 7 to 10 minutes. Monitor the water level in the roasting pan to make sure it never falls below ¼ inch. Turn the pork, brush with the reserved marinade, and broil until the meat is just beginning to char, 7 to 10 minutes, or until pork registers 155 degrees when tested with a meat thermometer. If pork is getting too charred, lightly cover with a small piece of aluminum foil.

Carefully remove barbecued pork from broiler and set on a cutting board to cool for 10 minutes. Slice ¼ inch thick and serve warm or at room temperature meat juices that have accumulated on the board

Serves 6 to 8 as part of a multicourse meal.

Barbecued Spareribs

Cantonese cooks are masterful at cooking spareribs, especially barbecued. These ribs are marinated overnight, which produces a tender and flavorful result. Just before roasting, they are rubbed with honey. As the ribs roast, the kitchen is filled with an intoxicating aroma from the rich barbecue sauce. A brief 5- to 10-minute broiling turns the honey coating into a delicious caramelized crust. The traditional way to make barbecued spareribs is to hang the spareribs with special hooks over a pan of water from the top rack of the oven. This certainly works, but it is dangerous hooking and unhooking the ribs from the hot oven rack. I have developed a simpler method that achieves the same result. It requires placing a cooling rack over a roasting pan filled with about 1/4 inch of water. The purpose of the pan of water is to keep the pork moist, as well as to prevent the marinade from burning and smoking in the oven. It is important to monitor the level of water in the pan to make sure it never falls below a depth of 1/4 inch.

2 pounds lean pork spareribs, well trimmed

1/4 cup sugar

1 tablespoon thin soy sauce

1 tablespoon black soy sauce

1 tablespoon hoisin sauce

1 tablespoon ground bean sauce

1 tablespoon Shao Hsing rice cooking wine

1 tablespoon oyster flavored sauce

1 teaspoon sesame oil

1/4 teaspoon ground white pepper

3 tablespoons honey

Cilantro sprigs, optional

Cut the spareribs into 2 equal pieces. Remove any visible fat pockets. Lightly score the spareribs on the meat side, and place them in a large, shallow bowl. Sprinkle sugar on both sides of the ribs, using more on the meaty side. Set aside to marinate for 15 minutes. Pour off any excess liquid.

In a small bowl, combine the thin and black soy sauces, hoisin sauce, bean sauce, rice wine, oyster sauce, sesame oil, and pepper, and stir to combine. Pour over the spareribs, making sure the spareribs are well coated. Loosely cover the ribs with plastic wrap and marinate overnight in the refrigerator.

Just before roasting, use your hands to spread honey on the spareribs, especially on the meaty side. Preheat the oven to 500 degrees. Place a rack in a roasting pan and add enough water so that the water reaches a depth of 1/2 inch in the pan. Place the marinated spareribs meat-side up on the rack, leaving about 1 inch of space between the two pieces.

Carefully place the pan in the oven and roast 30 minutes. Monitor the water level in the broiler pan to make sure it never falls below 1/4 inch. Carefully remove the roasting pan of ribs from the oven.

Preheat the broiler. Place the roasting pan of ribs 4 inches from the heat and broil 5 to 10 minutes, or until the spareribs have a sugar crust similar to the crust on a baked ham. Carefully remove the spareribs from the oven and set on a platter to cool 15 minutes.

Cut the spareribs into individual ribs and serve immediately or at room temperature. Garnish with cilantro if desired.

Serves 4 to 6 as part of a multicourse meal.

Roast Duck

Rich golden brown with crisp skin and succulent meat, Roast Duck has an aromatic flavor that comes from a mixture of Sichuan peppercorns, ginger, garlic, scallions, ground bean sauce, rice wine, and soy sauce. Most families never make this at home, but if you do not live near a Chinese deli it is simple to roast and even more delicious.

The most challenging procedure is "drying" the duck for three hours in a room that is cool and breezy. Never make this on a hot day or in a room that is well heated, or you will run the risk of spoiling the duck. Traditional Chinese cooks feel that air-drying is essential; the drier the duck, the better it will absorb the flavors of the marinade and produce a skin that is crisp.

One 3-pound duck

2 teaspoons salt

1½ teaspoons Sichuan peppercorns (fa ziu)

2 tablespoons ground bean sauce

1 tablespoon thin soy sauce

1 tablespoon black soy sauce

1 tablespoon Shao Hsing rice cooking wine

2 teaspoons sugar

⅓ cup cilantro sprigs, plus additional for garnish

1 teaspoon vegetable oil

5 cloves garlic, smashed

3 slices ginger

3 whole scallions

1 tablespoon honey

Remove any fat pockets from the duck and rub it all over with salt. Rinse the duck in cold water and thoroughly pat it dry with paper towels. Thoroughly pat dry the duck cavity and skin with paper towels and set on a roasting rack breast-side up.

In a small skillet, heat the peppercorns over medium heat, stirring, 3 to 5 minutes, or until the peppercorns are fragrant and just beginning to smoke. Remove from heat, and place in a mortar and crush until ground. Set aside.

In a small bowl, combine the bean sauce, thin soy sauce, black soy sauce, rice wine, sugar, ground Sichuan pepper, and ⅓ cup cilantro sprigs.

Heat a 14-inch flat-bottomed wok or skillet over high heat until hot but not smoking. Add the oil, garlic, ginger, and scallions, and stir-fry 10 seconds. Add the soy sauce mixture and bring it to a boil. Reduce heat to low, cover, and simmer 5 minutes. Remove from heat, uncover, and cool completely.

Pour ¼ cup boiling water into a small bowl and stir in the honey until dissolved. Set aside to cool.

Line a roasting pan with several sheets of heavy-duty aluminum foil and set the rack holding the duck in the pan. Add enough water to the roasting pan so that it reaches a depth of ½ inch. Lightly brush the entire duck, including the back side, with the cooled honey water.

When the scallion soy mixture has cooled, carefully spoon the cooled mixture into the cavity of the duck. Close the cavity with a bamboo skewer, weaving the skewer through the flaps of skin at the two sides of the opening to "sew" them together. Finish by tucking the tail end in. Air-dry the duck for 3 hours, preferably in front of a fan in a cool breezy room, turning the duck once, until the skin feels dry to the touch.

Preheat the oven to 450 degrees.

Place the pan with the duck in the oven and roast 20 minutes. Reduce the temperature to 350 degrees and roast 20 more minutes, monitoring the color of the duck as it roasts. If any area begins to brown too quickly, lightly cover it with a piece of aluminum foil. Using several thicknesses of paper towels to grip the duck, carefully turn duck breast-side down and roast an additional 20 minutes. Increase the temperature of the oven to 450 degrees and roast 12 to 15 more minutes, or until a meat thermometer registers 170 degrees when inserted at the meatiest point of the thigh but not touching the bone, and the duck is a rich brown color.

Carefully transfer the duck to a platter. Remove the skewer and slowly pour the juices out of the duck. Allow the duck to rest for 15 minutes while you defat the juices. With a meat cleaver, chop the duck through the bone into bite-sized pieces (or disjoint into serving pieces), reserving any juices. Garnish with fresh cilantro if desired. Serve immediately, while the skin is crisp, with the defatted juices.

Serves 4 to 6 as part of a multicourse meal.

Chinese Bacon

Chinese Bacon (*lop yok*) has a denser and richer flavor than Western bacon. It is never eaten alone but, because it has such depth of flavor, it is added to dishes as varied as Flavored Sweet Rice (page 8), Turnip Cake (page 128), Stir-Fried Chinese Broccoli and Bacon (page 88), and Taro Root Cake (page 130). Chinese Bacon is found in Chinese butcher shops and some Chinese markets. You must ask for it by its Cantonese name, *lop yok*, for no Chinese person calls it Chinese Bacon.

For those who do not live near a Chinatown, Chinese Bacon can be made at home. The process is not difficult, but you must have an outside area where you can dry the bacon. In recent years, because they have more time, my parents and I have occasionally made bacon at home.

Mama recalls that in China this was never made in the summer because the weather is too hot. Chinese Bacon is air-dried, and you must wait until the twelfth lunar month, around January on our calender, when the north wind (*buck fung*) is strong, so that the *lop yok* will have the "fragrance from the wind." Mama always tells me to make this in New York where she imagines the winter wind to be ideal, but I am reluctant to try, feeling the wind may be perfect, but that the city's pollution would destroy any tangible fragrance. My parents feel San Francisco's weather is not the best for making *lop yok*; it's neither cold nor dry enough.

One 1¾-pound pork belly, as meaty as possible

1 tablespoon Shao Hsing rice cooking wine

1 tablespoon thin soy sauce

1½ teaspoons sesame oil

1 teaspoon black soy sauce

1 teaspoon dark brown sugar

1 teaspoon salt

½ teaspoon ground white pepper

Rinse the pork belly and pat it dry. Cut lengthwise through the layers of fat and meat into ½-inch-thick slices to make about 6 slices. Remove the tough rind and any fat attached to it. (The weight after the fat is removed should be about 1 pound.)

On a large plate, combine the rice wine, thin soy sauce, sesame oil, black soy sauce, brown sugar, salt, and pepper. Place the dried ginger, star anise, and tangerine peel in a mortar, and grind as finely as possible. Add it to the liquid mixture and stir to combine. Add the pork and thoroughly coat all sides of the pork with the mixture. Cover with plastic wrap and refrigerate 24 hours, occasionally turning the pork, so that the marinade penetrates on all sides.

One inch in from the short edge of each slice, poke a small hole with a skewer and pull about 6 inches of kitchen string through the hole.

- 1 piece dried ginger (*sa geung*)
- 1 star anise (*bot guok*)
- 1 small piece dried tangerine peel (*guo pay*), about 1-inch diameter

Tie all 6 slices on an 18-inch pole, leaving about a ½-inch space between each piece, and hang outside in the sun to dry. The slices can also be placed on a large rack set over a roasting pan. Loosely cover the slices with cheesecloth or a food screen, if desired, and set outside. Discard the marinade.

Whichever method you choose, bring the meat in once the sun has gone down and let stand at room temperature. Set the meat outside the next morning until the sun sets, and continue doing so for 4 to 7 days, or until it is completely dry and hard. If the weather is cloudy, it could take longer. Store covered and refrigerated until ready to use; it should last several months.

Makes 6 bacon strips.

Uncle Tommy's Roast Turkey

My Uncle Tommy was a fusion cook long before anyone coined the term. He loved to experiment in the kitchen, and was known in the family for his fabulous cooking, most notably his roast turkey. Uncle Tommy used classic Asian ingredients to marinate his turkey, a basic Western approach to roast it, and a Cajun technique of browning the flour to make the gravy; I'm quite sure he had never had Cajun food, but Uncle Tommy had creative instincts, especially when it came to cooking. My cousins Sylvia, Kathy, and David have tried to duplicate their father's recipe and this comes closest in taste to the delicious turkey we remember.

One 12-pound turkey

2 tablespoons Chinese dried black beans

2 tablespoons finely minced ginger

1 tablespoon finely minced garlic

3 tablespoons ground bean sauce

3 tablespoons hoisin sauce

2 tablespoons thin soy sauce

1 carrot, cut into 1-inch chunks

1 celery stalk, cut into 1-inch chunks

2 scallions, cut into 2-inch pieces

2 tablespoons butter, melted

1/4 cup all-purpose flour

The day before, remove any fat pockets from the turkey, and remove giblets and neck, and refrigerate, covered, until ready to use. Rinse and pat dry the turkey with paper towels. Set it on a rack to air-dry.

Rinse the black beans in several changes of cold water and drain. In a medium bowl, mash the black beans with the back of a wooden spoon. Stir in the ginger, garlic, ground bean sauce, hoisin sauce, and soy sauce, and stir to combine. Place the turkey in a large pan and rub the mixture over the entire turkey and in the cavity. Cover the turkey with plastic wrap and refrigerate overnight.

One hour prior to roasting the turkey, remove from the refrigerator and allow it to come to room temperature. When ready to roast, preheat the oven to 325 degrees, and place the oven rack at the lowest position in the oven.

Spread the carrots, celery, and scallions in the bottom of a roasting pan. Place a roasting rack on top of the vegetables. Place the untrussed turkey breast-side up on the roasting rack at its flattest setting. Pour 1 cup of water into the pan and roast 1 hour.

Meanwhile, place the giblets (the gizzard, heart, and neck; discard the liver) in a 1½-quart saucepan and add 3 cups cold water. Bring to a boil, then reduce heat to low and simmer, partially covered, until reduced to about 2 cups. Discard the solids.

Brush the turkey with the butter and roast 1½ to 2 hours, or until a meat thermometer registers 170 degrees when inserted at the meatiest point of the thigh but not touching the bone, and the turkey is a rich mahogany color.

Transfer the turkey to a cutting board and allow to rest for 20 minutes. Meanwhile, pour the giblet broth into the roasting pan and stir to scrape up the browned bits, discarding the vegetables. Pour these pan juices into a gravy separator and skim the fat.

In a medium, heavy skillet, cook the flour over medium heat, stirring constantly until the flour begins to brown, 5 to 6 minutes. Remove from heat and gradually stir in 1 cup of the pan juices with a whisk, whisking until smooth. Return to stove and gradually add about 1 cup of the pan juices and cook, stirring, over medium heat until thickened, 1 to 2 minutes. If gravy is too thick, add chicken broth or water until the gravy reaches the desired consistency. Add salt to taste and serve gravy with the turkey.

Serves 12 to 16 as part of a multicourse meal.

Mama's Rice Stuffing

Mama and I used to sit every Thanksgiving morning watching the Macy's Thanksgiving Day Parade on television, while shelling the blanched fresh chestnuts for this stuffing. I believe this is where my love of cooking was born. The hard chestnut shell is not difficult to peel, but the thin skin that sticks to the chestnut can be awful to remove. The labor-intensive process did not discourage me; I always thought our hard work was worth it for the delicious results. Now, Mama soaks the chestnuts in cold water for half a day before cooking them and she says the skin comes off much more easily. Some Chinese families cook Flavored Sweet Rice (page 8) to accompany their turkey, but we always preferred Mama's Rice Stuffing. Dried chestnuts can be used, but fresh chestnuts are the best, and always in season for Thanksgiving.

½ pound fresh chestnuts, about 15

4 Chinese dried scallops (*gawn yu chee*)

6 Chinese dried mushrooms

2 Chinese sausage (*lop cheung*)

2 cups long grain rice

3 teaspoons vegetable oil

1 celery stalk, cut into ½-inch dice

¼ cup chopped cilantro

2 to 3 tablespoons thin soy sauce

Using a paring knife, make a 1-inch slash through the skin of each chestnut. Place the chestnuts in a 2-quart saucepan with enough cold water to cover. Set aside for about 6 hours.

In a small bowl, soak the scallops in about ⅓ cup cold water for about 2 hours, or until softened. Drain, reserving the soaking liquid. Remove the small hard knob from the side of the scallops and discard. Finely shred the scallops.

In a medium bowl, soak the mushrooms in ⅓ cup cold water for 30 minutes, or until softened. Drain and squeeze dry, reserving the soaking liquid. Cut off and discard the stems and mince the caps.

Bring the chestnuts and water to a boil over high heat, uncovered. Reduce heat to low, and simmer 20 to 25 minutes, or until chestnuts are tender when pierced with a knife. Drain and cool them under cold water. When cool enough to handle, peel the shell and inner skin with a paring knife, discarding any chestnuts with mold.

Finely chop the sausage.

Wash the rice in several changes of cold water until the water runs clear. Drain well, and place in a 3-quart saucepan. Pour the reserved mushroom and scallop soaking liquids into a 1-quart measuring cup, and add enough cold water to measure a total of 3¼ cups water. Add the liquid to the rice in the saucepan and bring to a boil, covered, over high heat, never stirring the rice. Reduce heat to low, and simmer covered, 7 to 10 minutes, or until the water almost completely evaporates.

Meanwhile, heat a 14-inch flat-bottomed wok or skillet over high heat until hot but not smoking. Add 1 teaspoon oil and the sausage, and stir-fry 10 seconds. Add the remaining 2 teaspoons oil, mushrooms, scallops, and celery, and stir-fry 1 minute. Add the chestnuts, breaking them into smaller pieces. Remove from heat.

After rice has cooked for 7 to 10 minutes, quickly add the stir-fried mixture, cover tightly, reduce the heat to low, and steam 7 to 10 minutes, or until all of the water is absorbed. Turn off the heat and let sit 5 minutes. Stir in cilantro and soy sauce. This stuffing can be served immediately or it can be used to stuff a turkey. For a 12-pound turkey roasted at 325 degrees, allow 12 to 15 minutes per pound stuffed. Stuffing should register 160 degrees to be safe to eat.

Serves 6 to 8 as part of a multicourse meal.

Turkey Porridge

The morning after Thanksgiving thousands of Chinese-American households cook Turkey Porridge, also known as congee or *jook*. Turkey is not eaten in China, but most Chinese-Americans enjoy cooking turkey on Thanksgiving. The following day, the meat is removed from the carcass for leftovers, then the carcass is placed in a large pot with water and rice, and cooked for 3 to 4 hours to make Americanized traditional Chinese porridge. The sweet aroma of stock fills the house and by lunchtime there is lovely porridge to eat. Porridge is traditionally eaten to cleanse the system of rich foods (see "Cooking as a Healing Art," page 191), so Turkey Porridge is welcomed as a soothing food the day after a rich Thanksgiving feast.

1⅓ cups long grain rice

1 turkey carcass

1 teaspoon salt

2 ounces Sichuan preserved vegetable, about ¼ cup

1 tablespoon vegetable oil

Wash the rice in several changes of cold water and drain. Place the turkey carcass and 3½ quarts cold water in a large pot. Bring to a boil over high heat. Cook 1 minute, skimming any scum that rises to the surface. Add the drained rice and return to a rolling boil over high heat. Cover, reduce heat to low, and simmer 3 hours, stirring occasionally, until the rice has "flowered" (the grains will swell and the ends seem to blossom out). Continue simmering 1 hour, or until the porridge is a thick soup. Remove any visible bones and add salt to taste.

Rinse the Sichuan preserved vegetable in cold water to remove the red chili paste, and pat dry. Finely chop and place in a small heat-proof bowl. In a small skillet, heat oil over high heat until hot but not smoking. Carefully pour the hot oil over the preserved vegetable. The oil will make a crackling sound as it hits the vegetable.

Spoon the porridge into bowls and sprinkle with preserved vegetable and oil. Serve immediately.

Serves 6 to 8 for a typical Chinese lunch.

THE CANTONESE COOKING TRADITION

has long recognized the connection between food and health. The following recipes provide a glimpse of what foods an old-fashioned Cantonese family integrates into its diet for optimum well-being. They range from refreshing and replenishing tonics to foods that stimulate and restore physical harmony. Many recipes require only a handful of ingredients and emphasize the importance of the pure flavors of healing foods, unadulterated by many seasonings. It is important not to overindulge in any one recipe and to eat moderate servings. In Chinese cooking, less is always more.

Achieving Yin-Yang Harmony

烹
飪
爲
醫
療

Pum Yum Wai Yee Liu

COOKING AS A
HEALING ART

Great-Grandmother Tong Ng Kwei-Foon, circa 1928.

THE WOMEN IN MY FAMILY HAVE ALWAYS struck me as being "body fortune-tellers." They can look at anyone and guess what their body is in need of. They will joke about being a fake doctor (*ga yee sung*), because a reputable Chinese herbalist performs a thorough exam before making a diagnosis. But my relatives' expertise is for keeping the body in harmony. It takes my female relatives only a moment to observe your chapped lips, hear you complain of insomnia, or watch you cough before they decide what you need to soothe your ills. You will think to yourself that your chapped lips need a lip balm, the street noise is keeping you up, and, in a few days, your cough will go away. But their interpretation is totally different and everything points to a body suffering from *yeet hay* (excessive internal heat), undoubtedly caused by a diet high in spicy foods or any one of the following fatty foods: chocolates, fast foods, fried dim sum, or rich restaurant meals. This heat must be neutralized with the proper foods to restore balance in the body. What you eat and the season in which you eat it is one of the central tenets of food as medicine in Chinese cuisine.

Most people have heard of yin and yang, a Taoist concept that is based on the idea of opposites in balance, whether cold/hot, water/fire, or female/male. Foods are said by the Cantonese to have a warming, cooling, or neutral nature. This is a reference not to the temperature of the food, but to the intrinsic nature of the food. Yang foods are warming, invigorating, and powerful; many are high in fat and spicy. Typical foods with a strong yang nature include butter, organ meats, chicken, ginger, and lamb, yet these foods also have some yin qualities. Yin foods are cooling, soothing, and mild, and characteristically more vegetarian, although they too can have yang qualities. Typical foods with a strong yin nature include crab, watermelon, cucumber, bean sprouts, tofu, and watercress. Rarely are foods purely yin or yang. The yin-yang balance is created by the natural contrast of the ingredients.

The inherent yin or yang nature of an ingredient can be altered by the foods it is cooked with, as well as by the method of cooking. Ginger, for example, is said to be warming and is therefore always cooked with vegetables that have a cooling nature, in order to neutralize the vegetables' cool properties. In another example, watercress soup is said to be so cooling that it can cause elderly people to faint if the watercress has only been simmered a few minutes. However, if the watercress has been simmered for three to four hours, the yin nature of the watercress is neutralized and the soup can be safely drunk. Stir-frying, deep-fat frying, and roasting impart a yang influence on food, while steaming, poaching, and boiling are all yin methods of cooking; cooks therefore serve a mixture of stir-fried and steamed dishes in a single meal to create harmony.

It is fundamental to the Cantonese system of eating to keep yin and yang foods (and yin and yang cooking methods) in balance. Every individual's age, digestive system, absorbing power, and metabolism are different and affected by the seasons of the year. Unlike the Western model of nutrition, which has very clear general guidelines, the Cantonese approach is very personalized and complex and takes into consideration numerous factors to achieve optimal health. To achieve the ultimate balance, my family, like many Cantonese families, prepares special tonic soups. The Cantonese realistically presume that no one eats a pure and fat-free diet (and no other culture probably enjoys rich food more than the Chinese, especially when it comes to special delicacies for special occasions). To offset the occasional indulgence (as well as deficiencies in the diet), specific soups are taken to restore balance. In fact, even if no signs of imbalance are evident, soups, tonics, and teas with mild herbs are drunk as a preventive measure.

My brother, Douglas, and I were told numerous times that if we didn't counter the consumption of rich fatty foods with *yun* (soothing) foods, the resulting imbalance could lead to a cold, skin problems, or other ailments. According to my cousin Fred, the Cantonese have learned through time and experience that these are signs that indicate the body's life force must be brought back to equilibrium. The Cantonese believe that young people are especially vulnerable to the imbalances caused by consuming too many warming, yang foods—such as spicy, deep-fried, stir-fried, or even pan-fried foods.

When, as children, we asked our parents what a *yun* food does, they would tell us that some foods cleanse your system, but a Chinese herbalist explained to me that it is not so much a question of "cleansing" as it is of restoring the overall harmony of the body. In the West, we do not have a tradition of eating foods that cleanse and replenish. Although we recognize that eating an excess of junk food or rich food has a negative effect on the body, there is no concept of how to cleanse the body of these foods—except maybe by drinking lots of water. In Cantonese culture, cleansing with water is not enough. My Auntie Frances once told me that water cleanses but it doesn't put enough back into your body to restore what your body is missing. "For this you need a *yun* soup." According to my Auntie Katheryn, my grandfather, Gunggung, who lived to the age of ninety-three, never drank a drop of plain water; he, like most traditional Cantonese, drank *yun* soups or tea.

Most *yun* foods are soups, and the Cantonese have developed the making of *yun* recipes into a high art form. Foods that are *yun* are said to be soothing, moist, and smooth, like a cough drop that soothes a parched throat. My Uncle Sam says, "The word *yun* carries a sense of benefit; one calls the rain after a drought *yun yue,* as it lubricates the parched earth." *Yun* soups or teas restore balance in the body and are also said to moisten and lubricate the internal organs. (The concept of internal organs becoming dry is unknown in the West, but for the Cantonese it is not desirable.) For instance, when I have a dry cough, my relatives often tell me it is a sure sign of internal dryness in my system.

I believe the real wisdom of the Cantonese diet lies with these *yun,* or harmonizing, soups. However, I found it difficult to pin down anyone in my family in order to get definitive information on the soups. They seem to cook them by instinct, and their explanations are vague and difficult to understand. If you press my parents or relatives to elaborate on the meaning of *yun,* they will tell you some soups clear excessive internal heat, some lubricate the respiratory system, some prevent the flu, some quench thirst, and some clear phlegm and coughs. How they know this has always baffled me, but I guess it is similar to Westerners knowing carrots are good for the eyes, or milk products benefit the teeth and bones. They will also warn you never to eat an excess of these tonic soups. To overindulge in a nourishing soup is to disrupt the balance of yin-yang forces. Everything must be eaten in moderation.

To my understanding, there are three main categories of *yun* foods prepared with a combination of mild herbs and foods, which the Cantonese believe have medicinal attributes. One group is vegetable soups; these soups are never served in a Chinese restaurant, but are home-made soups (and, generally speaking, an acquired taste). They are called *lo faw tung* in Cantonese, meaning slow-simmering soups, and come from a distinctly Cantonese tradition. When we were children, Douglas and I liked canned chicken noodle soup and cream of mushroom soup and we would cringe at the thought of drinking those weird Chinese soups our parents served every night at dinner. Baba and Mama, appalled by the notion that the canned goop mixed with water was called soup, instead cooked us Mustard Green Soup (page 221) in the autumn to fortify us against flus, Herbal Winter Melon Soup (page 220) to cool us from the summer heat, Watercress Soup (page 218) because it was just plain good for any time of the year, and various other soups. The main purpose of these vegetable-based *yun* soups was to correct and restore the proper yin-yang balance. Some of the soups tasted bland, while others, cooked with pork, tasted better. Still, since most were simmered for three to four hours, the vegetables were cooked to death and not in the least bit appealing to us. My cousin Cindy remembers that her mom would tell her the soups would make her beautiful—anything to get Cindy and her sister Kim to drink the soups. Even today, my parents cook these soups according to the season and eat them in moderation (no more than one or two bowls per day). A bowl of *yun* soup is often served at the beginning and end of a meal. My parents and grandmother will often smile contentedly drinking the soup, commenting on how refreshed the soup makes them feel. No water, milk, or soda has ever been served at mealtime in my family's home.

The second kind of *yun* food is legume-, fruit-, and nut-based soups, called *tong shui* in Cantonese. These soups are made with one or more of the following ingredients: Chinese red beans, green mung beans, walnuts, black sesame seeds, lotus seeds, almond seeds, papayas or Asian pears, dried figs, and dried dates. These ingredients are said to invigorate the kidneys and detoxify and moisten the internal organs, depending on the ingredient. Soups like Almond Soup (page 203), Walnut Soup (page 196), and Peanut Soup (page 202) are probably the most appealing to the Western palate, while some *tong shui* like Fresh Fig and Honey Date Soup (page 211) and Lotus Seed "Tea" (page 200) may require getting used to. Most are sweet, and eaten as late-afternoon snacks or as an after-dinner treat, and come closest to the Chinese notion of dessert, like Double-Steamed Asian Pears (page 208). Generally they are sweetened with rock sugar or brown candy, both of which are said to remove toxins from the body.

The third category of *yun* food is *jook* (rice porridge or congee). Although *jook* can be the basis of a recipe with highly flavored ingredients (see Chicken Porridge, page 13, or Turkey Porridge, page 188), it is also used as a cleansing soup to remedy a fever, a stomach-ache, diarrhea, or the flu. It is also said to cleanse the intestines (*ching cheung wai*), and is used to restore balance after a period in which very rich foods have been eaten. This cleansing version of *jook*, called white porridge or *bock jook,* is very plain. For white porridge, the rice is cooked in water with no seasonings at all. When, as children, we were sick, Mama and Baba would feed us this soothing rice porridge made from a few spoonfuls of rice cooked slowly, for three or four hours, in several quarts of water. My Uncle Sam says my Auntie Helen automatically cooks white porridge whenever someone in their family is ill. Similarly, in the West, there are those who believe when one has the flu that one must starve a fever and drink only fluids until the body can handle solid foods. The Cantonese firmly believe not only that *jook* is the easiest food for the body to digest but that it also cleanses the system of toxins and protects the body from dehydration. All cleansing *jook* are not necessarily plain, as in Gingko Nut Porridge (page 222). In China, *jook* is also the most common breakfast food, much the way oatmeal or cream of wheat is consumed by Westerners. It is also a favorite of women on diets, as it is low in calories yet filling.

As a footnote to this, last summer I developed a horrible cough that lasted four months, one that neither codeine cough syrup nor health-food-store remedies could cure. Mama made me seek acupuncture treatments and drink Dried Fig, Apple, and Almond Soup (page 213)— which I had hated as a child. Within the first day, the cough subsided! This past autumn, in preparation for this book, I cooked the Mustard Green Soup that I had disliked as a child. To my surprise, I found it soothing and comforting. It has taken nearly thirty-five years to cultivate a respect and taste for these mysterious *yun* soups, but it is my goal to someday master the mysteries of *yun* soups so that I, too, can be a *ga yee sung* (fake doctor), and know as well as my mother and aunties which soups to prescribe.

The following *yun* recipes restore balance, especially to correct *yeet hay*—excessive heat from too many yang foods. In my family, all of these soups are consumed in an effort to harmonize the body, not as a substitute for professional medical advice.

Walnut Soup

Walnut Soup (*Hup Tul Woo*) is a favorite snack soup, often eaten in place of dessert. The Chinese believe walnuts resemble the shape of the brain and, thus, are good for nourishing the brain. Any foods that resemble the shape of a body organ are said to be good for that organ. Walnuts are also associated with longevity, since walnut trees live for hundreds of years. Regardless, this is a delicious soup. The oven-roasting brings out the fragrance of the walnuts, and it is rich and creamy despite the fact that there is no dairy added. I think Walnut Soup is a wonder because it tastes so good while also being good for you. Be sure to use rice flour and not glutinous rice flour.

2 cups shelled walnuts, about 8 ounces

¼ cup rice flour

1½ slabs brown candy (*peen tong*), about 3 ounces

Preheat oven to 350 degrees. In a large saucepan, bring 1 quart water to a boil over high heat. Add the walnuts and boil, uncovered, 1 minute. Drain well. Spread the walnuts on a cookie sheet lined with aluminum foil. Bake 15 to 20 minutes, or until golden and fragrant. Cool on a rack.

Place the cooled walnuts in a food processor or blender with ½ cup cold water, and process until almost a smooth paste, scraping down sides of work bowl. Add ½ cup cold water and process until almost smooth.

In a 2-quart saucepan, whisk the rice flour and 1 cup water until smooth. Whisk in the walnut puree and 2½ cups cold water. Heat over medium-high heat, whisking constantly, until mixture comes to a boil. Cut the brown candy into smaller pieces. Add the brown candy, reduce heat to low, and simmer 10 minutes, whisking occasionally. The soup should be the consistency of a light cream soup. If mixture is too thick, whisk in up to ½ cup more water. Serve piping hot (no more than 1½ cups per person).

Makes 4 servings as a tonic.

Green Mung Bean Soup

Mung bean soup is one of the tonics recommended for skin problems, such as acne or a rash. Baba says that it is a *hon leung* soup, one that cools the body of heat inflammations, and it is popular in the summer. My father no longer drinks this, as its cooling properties are too dangerous for older people. I am told that in China women often stop drinking mung bean soup after they are in their forties, because the soup is reputed to have such a strong cooling energy that it may cause them to faint.

My parents advise me that with my constitution, which is cool, or *hon dai,* I cannot consume foods that are too cooling. So, if I make this soup, I need to add some red beans (*hoong dul*), which have a warming quality that neutralizes the cooling properties to create a healthier yin-yang soup for me. *Look dul sah* is said to be the perfect tonic if one's diet has been filled with rich or fried food, as it helps to cleanse the body of toxins. Mung beans come in two forms: green and yellow. Use the jade-green dried mung beans that are unpeeled and the size of barley.

I cup dried green mung beans, about 7 ounces

¼ cup lotus seeds with skins, rinsed

I ½ slabs brown candy (*peen tong*), about 3 ounces

Pick through the beans and rinse them in several changes of cold water. In a 2½-quart saucepan, bring the mung beans and 1½ quarts of cold water to a boil over high heat. Cover, reduce heat to low, and simmer 1 hour, stirring occasionally. Remove from heat and cool slightly. Using a slotted spoon, place the solids in a food processor or blender and process until smooth. Combine with cooking liquid and return puree to saucepan, add the lotus seeds, and return to a boil over high heat.

Reduce heat to low and simmer 1 hour, stirring occasionally, until soup is a rich brown color and the consistency of lentil soup. Add more water, if necessary. Cut the brown candy into smaller pieces. Stir in the brown candy and cook until dissolved, 2 to 3 minutes. Serve piping hot (no more than 1½ cups per person).

Makes 4 servings as a tonic.

Foxnut Soup

My Auntie Lil makes this soup for her family at least once a month. She says it's good for one's skin and is *yun*, balancing, for the entire body. The Chinese herb foxnut (*chee sut*) expands like popcorn as it cooks, so her children called this popcorn soup when they were young. Foxnut is found in Chinese grocery stores and herb stores. It resembles lotus seeds with skin, but the skin has a brighter red color and the flesh of the nuts is whiter. (See "Foods with Medicinal Attributes" in the photo insert.) Refer to Glossary for information on shopping for sheet dried bean curd, page 261.

⅓ cup foxnut (*chee sut*), rinsed

I sheet dried bean curd (*bien foo jook*)

I ounce rock sugar, about 2 tablespoons

I large egg, beaten

In a 1½-quart saucepan, bring 1 quart cold water to a boil. Add the foxnut and return to a boil. Cover, reduce heat to low, and simmer 1 hour, or until the foxnut opens like popcorn.

Rinse the bean curd sheet under cold water. Return the soup to a boil over high heat. Tear the bean curd sheet into bite-sized pieces and add it to the soup. Cover, reduce heat to low, and simmer 20 to 30 minutes. Add the rock sugar and cook, stirring, until the sugar is fully dissolved, about 5 minutes. Add the beaten egg and remove from heat. Serve piping hot (no more than 1 cup per person).

Makes 4 servings as a tonic.

Sesame Tong Shui

Black sesame seeds are unhulled sesame seeds, and the Chinese believe that the seeds are extremely nutritious, nourishing the skin, preventing constipation, and protecting one's hair from graying. This classic *tong shui* soup is eaten between meals or as a late-night snack. The first time I made this, I bought a bag of black sesame seeds imported from China and prepared the recipe without realizing that the bag had lots of tiny pebbles and twigs mixed in with the sesame seeds. The soup was inedible, to say the least. The sesame seeds from Japan are superior in quality to those from China, although you should still keep an eye out for tiny pebbles, in much the same way you would examine dried beans. Black sesame seeds are available in some gourmet and health-food stores, but are more expensive there than in Chinese markets. Make sure you use rice flour and not glutinous rice flour for this recipe.

½ cup black sesame seeds (*hock zeema*)

¼ cup sugar

½ cup rice flour

2 ounces rock sugar, about ¼ cup

Examine and pick through the sesame seeds, removing any visible tiny twigs or pebbles. Do *not* rinse.

Heat a 14-inch flat-bottomed wok or skillet over high heat until hot but not smoking. Add the sesame seeds and stir-fry 45 seconds to 1 minute, until fragrant, the crackling sound subsides, and wok begins to smoke. Turn off the heat and continue stir-frying 15 seconds. Set aside to cool.

Place cooled sesame seeds in a food processor or blender, and process until finely ground; the aroma of the sesame will be very fragrant. Add the sugar and process 5 seconds until well combined; this mixture will resemble salt and pepper. With the machine running, gradually add ¼ cup cold water and process until smooth and pale gray.

In a medium saucepan, combine the rice flour and 5 cups cold water. Bring to a boil over medium heat, whisking constantly until smooth. Add the pureed sesame and rock sugar to the saucepan. Bring to a boil over medium heat, stirring constantly, until mixture is thickened and sugar is dissolved. Serve piping hot (no more than 1 cup per person).

Makes 4 servings as a tonic.

Lotus Seed "Tea"

My Auntie Katheryn is very fond of making Lotus Seed "Tea," since the combination of lotus seeds and eggs is very nutritious. The word *tea* in Cantonese can mean a hot beverage, as it does here, or brewed tea from tea leaves. Many Chinese believe lotus seeds are excellent for the kidneys, while eggs are prized as the perfect food. Eggs are regarded as the embodiment of yin and yang (the yolk represents the dark while the white represents light), and they are an ancient Chinese symbol for the beginning of life. When babies are one month old, hard-boiled eggs are dyed red and eaten at their one-month-old birthday party.

1 ⅓ cups lotus seeds with skins, rinsed

1 ounce rock sugar, about 2 tablespoons

4 medium eggs

In a medium saucepan, combine 6 cups cold water and the lotus seeds. Bring to a boil over high heat. Cover, reduce heat to low, and simmer about 30 minutes, or until lotus seeds are tender. Add the rock sugar and cook, stirring, until dissolved, about 5 minutes. Add eggs one at a time and poach on low heat, uncovered, until the eggs are just set, but still slightly soft in the yolk, 3 to 4 minutes. Serve piping hot, allowing 1 egg per person, along with sweet broth and lotus seeds.

Makes 4 servings as a tonic.

Hoong Dul Sah

紅
豆
沙

Sweetened Red Bean Soup

Sweetened Red Bean Soup (*Hoong Dul Sah*) is recommended in the winter, when the weather is cold, to warm the body. Some people will also drink this chilled in the summer, but it is more popular in cold weather. The soup is reminiscent of lentil soup in texture. The brown candy (*peen tong*) must always be added when the soup is at a rolling boil or, it is believed, the sugar can cause fainting. Note these red beans are different from the elongated adzuki beans; choose the small, ¼-inch round red beans sold in Chinese supermarkets. (See "Foods with Medicinal Attributes" in the photo insert). Chinese pearl tapioca is available in Chinatown.

1⅓ cups small dried red beans (*hoong dul*), about 4 ounces

1 piece dried tangerine peel (*guo pay*) about 3 inches wide

¼ cup lotus seeds with skin, rinsed

¼ cup Chinese pearl tapioca

1 slab brown candy (*peen tong*), about 2 ounces

Rinse the red beans in several changes of cold water, and cover with at least 2 inches of cold water to soak overnight. Drain the soaked beans and discard the water.

In a small bowl, soak the tangerine peel in ¼ cup cold water for 30 minutes. Discard the water.

In a 2-quart saucepan, bring the beans, 1 quart cold water, and tangerine peel to a boil over high heat. Cover, reduce heat to medium-low, and simmer until very soft, about 1 hour. Drain and reserve the water. Place the drained beans and tangerine peel in a food processor and process until as smooth as possible.

Return the bean paste to the saucepan with the reserved cooking water. Add the lotus seeds to the saucepan, and bring to a boil over high heat, stirring constantly. Cover, reduce heat to low, and simmer until the lotus seeds are tender, about 30 minutes.

Meanwhile, in a small bowl, combine the pearl tapioca and ½ cup cold water and set aside to soak for 10 minutes. Cut the brown candy into smaller pieces. Return mixture to a boil over high heat. Add the softened tapioca and brown candy, reduce heat to medium, and cook, stirring constantly, until tapioca is translucent and sugar dissolves, about 10 minutes. Serve piping hot (no more than 1½ cups per person).

Makes 6 servings as a tonic.

Peanut Soup

Peanut Soup (*Fa Sung Woo*) is marginally a *yun* soup. When eaten in moderation, it is soothing to the system, but when eaten in excess, peanuts can cause *yeet hay* (excessive internal heat), as they are very rich. This soup has that incredible quality of tasting too delicious to be good for you, but the Chinese believe peanuts are a longevity food. In the West, studies have shown that peanuts contain resveratol, a plant chemical also found in red wine, which may have a protective effect against cancer and heart disease. Be sure to use rice flour and not glutinous rice flour.

¾ cup raw, skinless peanuts
½ cup sugar
½ cup rice flour

Heat a 14-inch flat-bottomed wok or skillet over high heat until hot but not smoking. Add the peanuts and stir-fry 30 seconds. Reduce heat to medium and stir-fry 3 to 5 minutes, or until the peanuts are golden and fragrant. Allow to cool thoroughly.

Place the cooled peanuts in a food processor and process until finely ground to the peanut-butter stage, about 1 to 2 minutes. Add the sugar and process 10 to 15 seconds, or just until combined.

In a 2-quart saucepan, combine the rice flour and 1 cup cold water, stirring until smooth. Add 1 cup cold water and the peanut mixture and stir again until smooth. Add 1 quart cold water and bring to a boil over high heat, stirring constantly until thickened. Remove from heat and serve piping hot (no more than 1 cup per person).

Makes 6 servings as a tonic.

Overleaf
Sesame Balls with
good luck New Year's
tangerine and photo of
Baba as a child.

Facing page
Rich panfried slices of
New Year's Cake (left)
and Taro Root Cake
served with tea.

Above
Jai (Buddha's Delight) is
the delicious Buddhist
vegetarian dish made
with gingko nuts,
mushrooms, oysters,
lily buds, cloud ears, and
cellophane noodles.

Right
Raw ingredients for
Buddha's Delight.

Facing Page
New Year's tray of togetherness filled with candied fruits and nuts signifying the sweetness of life.

Left
Traditional New Year's centerpiece of pomelos, oranges, and tangerines with *lysee*, lucky money.

Below
Preparing New Year's Cake to be panfried.

Facing Page
Stir-Fried Clams in Black Bean Sauce symbolizes prosperity, because the clam shells are said to resemble Chinese coins.

Right
Mama prepares bok choy, removing flowers.

Below
Stir-Fried Bok Choy.

炒白菜

魚翅湯

Above
Chinese culinary genius
is best exemplified
by Shark's Fin Soup,
an extraordinary
combination of
texture and flavor.

Left
Delicately flavored
Almond Soup is drunk
after the dramatic shift in
season from winter to
spring. The soup fortifies
the body against the
abrupt changes of weather
that can cause illness.

Facing Page
Dried Fig, Apple, and
Almond Soup is a classic
yun or harmonizing soup,
suitable for any season.

Left
Savory Rice Tamales
wrapped with bamboo
leaves for the Dragon
Festival.

Below
Unwrapped and cut
open, the tamale reveals
its filling of sweet rice,
yellow mung beans, pork,
salted duck egg, shrimp,
and Chinese sausage.

浸鯨魚

Above
Poached Steelhead Fish is an auspicious dish that must be served on both New Year's Eve and New Year's Day to ensure a proper beginning and ending to the year.

Left
Baba demonstrates the art of shredding ginger into fine delicate pieces.

Chinese Staples

1. Sweet rice
2. Long grain rice
3. Expensive Chinese dried mushrooms
4. Inexpensive Chinese dried mushrooms

5. Dried chestnuts
6. Black moss
7. Salted turnip, *teem choy poe*
8. Salted turnip, *chung choy zack*

9. Brown candy
10. Rock sugar
11. Dried shrimp
12. Sichuan peppercorns
13. Dried scallops
14. Dried oysters

15. Sheet dried bean curd
16. Stick dried bean curd
17. Rice flour
18. Glutinous rice flour
19. Wheat starch

20. Tapioca starch

21. Water chestnut flour

22. Cellophane noodles

23. Rice vermicelli

24. Shark's fin

25. Black vinegar

26. Red rice vinegar

27. Sweetened black vinegar

28. Thin soy sauce

29. Black soy sauce

30. Hoisin sauce

31. Plum sauce

32. Chili garlic sauce

33. XO sauce

34. Chinese dried black beans

35. Sesame oil

36. Oyster flavored sauce

37. Shao Hsing rice cooking wine

38. Ground bean sauce

39. Wet bean curd (white)

40. Wet bean curd (red)

Foods with Medicinal Attributes

1. Dried brown dates
2. Dried black dates
3. Dried red dates
4. Dried dragon eye
5. Shelled dragon eye
6. Dried figs
7. Dried sweet potato
8. Dried yam, *wai san*
9. Korean ginseng, sliced
10. Korean ginseng, whole
11. Chinese ginseng
12. American ginseng
13. Wolfberries
14. Licorice root
15. Lily bulbs
16. Lily buds
17. Peeled almond seeds, *buck hung*
18. Peeled almond seeds, *nom hung*
19. Dried ginger
20. White sesame seeds
21. Black sesame seeds
22. Dried tangerine peels
23. Gingko nuts
24. Seaweed
25. *Ching bo leung*
26. Lotus seeds with skin
27. Blanched lotus seeds
28. Snow fungus
29. Wood ears
30. Cloud ears
31. Star anise
32. Cinnamon bark
33. *Dong quai,* knobs
34. *Dong quai,* sliced
35. Red beans
36. Adzuki beans
37. Foxnut
38. Job's Tear barley
39. Yellow mung beans
40. Green mung beans
41. Dried soybeans

Fresh Vegetables

1. Long beans, light green
2. Long beans, dark green
3. Flowering garlic chives
4. Chinese chives
5. Yellow chives
6. Young bok choy
7. Winter melon
8. Taro root
9. Luffa
10. Cilantro
11. Bitter melon
12. Chinese eggplant
13. Water chestnuts
14. Ginger
15. Water spinach
16. Chinese broccoli
17. Broad-leaf mustard greens
18. Scallion
19. Snow peas
20. Fuzzy melon
21. Napa cabbage
22. Soybean sprouts
23. Mung bean sprouts
24. Chestnuts
25. Watercress
26. Green turnip
27. Chinese turnip
28. Chayote
29. Snow pea shoots
30. Lemongrass
31. Lotus root

Fresh Foods

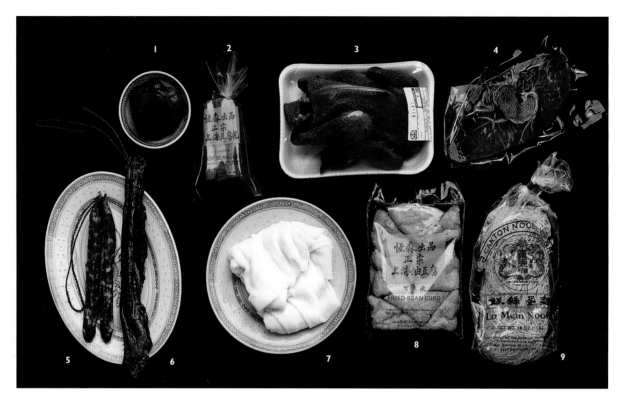

1. Sichuan preserved vegetable
2. Five spice tofu
3. Black chicken
4. Smithfield ham steak
5. Chinese sausage
6. Chinese bacon, *lop yok*
7. Fresh broad rice noodles
8. Fried bean curd, *dul foo gock*
9. Fresh egg noodles

Almond Soup

Almond Soup is one of the most delicious yin-yang concoctions. The flavor of this combination of almond seeds (which actually are not almonds at all, but apricot kernels) is fragrant and unique. *Nom hung* almonds are from Southern China and are marginally bigger in size and are known for their sweetness. *Buck hung* are from the North and are slightly bitter, but they bring out the flavor of the *nom hung* almonds. (See "Foods with Medicinal Attributes" in the photo insert). When you buy these almonds in Chinatown, the two varieties are not distinguished in English. You must ask for them by their Cantonese names. These almonds are excellent for lubricating one's system, moistening the lungs, and clearing the skin. Traditionally, this mixture was strained through cheesecloth after it was cooled, but my family doesn't mind the ground almonds and feels that it's more nutritious to eat everything.

1 cup peeled almond seeds (*nom hung*), 4½ ounces, rinsed

10 to 15 peeled almond seeds (*buck hung*), rinsed

1 tablespoon long grain rice, rinsed

3 pieces rock sugar, about 1½ ounces or ⅓ cup

Soak all the almonds and rice in 1½ cups cold water overnight to soften almonds and rice. Drain, reserving the soaking water.

Place the almonds and rice in a blender or food processor and process, adding the reserved water in ¼-cup increments; the mixture will be a smooth paste.

In a 3-quart saucepan, bring 3 cups cold water to a boil over high heat. Reduce heat to medium, and gradually stir in the almond paste. The mixture should be the consistency of a light pureed soup, so add more water, if necessary. Cover, reduce heat to medium-low, and simmer 30 to 40 minutes, stirring frequently, or until the almonds lose their raw flavor. If the mixture becomes too thick, add more water. Set aside and cool completely. Strain through cheesecloth or muslin, discarding the solids. Return to the saucepan over medium heat, add the rock sugar, and cook until sugar has melted, about 3 to 5 minutes. Serve piping hot (no more than 1 cup per person).

Makes 4 servings as a tonic.

豬
仔
薯
片
湯

Dried Sweet Potato Soup

The Cantonese believe this soup is especially good for soothing itchy skin conditions because it is a cooling soup. Dried sweet potato (*zhu zai shu peen*) is available in Chinese supermarkets. Brown candy (*peen tong*), a kind of Chinese sugar, is said to be beneficial for removing toxins from your system. My Auntie Katheryn taught me that brown candy can also be finely chopped, dissolved in cold water, and made into a paste. Smear it in globs on heat rash or mosquito bites, and allow it to dry for 15 minutes before rinsing it off with cold water. Indeed, it removes itchiness and swelling, although the sticky sugar feels strange when applied to the skin.

1 1/3 cups dried sweet potato (*zhu zai shu peen*), about 6 ounces

1/3 cup Job's Tear barley, rinsed

1 slab brown candy (*peen tong*), about 2 ounces

Rinse the dried sweet potato in several changes of cold water. In a medium bowl, soak the sweet potato in 2 cups cold water for 2 hours to soften.

In a 2-quart saucepan, combine the sweet potato and the soaking liquid, barley, and 2 cups cold water, and bring to a boil over high heat. Cover, reduce heat to low, and simmer 1 hour. Cut the brown candy into smaller pieces. Add the brown candy and cook, stirring, until dissolved. Serve piping hot (no more than 1½ cups per person).

Makes 4 servings as a tonic.

蕃
薯
蓮
子
湯

Sweet Potato and Lotus Seed Soup

The Chinese believe sweet potatoes are very nourishing and moisten the internal organs while they aid in easing constipation. In the West, we know that sweet potatoes are high in fiber and beta carotene. This is a simple, mildly sweet tonic soup with the flavor and texture of sweet potatoes and many Cantonese families make this year-round. The lotus seeds nourish the kidneys, and the brown candy removes toxins.

4 medium sweet potatoes, about 2 pounds

⅓ cup lotus seeds with skins, rinsed

½ slab brown candy (*peen tong*), about 1 ounce

Peel and cut the sweet potatoes into ½-inch cubes.

In a 2½-quart saucepan, bring 6 cups cold water to a boil over high heat. Add the sweet potatoes and lotus seeds, and return to a boil. Cover, reduce heat to low, and simmer 1½ hours. Add the brown candy and cook, stirring, until candy is dissolved. Serve piping hot (no more than 1½ cups per person).

Makes 6 servings as a tonic.

Dragon Eye and Lotus Seed "Tea"

Dragon Eye and Lotus Seed "Tea" is said to be calming and good for insomnia. Like the Lotus Seed "Tea," this is not a traditional brewed tea, but a hot beverage the Cantonese also call *tea*. Dragon eye (*longan*) is a fruit that is available fresh in the months of July and August in America, but it is the dried *longan* that is used for this tonic. Dried dragon eye is delicious uncooked; the fruit has a sweet and slightly smoky taste. It is sold in two forms in Chinese supermarkets: in the shell where the fruit has a small black pit, or shelled and pitted.

The method of cooking used here is double-steaming ("The Art of Steaming," page 33). The ingredients and cold water are placed in a traditional Chinese-style tureen or a heatproof bowl with an airtight lid. The bowl is then set on a rack in a very large pot (such as a canning kettle) and about two inches of cold water is poured in. The water both inside and outside the tureen must be cold, otherwise the tureen might crack. The water in the pot is brought to a boil and the covered tureen steams, retaining both flavor and nutrients. For herbal soups, especially, this method extracts the most from the ingredients and is therefore the most healthful.

1 1/3 cups lotus seeds with skins, rinsed

1/2 cup pitted dried dragon eye (*longan*), rinsed

1 ounce rock sugar, about 2 tablespoons

Place the lotus seeds, dragon eye, rock sugar, and 1 quart cold water in a Chinese-style tureen (or a deep heatproof bowl) and cover with an airtight lid.

Place about 2 inches of cold water in a pot (such as a canning kettle or lobster pot) that is large enough to fit the tureen *without touching the sides of the pot*. Place a cake rack on the bottom of the pot, and carefully place the tureen on the rack. Cover the pot and bring to a boil over medium-high heat. Steam on medium-high heat 2 hours. Check the water level often and replenish with boiling water, never letting the depth of the water fall below 2 inches. Remove from heat and carefully remove the tureen from the pot. Serve piping hot (no more than 1½ cups per person).

Makes 4 servings as a tonic.

Double-Steamed Papaya and Snow Fungus Soup

Papaya is soothing (*yun*) and, when combined with snow fungus, almonds, and rock sugar, it is said to benefit the entire body. Papaya can be found almost year-round, but the best time is from the late spring through the summer. Do not choose papayas that are ripe for this soup; they should have a hint of green. This soup is double-steamed (see Dragon Eye and Lotus Seed "Tea," page 206). It is critical when double-steaming to start with cold water in both the tureen and the pot to prevent the tureen from cracking. See Almond Soup (page 203) for information on almonds.

6 dried snow fungus (*shoot yee*), about 1 ounce

⅓ cup peeled almond seeds (*nom hung*), rinsed

6 peeled almond seeds (*buck hung*), rinsed

2 papayas, 12 ounces each

2 ounces rock sugar, about ¼ cup

Place the snow fungus in a small bowl and cover with water; the snow fungus will immediately expand. Soak it overnight, until softened. Remove any dark or yellow hard spots from the bottom of the snow fungus by hand and rinse thoroughly. Break into smaller pieces.

Soak all the almonds in ½ cup cold water overnight. Drain the almonds, reserving the soaking water. In a small saucepan, bring 1 cup cold water to a boil over high heat. Add the almonds and their soaking liquid and return to a boil. Cover, reduce heat to low, and simmer 4 hours, or until the almonds turn pale yellow and are tender when pierced with a knife. Check the saucepan from time to time to make sure the liquid does not evaporate. Set aside the almonds and cooking liquid.

Peel and seed the papayas. Cut into ½-by-2-inch pieces. Place the papaya, snow fungus, almonds and their cooking liquid, rock sugar, and 3 cups cold water in a Chinese-style tureen (or a deep heatproof bowl) and cover with an airtight lid.

Place about 2 inches cold water in a pot (such as a canning kettle or lobster pot) that is large enough to fit the tureen *without touching the sides of the pot*. Place a cake rack on the bottom of the pot and carefully place the tureen on the rack. Cover the pot and bring to a boil over medium-high heat. Steam on medium-high heat 2 hours. Check the water level often and replenish with boiling water, never letting the depth of the water fall below 2 inches. Remove from heat, and carefully remove the tureen from the pot. The soup will be a beautiful pale-orange color. Serve this sweet broth with pieces of piping hot snow fungus, almond seeds, and papayas (no more than 1½ cups per person).

Makes 4 servings as a tonic.

Double-Steamed Asian Pears

The Cantonese believe double-steamed pears are *yun fay,* or soothing for the lungs. The cooked pears are excellent all year round and especially good for coughs, or when one is recovering from an illness. Asian pears come in many varieties, but the most common ones have a round unpearlike shape and a rough skin. They are crisp and sweet like an apple, and are delicious raw. Again, this recipe involves double-steaming (see Dragon Eye and Lotus Seed "Tea," page 206).

¹/₃ **cup peeled almond seeds (*nom hung*), rinsed**

6 peeled almond seeds (*buck hung*), rinsed

4 firm Asian pears, about 2¹/₂ pounds, rinsed

2 ounces rock sugar, about ¹/₄ cup

Soak all the almonds in ½ cup cold water overnight. Drain the almonds, reserving the soaking water. In a small saucepan, bring 1 cup cold water to a boil over high heat. Add the almonds and their soaking liquid and return to a boil. Cover, reduce heat to low, and simmer 4 hours, or until the almonds turn a pale yellow and are tender when pierced with a knife. Check the saucepan from time to time to make sure the liquid does not evaporate. Set aside the almonds and their cooking liquid.

Core the pears and peel them. Place the pears in a Chinese-style tureen (or a deep heatproof bowl) large enough to snugly fit all 4 pears upright. Add the rock sugar, 2 cups cold water, and the cooked almonds with the reserved cooking liquid, and cover with an airtight lid.

Place about 2 inches cold water in a pot (such as a canning kettle or lobster pot) that is large enough to fit the tureen *without touching the sides of the pot.* Place a cake rack on the bottom of the pot and carefully place the tureen on the rack. Cover and bring to a boil over medium-high heat. Steam on medium-high heat 2 hours. Check the water level often and replenish with boiling water, never letting the depth of the water fall below 2 inches. Remove from heat, and carefully remove the tureen from the pot. Serve the pears with the almonds and sweet broth, piping hot.

Makes 4 servings as a tonic.

豆漿

Homemade Soy Milk

I am very fond of soy milk and buy it once a week in Chinatown. Mama, who has more time, makes it herself from dried soybeans. Dried soybeans (*wong dul*) are inexpensive and available in all Chinese grocery stores and health-food stores. Recent studies show a diet high in soybeans lowers cholesterol, fights heart disease, and can decrease the chances of some cancers from forming. Rich in *isoflavones,* an important phytoestrogen, soybeans may also be beneficial for menopausal women.

Traditionally, soy milk is made by pureeing the beans with water, then straining through a muslin cloth to extract the milk. Mama does not strain her soy milk. She feels that it is more nutritious to drink everything, but she shakes the bottle well before pouring. I should say that I think the name *milk* is misused. Although soy milk is white like dairy milk, real soy milk is watery and bean-y tasting. Some soy milk sold in cartons has added ingredients like malted cereal extract and barley and flavorings to make it seem more dairy-like and creamy, but it is inappropriate for Chinese recipes.

½ cup dried soybeans, about 3 ounces

Wash the soybeans in several changes of cold water. In a small bowl, cover the soybeans with about 1 cup cold water. Cover the soybeans, refrigerate, and soak for 1 day. Remove any hulls that float to the surface. Place the beans and their soaking water in a medium saucepan and bring to a boil over high heat. Cover, reduce heat to low, and simmer 1 hour, or until beans are tender. Check occasionally to make sure the liquid does not completely evaporate.

Drain the beans, reserving any cooking liquid. Process the beans in a food processor or blender, adding the reserved cooking water and ½ cup cold water in small increments; the mixture will be a smooth paste, resembling pureed vegetables.

In a 4-quart saucepan, bring 4½ cups water to a boil over high heat. Carefully add the soybean paste, and return to a boil over medium heat, stirring constantly. Reduce heat to low, cover, and simmer 15 to 20 minutes. The milk will have a lot of foam. Remove it from the heat and allow to cool. If desired, strain through a muslin cloth, squeezing the cloth to extract as much milk as possible, and discard the solids. Pour mixture into a bottle and refrigerate. Shake the mixture before using. Soy milk will keep for about 4 to 5 days.

Makes about 1 quart.

咸豆漿

Savory Soy Milk

Soy milk cooked with savory ingredients is popular as a breakfast item in China, especially in Shanghai. It is often eaten with an unsweetened Chinese fried doughnut (*yul tew*), which is dunked into the hot soy milk. *Yul tew* are freshly made every day and are available in Chinatown bakeries.

Use only unsweetened soy milk purchased in a Chinese market or a health-food store, or Homemade Soy Milk (page 209) for this recipe. In Chinatown, make sure you ask which bottles are unsweetened, because most people buy the more popular sweetened version. Never use soy milk sold in cartons for this recipe, because it often includes malted cereal extract and barley, and is also available flavored with vanilla or carob, giving the soy milk a taste and consistency that would not be suited to this recipe.

1 tablespoon Sichuan preserved vegetable (*cha choy*), optional

1 tablespoon vegetable oil

2 tablespoons Chinese dried shrimp, rinsed

3 tablespoons finely minced scallions

1 quart unsweetened soy milk, store-bought or homemade (page 209)

¼ teaspoon salt

If using, rinse the preserved vegetable under cold water to remove the red chili paste coating; pat dry. Finely mince and set aside.

Heat a 1½-quart saucepan over high heat until hot but not smoking. Add the oil, shrimp, scallions, and preserved vegetable, and stir-fry 30 seconds.

Add the soy milk, bring to a boil over high heat, and immediately remove from heat. Stir in salt. Serve piping hot (no more than 1 cup per person).

Makes 4 servings as a tonic.

Fresh Fig and Honey Date Soup

My Uncle Sam remembers drinking this soup in Shanghai and thinking that it was odd to have a soup made from figs and dates. Many Chinese people are not aware of this *tong shui* and its ability to moisten the internal organs. Mama says that in Shanghai they would poke the fresh figs with pins to release the white liquid called *"milk."* She cannot give me an explanation of why the milk must be released, but this is how she remembers it was always prepared. There is no need to pit the dates before cooking.

12 ounces fresh figs

1 pound pork neck bones, rinsed

2 Chinese dried brown dates (*mut zoe*), rinsed

Cut off ¼ inch from the tips of the figs. Set aside to allow the milk to be released, about 15 minutes. Rinse and drain.

In a 2½-quart saucepan, combine the pork bones and 6 cups cold water and bring to a boil over high heat. Skim any scum that rises to the surface. Add the figs and return to a boil. Add the brown dates, cover, reduce heat to low, and simmer 3 hours. Serve piping hot (no more than 1½ cups per person).

Makes 4 servings as a tonic.

Soybean and Sparerib Soup

Dai Dul Gna Choy Pie Qwat Tong

大
豆
芽
菜
排
骨
湯

In Shanghai, when the summer heat was strong, my Auntie Katheryn remembers her parents making this soup to stay cool. In the West, we drink cold fluids to combat heat, but in China certain hot soups are said to cool the body. The spareribs must be very lean for the soup to be sweet and flavorful. They are blanched before the sprouts are added to remove any impurities. Choose fat, creamy colored soybean sprouts that are not limp (See Sprouting Soybeans, page 80).

I pound soybean sprouts, about 6 cups

I pound lean pork spareribs

2 thick slices ginger

Salt, optional

Wash soybean sprouts in several changes of cold water and drain thoroughly in a colander.

In a 2½-quart saucepan, bring 2 quarts water to a boil over high heat. Add the spareribs and return to a boil. Drain and rinse the spareribs under cold water, and cut them into individual ribs. Wash the pot and bring 1½ quarts water to a boil over high heat. Add the spareribs, soybean sprouts, and ginger, and return to a boil. Cover, reduce heat to medium, and simmer 3 hours. Add salt to taste. Serve piping hot (no more than 1½ cups per person).

Makes 6 servings as a tonic.

Dried Fig, Apple, and Almond Soup

Mo fa guo is the Cantonese name for a variety of dried figs used in cooking. They are reputed to be good for moistening the lungs, and therefore recommended to combat coughs. These figs are different from the figs eaten in the West. They are ivory colored and are smaller, with more delicate seeds. If these figs are not available, regular dried or fresh figs can be substituted in this recipe. However, there is no substitute for the almond seeds; there are two different almond seeds called for here. For an explanation, see the introduction to Almond Soup (page 203).

I have tried this soup with Granny Smith apples, but I prefer the Red Delicious apples. This is the soup that helped cure a persistent cough I had after months of trying codeine cough syrups, throat-coat teas, and every lozenge on the market.

¼ cup peeled almond seeds (**nom hung**)

4 to 5 peeled almond seeds (**buck hung**)

3 medium Red Delicious apples, unpeeled

8 ounces pork loin, well trimmed

10 Chinese dried figs (**mo fa guo**), rinsed

Rinse all of the almonds in several changes of cold water, and soak them in ½ cup cold water overnight to soften.

Core the apples and cut into 1-inch-thick wedges.

In a 4-quart saucepan, bring 2 quarts water to a boil over high heat. Add the pork and return to a boil, skimming any scum that rises to the surface. Add the apple wedges, dried figs, and almonds with their soaking water. Return to a boil over high heat. Cover, reduce heat to medium-low, and simmer 3 hours. Serve piping hot (no more than 1½ cups per person).

Makes 6 servings as a tonic.

Ching Bo Leung Soup

Ching bo leung is one of the most popular all-purpose tonic soups. It is a special combination of seven Chinese herbs: Job's Tear barley (*yee mai*), lotus seeds (*leen zee*), dried dragon eye (*longan*), lily bulbs (*bock hup*), foxnut (*chee sut*), Solomon's Seal (*yook jook*), and Chinese dry yam (*wai san*). Available in Chinese supermarkets, the herbs come premeasured in an inexpensive package sometimes labeled *ching bo leung,* but often labeled only with Chinese characters. The package comes with the loose herbs and two separate sealed packets of barley and dragon eye. (Traditional Chinese families buy the herbs for *ching bo leung* individually, instead of in prepackaged form.) This soup is popular to drink all year round, as it is believed to detoxify the body, nourish the kidneys and lungs, and build up the blood. If desired, the pork can be omitted and chicken can be substituted. Some families cook the soup without any meat and, instead, add a little rock sugar and serve it as a sweet soup.

One 6-ounce package *ching bo leung*

8 ounces pork loin, well trimmed

Empty the contents of the herb package (including the barley and dragon eye packets) into a colander and rinse under cold water.

In a 2½-quart saucepan, combine the pork and 6 cups of water, and bring to a boil. Skim any scum that rises to the surface. Add the herbs and return to a boil. Cover, reduce heat to low, and simmer 2 hours. Serve piping hot (no more than 1½ cups per person).

Makes 4 servings as a tonic.

青蘿白湯

Green Turnip Soup

Shanghai in the winter could be bitterly cold. Mama would describe how coal was burned throughout the city to keep homes and buildings warm, but this, in turn, left the air polluted. Her family often made Green Turnip Soup to cleanse pollutants from their bodies. Green turnip (*chang law bock*) is one of the most commonly used vegetables for soups. It has a cooling effect, which is balanced by the warmth provided by the carrots. The turnips are about 6 to 8 inches long and 3 inches wide and are in season in the winter. Two-thirds of the turnip is pale green, the rest of it creamy white. Green turnip is also said to be beneficial if you have shortness of breath. Be forewarned that the cooking of green turnip produces a strong cabbagelike smell that is not appealing to most people. However, the flavor of the soup is rich from the pork and sweet from the vegetables, and is one of my favorites.

1 green turnip, about 1 pound

3 medium carrots

8 ounces pork neck bones

Trim the ends of the turnip and peel it. Cut the turnip lengthwise into quarters, then cut crosswise into 1-inch pieces. Trim the ends of the carrots and cut on the diagonal into ½-inch-thick slices.

In a 2½-quart saucepan, bring 2 quarts water and the pork to a boil over high heat. Skim any scum that rises to the surface. Add the turnip and carrots, and return to a boil. Cover, reduce heat to low, and simmer 3 hours. Remove pork bones and discard. Serve piping hot (no more than 1½ cups per person).

Makes 6 servings as a tonic.

四
味
湯

Four Flavors Soup

Four Flavors Soup (*Say May Tong*) is one of the most famous of the Cantonese herbal soups for balancing yin and yang. The *four* in the title refers to the four Chinese herbs used. My family likes to include lotus seeds (*leen zee*), Chinese yam (*wai san*), lily bulb (*bock hup*), and wolfberries (*gay zee*), but there are many recipes for this, each with different variations. This combination is said to be nourishing for the kidneys, liver, eyes, digestive system, and lungs, making this soup a popular tonic all year round. All these herbs are found in Chinese herb shops and supermarkets.

⅓ cup blanched whole lotus seeds (*leen zee*), about 2 ounces, rinsed

12 ounces pork neck bones

½ cup dried Chinese yam (*wai san*), about 1 ounce, rinsed

⅓ cup dried lily bulb (*bock hup*), about 1 ounce, rinsed

⅓ cup wolfberries (*gay zee*), about 1 ounce, rinsed

Cover the lotus seeds with cold water for 3 hours. Drain, discarding the water. Remove the tiny green sprout in the center of the seeds.

In a 2½-quart saucepan, combine the pork bones and 7 cups cold water and bring to a boil over high heat. Skim any scum that rises to the surface. Add the Chinese yam and return to a boil over high heat. Cover, reduce heat to medium-low, and simmer 1 hour.

Add the lotus seeds and lily bulb to the soup, and return to a boil. Cover, reduce heat to medium-low, and simmer another 1 hour.

Add the wolfberries and return to a boil. Cover, reduce heat to medium-low, and simmer a final 1 hour. Remove pork bones before serving. Serve the soup piping hot (no more than 1½ cups per person; all the Chinese herbs can be eaten, including the wolfberries, except for the small pits in them).

Makes 4 servings as a tonic.

Chayote Carrot Soup

Chayote (*hup cheung qwa*), also known as mirliton, is a vegetable the Chinese believe cleanses the system of toxins but is not a cooling vegetable. It is therefore especially suitable for the elderly, who should avoid eating foods that are too cooling, as those foods might weaken them. This is a simple soup my parents often make in the spring and eat at the conclusion of their meal. No matter how long the chayote is cooked, the peel is always tough unless the chayote is very young; therefore, chayote must be peeled before cooking.

2 chayotes, about 1¼ pounds

4 medium carrots

8 ounces pork loin, well trimmed

Peel the chayotes. Halve and remove the flat, pale seed (if there is one). Quarter lengthwise and cut crosswise into ¼-inch-thick slices. Trim the carrots and cut them into 1½-inch lengths.

In a 3-quart saucepan, combine the pork with 2 quarts of cold water. Bring to a boil over high heat, skimming any scum that rises to the surface. Add the chayote slices and carrots, and return to a boil. Cover, reduce heat to medium-low, and simmer 3 hours, or until broth is no longer pale in color, but has a slight orange blush and has cooked down to about 1½ quarts. Serve piping hot (no more than 1½ cups per person).

Makes 4 servings as a tonic.

Watercress Soup

The Cantonese say that it is critical that watercress always be added to water that has been brought to a boil. If the water is not boiling, the watercress becomes bitter. The long cooking removes watercress's extreme yin (cooling) nature. Without the long cooking, the coolness of the vegetable is thought to lead to fainting spells, and is therefore considered dangerous for the elderly to drink. This is a favorite soup for cleansing the system of toxins year-round. My parents also remind me to drink Watercress Soup in cold weather when my throat tends to feel dry.

1 piece of dried tangerine peel (*guo pay*), about 3 inches wide

2 bunches watercress

1 pound pork neck bones

½ teaspoon salt

In a small bowl, soak the tangerine peel in ¼ cup water 30 minutes. Drain, and discard the water.

Wash the watercress in several changes of cold water and drain in a colander. In a 4-quart saucepan, bring 1 quart cold water to a boil over high heat. Add the pork neck bones and boil 1 minute. Drain the pork bones, and rinse under cold water.

Return the pork bones to the pot and add the tangerine peel and 2 quarts cold water. Bring to a boil over high heat. Add the watercress. Cover, reduce heat to low, and simmer 3 hours. Discard the pork bones and stir in the salt. Serve piping hot (no more than 1½ cups per person).

Makes 4 servings as a tonic.

Yen Yen's Winter Melon Soup

The importance of winter melon, *doong qwa,* in the Cantonese diet cannot be overemphasized. My eldest aunt, Yee Gu Ma, who is ninety-two, has her granddaughter Cindy make this for her nearly every week. She wants the winter melon to be very mature, with lots of white powder on it when it is purchased. The powder indicates maturity but must be thoroughly scrubbed off before cooking. Winter melon is sold whole or by the wedge. Cindy cooks it with the rind, because the rind is said to cleanse the blood. Winter melon is considered to be cooling, which is why ginger is added to the soup to give warmth, and to neutralize the melon's cooling properties. Except for the fact that she is too frail to walk much, Yee Gu Ma is in excellent health. I have always suspected that my aunt's remarkable health is due in part to her fondness for this soup. My auntie has thirteen grandchildren and seventeen great-grandchildren (the eldest being twenty-one years old and the youngest fifteen months old), and she is known to them as Yen Yen.

One 3-pound wedge mature winter melon

1 pound pork loin, well trimmed

One 1-inch-thick slice of ginger, smashed

Salt

Scrub the winter melon rind and wash off the powdery white film. Discard the seeds and string pulp. Cut the winter melon into 3-inch cubes, leaving on the rind.

In a large pot combine the pork and 3 quarts cold water, and bring to a boil over high heat. Skim any scum that rises to the surface.

Add the winter melon and ginger, and return to a boil over high heat. Cover, reduce heat to medium-low, and simmer 4 hours. Add a little salt to taste. Serve the soup piping hot (no more than 1½ cups per person; the rind on the winter melon is not to be eaten).

Makes 8 servings as a tonic.

Herbal Winter Melon Soup

This is the most cleansing of the four winter melon soups offered in this book. The soup is cooked with the rind, seeds, and flesh, which are all said to have medicinal properties. The rind cleanses the blood, the seeds prevent constipation, and the flesh soothes the lungs. The winter melon is a cooling, vegetable and the adzuki beans are warming; together, they create a neutral soup that is balancing to the body. The long 5-hour cooking also neutralizes the cooling quality of the winter melon. Do not confuse adzuki beans (*zeck siu dul*) with Chinese red beans; adzuki are small, oblong red beans available in Chinatown and in some gourmet and health-food stores. This soup has an earthy clear taste that is probably too plain for the Western palate.

The final color of the soup is a blush red. Auntie Katheryn recalls that when it was so hot in Shanghai that you "stuck to the furniture," this soup was drunk to quench thirst and to cool you down. Unlike the Western practice of drinking iced beverages to cool the body, hot soups are often drunk in the summer in China. Meat is deliberately not used, as the Chinese believe fatty foods prevent the body from being cleansed. If desired, one Chinese salted duck gizzard (*hom op sun*) that has been rinsed of salt can be added for flavor; these are found in Chinese butcher shops.

One 1½-pound wedge mature winter melon

⅓ cup adzuki beans, about 2 ounces, rinsed

Scrub the winter melon rind and wash off the powdery white coating. Cut the winter melon into 3-inch cubes, leaving the rind, seeds, and string pulp. Place the winter melon in a 3-quart saucepan. Add 6 cups cold water and the adzuki beans, and bring to a boil over high heat. Cover, reduce heat to low, and simmer for 4 hours. Serve the soup piping hot (no more than 1½ cups per person; neither the rind nor the seeds should be eaten).

Makes 4 servings as a tonic.

芥
菜
湯

Mustard Green Soup

My Auntie Lil says Mustard Green Soup is best to drink in October, when mustard greens are ideal for balancing your system and preventing the flu. Perhaps its flu-fighting attributes are because it is a nutrient-potent vegetable being high in calcium, beta carotene, and folate, with a respectable amount of vitamin C. There are two popular mustard green soups. One is made with only pork and mustard greens, but the meatless version offered here is preferred, because the slightly bitter taste of the mustard greens is balanced by the sweetness of the sweet potato.

There are many varieties of mustard greens, but the two most popular varieties found in Chinatown are *dai gai choy,* big bunches with broad leaves and stems, and *gai choy sum,* smaller bunches with skinny stems. The bigger mustard greens tend to be less pungent.

This is the soup I dreaded the most as a child, but I have finally acquired a taste for, and appreciation of, it. Be forewarned that the cooking of mustard greens does produce a strong cabbagelike smell that is not appealing to most people. Salt is never added.

1 pound broad-leaf mustard greens (*dai gai choy*)
1 large sweet potato

Rinse the mustard greens in several changes of cold water and drain thoroughly in a colander. Cut the mustard greens into 1-inch pieces. Peel the sweet potato and cut into large chunks.

In a 3-quart saucepan, bring 1½ quarts water to a boil over high heat. Add the mustard greens and sweet potato, and return to a boil. Cover, reduce heat to low, and simmer 3 hours. Serve piping hot (no more than 1½ cups per person).

Makes 4 servings as a tonic.

Gingko Nut Porridge

Of the three porridge, or *jook,* recipes offered in this book, this is the most therapeutic. It is a congee like the others you've read about, but prepared with gingko nuts (*bock guo*), dried bean curd sticks (*foo jook*), and Chinese dried scallops (*gawn yu chee*). The combination is plain by Western standards, but the Chinese appreciate the purity and delicacy of flavor. Whenever I fly home, my parents have a big pot on the stove (about four times the amount of this recipe) so that, the moment I arrive, we can have this as a late-night snack (*siu ye*). They feel it helps to restore the body after the damaging effects of flying. Baba likes to place a few thin slices of raw beef or fish with finely shredded ginger on the bottom of the bowl before ladling on the piping-hot porridge, but it is also eaten plain.

My parents can make this year-round because gingko nuts are almost always available in San Francisco. In New York, I am only able to make this when they are in season, from December until April. The nuts are said to be beneficial for relieving coughs and reducing phlegm. Gingko biloba, which is reputed to be good for memory functions, is from the gingko leaves and not the nuts.

½ cup long grain rice

¼ teaspoon vegetable oil

½ teaspoon salt

1 stick dried bean curd (*foo jook*)

¼ cup unshelled gingko nuts (*bock guo*), about 1½ ounces

¼ cup Chinese dried scallops (*gawn yu chee*)

4 ounces flank steak, well trimmed, optional

2 tablespoons finely shredded ginger, optional

Wash the rice in several changes of cold water. Drain the rice and soak overnight in 1 quart cold water with oil and salt.

In a 1½-quart saucepan, bring 3 cups cold water to a boil over high heat. Break up the bean curd sticks into 2-inch pieces, and add them to the boiling water. Cook, turning the pieces, 1 to 2 minutes, or until almost ivory colored and softened. Drain and rinse under cold water.

Meanwhile, crack the gingko nuts lightly with a hammer, tapping on the opening and removing the shells. In a small saucepan, bring about 1 cup water to a boil over high heat. Blanch the shelled gingko nuts for about 1 minute. Drain, rinse under cold water, and remove the skins.

Place the rice and soaking water in a large pot. Add the gingko nuts and blanched bean curd sticks, and bring to a boil over high heat.

Cover, reduce heat to low, and simmer 2 hours, stirring occasionally, until the rice has "flowered" (the rice grains will swell and the ends will look blossomed out).

Meanwhile, in a small bowl, soak the dried scallops in ½ cup cold water for 2 hours, or until softened. Drain, reserving the scallop liquid. Remove and discard the small hard knob from the side of the scallops.

Add the scallops and reserved soaking liquid to the rice in the saucepan, and continue simmering 1 hour, or until scallops are tender and porridge is almost smooth. Add a little salt to taste. Serve piping hot.

If desired, serve with beef and ginger. Halve the flank steak with the grain into 2 strips. Cut each strip across the grain into scant ¼-inch-thick slices. Divide the slices and ginger among large soup bowls. Bring porridge to a boil over medium heat. Ladle hot porridge over beef and serve immediately. The hot porridge will cook the beef to the medium-rare stage.

Serves 4 to 6 as part of a multicourse meal.

Snow Fungus Soup

Snow fungus (*shoot yee*), also known as *white* or *silver fungus,* is said to be good for insomnia, constipation, and lubricating the lungs. The fungus looks like small, hard sea sponges. The best quality is light golden in color, not pure white. It is hard and dry, but after soaking and cooking, it can become so silky in texture that it almost melts in your mouth. Snow fungus has no flavor in itself but absorbs the rich flavors of the Homemade Chicken Broth (page 234) and Smithfield ham.

6 dried snow fungus (*shoot yee*), 1 ounce

1 ounce Smithfield ham

1 teaspoon light brown sugar

1 quart Homemade Chicken Broth (page 234)

Place the snow fungus in a small bowl and cover with water; the snow fungus will immediately expand. Soak the fungus overnight, until softened. Remove any dark or yellow hard spots from the bottom of the snow fungus by hand and rinse thoroughly. Break into smaller pieces.

Rinse the ham in cold water. In a small saucepan, bring 1 cup cold water to a boil over high heat. Add the ham and return to a boil. Reduce heat to medium-low, cover, and simmer 20 minutes. Drain the ham and rinse it under cold water. Pat dry with paper towels, place the ham in a small heatproof dish, and add brown sugar.

Bring water to a boil over high heat in a covered steamer. Carefully place the dish into the steamer, cover, reduce heat to medium, and steam 20 minutes, or just until ham is softened. Check the water level and replenish, if necessary, with boiling water. Carefully remove the dish from the steamer, set aside the ham, discarding any juices that have accumulated in the dish.

In a 2-quart saucepan, bring the chicken broth to a boil over high heat. Add the snow fungus, reduce heat to medium-low, cover, and simmer about 30 minutes if you prefer the texture crisp, or 1 hour or more if you prefer the texture silky and soft.

Slice the ham into paper-thin slices. Stack a few slices at a time and cut into paper-fine shreds, then cut the shreds to make a superfine dust of ham. When ready to serve, ladle the piping-hot soup into individual bowls and garnish with a sprinkling of ham dust. Serve piping hot (no more than 1½ cups per person).

Makes 4 servings as a tonic.

American Ginseng Chicken Soup

American ginseng (*fa kay sum*) is completely different from Chinese and Korean ginseng (see Korean Ginseng Soup, page 232). It is considered cleansing to the system, especially in ridding the body of alcohol and nicotine. American ginseng is also an excellent tonic to drink if you have acne, and it is said to help many people to sleep more soundly (although it makes my Auntie Elaine restless, proving that herbs affect everyone differently).

Fa kay sum is available "wild" or cultivated. The wild form, which is more potent, is a stimulant and is extremely expensive—it can cost well over $100 an ounce. Cultivated ginseng can be purchased for as little as $1 per ounce. If the ginseng is too hard to chop, it can be steamed briefly to soften before chopping. The Cantonese believe that when you drink ginseng soup you cannot eat fruit or vegetables at the same time, as they counteract the positive effects of the ginseng.

2½ ounces Smithfield ham, preferably Chinese-style with bone

1 ounce American ginseng, rinsed

1½ pounds skinless chicken parts

Rinse the ham in cold water. In a small saucepan, bring 2 cups cold water to a boil over high heat. Add the ham and return to a boil. Reduce heat to medium-low, cover, and simmer 20 minutes. Drain the ham and rinse it under cold water.

Chop the ginseng into ¼-inch pieces.

In a 3-quart nonreactive (such as enamel-coated) saucepan, combine the ham, ginseng, chicken, and 2 quarts water. Bring to a boil over high heat. Skim off any scum that rises to the surface. Cover, reduce heat to low, and simmer 3 hours. Remove any visible fat. Serve the soup piping hot (no more than 1½ cups per person; this includes chicken but, of course, it tends to be a little tough). The ginseng can be eaten but the flavor is very strong.

Makes 4 servings as a tonic.

BABA'S MAMA'S DONG QUAI AND RESTORATIVE FOODS

Mama, Douglas, Grandmother Young Gee She, and Baba. San Francisco, California, 1952.

DONG QUAI, KNOWN IN ENGLISH AS angelica, or *Angelicae sinensis,* is the well-known Chinese herb for women. For centuries, women have taken this herb after their menstrual cycle or after childbirth to invigorate the reproductive system. I first heard about *dong quai,* not from my parents, but from a massage therapist who recommended a line of synthetic Chinese herbs to me. She praised *dong quai*'s ability to cleanse blood, improve circulation, and relieve menstrual pain, while discussing its importance in ancient China. I thought to myself, "If it's so famous, why hasn't my family ever mentioned it?"

I asked my parents if they had ever heard of *dong quai* and, of course, they'd had it in their kitchen cabinet for years. They had never thought I would be interested. Baba's Mama had liked *dong quai* and, when she passed away, Baba brought her jar of it home and there it sat in our cupboard for years. It seemed to please Baba that I had asked about it, as if the herb somehow connected his mother to the granddaughter she never knew. On a subsequent visit home, Baba and I went together to buy the knobs of *dong quai* along with the Chinese dried dates that are always cooked in combination with it. It is now a ritual. Even though I could buy the same herbs in New York, it has more meaning to do this with Baba. The *dong quai* knobs look like long, ivory-colored stones, and they feel heavy, although they weigh about one ounce each. I store them in a jar in a cool, dark, dry cupboard where they keep indefinitely.

Do I think *dong quai* is effective beyond its connection to my grandmother? Indeed, I feel that it helps to regulate my cycle and balance my system. For some women, however, this herb may be of no benefit or even too stimulating. *Dong quai* is regarded as an herb suitable for women throughout their lives. According to some herbalists, *dong quai* has phytoestrogens, which accounts for its ability to relieve menopausal problems. Again, every individual's reaction is unique and one must monitor one's own response. Health-food stores carry menopause supplements and female toners that often include *dong quai* as an ingredient. When in doubt, it's best to consult with a reputable Chinese herbalist for use and dosage. *Dong quai* is considered to be quite mild as an herb but, when cooked, it fills the home with a strong aroma. It has a slightly bitter flavor, but it is not as medicinal tasting as some Chinese herbs can be, and even has a sweet, smoky taste. *Dong quai* is also beneficial for men, and it is used in Chinese medicine in combination with other herbs for treating many different ailments.

My parents first taught me to simmer *dong quai* with water and Chinese dried red dates (*hoong zoe*) for several hours (see Dong Quai Soup, page 230). Later my Auntie Lulu and Auntie Katheryn informed me that the traditional combination is *dong quai* with dried black dates (*hock zoe*). A Chinese herbalist explained to me that red or black dates can be used; each has a different purpose and a herbalist should determine what's best for you. The only instruction my parents gave me was to drink the hot tonic for a few days after each menstrual cycle.

The Dong Quai Soup recipe is only one of many Cantonese restorative, or *bow*, recipes. The word *bow* in Cantonese means to replenish or repair, and these recipes help restore strength after an illness, childbirth, or whenever an individual is lacking in energy. The Cantonese have a strong tradition of making special recipes that have ingredients such as beef, chicken, ginger, Chinese dried red dates, lotus root, wolfberries, and Korean ginseng, which are reputed by the Cantonese to be blood builders. These ingredients can be beneficial when a body is tired or in need of an energy boost. Contrary to the notion that chicken broth (Jewish penicillin) is a cure for colds and the flu, the Cantonese believe a sick body is not able to assimilate a restorative food like chicken broth. It is said to be too rich and difficult for an ailing body to digest (and they also feel it dries the internal organs). Instead, the Cantonese feel that an ailing person should first consume balancing (*yun*) foods (see "Cooking As a Healing Art," page 191) that are fat free and easy to digest, such as rice porridge (Gingko Nut Porridge, page 222), which is said to cleanse the intestines, hydrate the body, and help remove toxins. Then, when you are convalescing and in need of invigorating nutrients, a replenishing food such as Homemade Chicken Broth (page 234) is drunk to restore energy and provide strength.

According to my family, my body type tends to be on the cool or weak side (*hon dai*), which is why Baba says I am susceptible to having cold hands and feet in the winter, and even an occasional dry night cough. Therefore, they feel it is important for me, in the cold weather, to eat restorative foods like Chicken Wine Soup (page 236) or Lotus Root Soup (page 231) and, occasionally, Korean Ginseng Soup (page 232) to increase my circulation, and to avoid cooling foods, such as salads or too much fruit. By the summer I must stop eating these dishes or my system will overheat. Restorative recipes should never be cooked in the summer, only in the winter. Auntie Katheryn once told me, "You cannot *bow* when you're perspiring; only when the autumn winds come can you begin to *bow*." Imagine eating a lamb stew, essentially a restorative food because lamb is considered a very warming ingredient, in the middle of a 95-degree summer day. The taste of the stew leaves your mouth almost feeling sticky from the richness. Yet, on a wintry cold day, the heaviness of eating a meat stew isn't noticeable because your body needs the stimulation of a warming, yang food. And, given my already cool constitution, Mama and my aunties warn me that, even in the summer, I should not eat or drink anything too cooling (*leung*), like Green Mung Bean Soup (page 197), for this could weaken me enough to cause fainting. Mama, on the other hand, has a body type that is warmer and stronger (*yeet dai*) than mine. In the winter, she seldom needs the supplement of a restorative food and, instead, requires more cooling foods to keep her in balance. She can drink Green Mung Bean Soup without a worry of ever fainting from its strong cooling properties. Women with a warm constitution may not need a restorative food like Chicken Wine Soup or Dong Quai Soup (page 230) after childbirth. Knowing your body type and its tendency toward being cool or warm is necessary when choosing the correct yin and yang foods to eat throughout the year.

You must be careful to consume restorative foods with moderation, and to monitor your body's reaction. Once, when I was asking Mama what other restorative foods I should eat, she said with concern, "You cannot overload your body with *bow* foods just because you have a *hon dai* tendency. You must eat a combination of warming and cooling foods, with a bit more emphasis on the warming foods. Do not shovel only hot coals into your system! If your mouth begins to feel dry or if you have an acne flare-up, then the restorative food is creating too much warmth in your body and developing into internal heat, or *yeet hay,* meaning you don't need this extra boost."

This summer Mama made Pickled Pig's Feet (page 238) for me so I could learn to cook the recipe. Pickled Pig's Feet is the classic recipe Cantonese mothers eat after giving birth to reinvigorate their bodies, but it is also eaten by gourmands in cold weather. Granted, San Francisco's summer weather is hardly hot weather by tropical standards, but nonetheless, it was too warming a food to eat in 65-degree weather. The recipe was delicious, so we ate more than we should have and, as Mama had predicted, my mouth started to feel dry and my lips became chapped. Within a few days, Mama broke out with a pimple, indicating that she too was showing *yeet hay* symptoms. To counter such a reaction, we balanced our bodies with *yun* foods like Chayote Carrot Soup (page 217) and Double-Steamed Asian Pears (page 208) to reduce our internal heat. The dance of harmonizing the body through foods requires moderation and constant adjustment.

Dong Quai Soup

Prepare this tonic soup and drink up to 1 cup a day for three to four consecutive days after a menstrual cycle, refrigerating the tonic between uses. It is said to rejuvenate the uterus, warm the female organs, and regulate menstrual flow; it is also drunk after childbirth, and to treat menopause. Some women's bodies may be balanced without *dong quai* and, for them, the herb may be overstimulating. *Dong quai* can also be cooked with chicken broth, which supposedly triples the tonic's blood-building quality while improving its flavor. This tonic should be taken in moderation, as too much can be overwarming to the body, and can produce the opposite effect desired, or *yeet hay* symptoms.

Dong quai is sold in herb stores and some Chinese supermarkets. It is sold in ivory-colored knobs with fine brown veins; each knob is about ¾ to 1½ ounces. It is also sold in fat pear-shaped paper-thin slices, about ½ ounce each. The price can vary according to the quality; very ordinary quality can cost about $10 a pound. If you use dried red dates, the dates must be soaked and the pits removed; black dates only need to be rinsed. Sometimes I double-steam the soup in individual portions, using the Chinese tureen with double lids to "contain" the aroma, as it can be strong. (For information on double-steaming, see Dragon Eye and Lotus Seed "Tea," page 206.)

2 to 4 *dong quai* knobs or 6 slices, about 3 ounces

8 Chinese dried red or black dates (*hoong zoe or hock zoe*)

In a 2½-quart saucepan, combine the *dong quai,* dates, and 2 quarts cold water, and bring to a boil over high heat. Cover, reduce heat to medium–low, and simmer about 3 hours, or until the soup has reduced to about 4 cups. Strain. Drink piping hot (no more than 1 cup per person). For the very adventuresome, the *dong quai* can be eaten, but be warned, it has a very powerful flavor even after 3 hours of cooking; the flavor is too strong for me.

Makes 4 servings as a tonic.

Lotus Root Soup

Lotus root is said to be excellent for purifying the blood. The root always comes in three connected pieces. You can use all three lotus root sections for soup, although the two smaller, rounder pieces are best for soups (see Lotus Root Stir-Fry, page 84). When you cut cooked lotus root, you will find many fine threads like the ones in okra, and the more threads there are, the better the quality of the lotus root. This soup has a mild, sweet aftertaste from the mushrooms, red dates, and scallops and is popular to drink starting in the autumn.

¼ cup **Chinese dried scallops** (*gawn yu chee*)

4 **Chinese dried mushrooms**

4 **Chinese dried red dates** (*hoong zoe*)

1 **pound fresh lotus root**

1 **pound pork neck bones**

¾ **teaspoon salt**

In a small bowl, soak the dried scallops in ½ cup cold water for 2 hours, or until softened. Drain, reserving the scallop liquid. Remove and discard the small hard knob from the side of each scallop. Shred the scallops into small pieces.

In a small bowl, soak the mushrooms in ¼ cup cold water for 30 minutes, or until softened. Drain and squeeze dry, reserving the soaking liquid. Cut off and discard the stems and thinly slice the caps.

In a small bowl, soak the red dates in ¼ cup cold water for 30 minutes, or until softened. Drain the dates, reserving the soaking liquid. Remove the pits from the dates.

Cut the lotus root sections apart, removing the rootlike strands dividing them. Using a vegetable peeler, peel the lotus root sections, and rinse under cold water to remove any mud. Cut in half lengthwise. Cut each section into ¼-inch-thick half-moon slices. Rinse thoroughly again and set aside in a colander.

In a 5-quart pot, bring about 1 quart cold water to a boil over high heat. Add the pork bones and boil 1 minute. Drain the pork bones in a colander, and rinse under cold water.

Return the pork bones to the pot, and add 3 quarts cold water, the lotus root slices, red dates and their soaking liquid, mushroom soaking liquid, and scallop soaking liquid, and bring to a boil, covered, over high heat. Reduce heat to medium-low and simmer 2 hours.

Add the sliced mushrooms and scallop pieces, and continue simmering 30 minutes, or until the lotus root can be easily pierced with a knife. The soup is ruddy in color when done. Remove the pork bones and add salt. Serve piping hot (no more than 1½ cups per person).

Makes 6 to 8 servings as a tonic.

Korean Ginseng Soup

Korean ginseng is completely different from American ginseng (page 225), and is eaten more for its restorative qualities than for its cleansing attributes. It is said to be good for your heart, a mild stimulant that helps to replenish *qi* energy and reduce stress. Korean ginseng is generally double-steamed to capture the flavor, and the resulting soup is strong in taste (see Dragon Eye and Lotus Seed "Tea" for information on double-steaming, page 206). My Auntie Margaret cooks this every other week for herself and my Uncle Stephen, alternating it with a batch of American Ginseng Soup. She makes it plain with water, although she tells me that a 4-ounce skinless chicken breast could be added to make this tastier. Looking at Auntie Margaret at the age of eighty is enough to convince anyone to follow this regimen. She claims that drinking Korean ginseng gives her an optimistic outlook on life and gives her youthful energy. She tries to get plenty of rest and not to think about sad or sorrowful matters.

Korean ginseng looks very different from all other ginseng; the roots resemble mahogany-colored squarish cigars. The herb is also available sliced, and Chinese herb shops will sell you as little as 1 ounce. Korean ginseng is the most expensive ginseng, costing from about $185 to over $300 a pound. Chinese ginseng (*gut lum sum*) can be substituted, for it is said to have similar attributes, but is considered to be inferior in quality and is, therefore, more affordable. In its most prized form, whole Chinese ginseng mimics the form of the human body. I am told that drinking Korean or Chinese ginseng is not recommended in the summer, as it is too invigorating for warm weather. Never use a metal saucepan, as that diminishes the power of the ginseng. Once the soup is ready, it should be served with a porcelain spoon to prevent one from contaminating the ginseng.

1 piece Korean ginseng, about 1 ounce

Rinse the ginseng and place it in a small nonreactive saucepan (such as enamel-coated), and add 2 cups cold water. Bring to a boil over high heat. Cover, reduce heat to low, and simmer 1 hour. Remove the ginseng, reserving the cooking liquid. When cool enough to handle, cut the ginseng into ¼-inch pieces.

Place the ginseng, the reserved cooking liquid, and 2 cups cold water in a Chinese-style tureen (or a deep heatproof bowl) and cover with an airtight lid.

Place about 2 inches cold water in a pot (such as a canning kettle or lobster pot) that is large enough to fit the tureen *without touching the sides of the pot*. Place a cake rack on the bottom of the pot and carefully place the tureen on the rack. Cover the pot and bring to a boil over medium-high heat. Steam on medium-high heat 4 hours. Check the water level often and replenish with boiling water, never letting the depth of the water fall below 2 inches. Remove from heat, and carefully remove the tureen from the pot. Ladle the soup with a porcelain serving spoon, and serve piping hot (no more than 1 cup per person). The ginseng can be eaten, but be warned, it has a very powerful flavor even after 4 hours of cooking.

Makes 4 servings as a tonic.

Gai Tong

鶏
湯

Homemade Chicken Broth

My parents' friend Mrs. K. L. Woo taught me that traditional Chinese cooks never cook their food in metal pots, especially when it comes to chicken broth or herb soups. The metal is said to diminish the restorative qualities of the broth. The classic utensil is the sandpot, the tall upright ones (larger than the ones used for braising; see equipment photo, page 244), which are inexpensive and available in Chinatown. As with Korean Ginseng Soup (page 232), serve this broth with a porcelain spoon to prevent the food from being contaminated by any metal. When using a clay pot, start on low heat and let the water and pot gradually heat. If you do not have a sandpot and a porcelain spoon, be assured that there are plenty of Chinese families who make their broth in a metal pot; sandpots are only for very particular cooks. Unlike the Western tradition of simmering stock uncovered, the Chinese always cook their stocks covered to seal in the flavor. The only other ingredient besides the chicken is ginger, although in the winter, some cooks will add a few Chinese red dates. This broth is a staple of my parents' lives. It is one of the only foods you will always find in their freezer. Homemade Chicken Broth is vital to good home cooking and is the ultimate tonic; canned chicken broth is not a substitute.

One 4-pound chicken
2 teaspoons salt
2 slices ginger, ½ inch thick

Remove any fat pockets from the chicken and rub the chicken all over with salt. Remove as much skin as possible, and rinse the chicken under cold water. Place the chicken in a pot large enough to hold it, and add 10 cups cold water, then place it over medium-high heat. As the water heats, skim the scum that rises to the surface, adjusting the heat so the broth never boils; skim until most of the scum has been removed. Add the ginger, and bring to a boil over high heat. Cover, reduce heat to low, and simmer 3 to 4 hours. Allow it to cool and then strain the broth, discarding the chicken and ginger; cover the broth and refrigerate. The next day, remove the hardened fat on top. Salt is not added, on the assumption that it will be added to the dish in which the broth is used.

Makes about 2 quarts.

Double-Steamed Black Chicken Soup

Black chicken (*zook see gai*), also known as silky or black meat chicken, is considered extremely restorative. A black chicken is, in fact, a game bird (weighing about 1½ to 2 pounds), and is originally from China. Today, the game birds are raised in South Carolina, Pennsylvania, and Canada. They are sold only in Chinese meat markets. The skin of the chicken is charcoal gray to black, and considered very nutritious, so it is never removed before cooking; the flesh has only dark meat. My family says this soup is one of the best over-all tonics, especially for building blood. This claim may not be far from the truth. Interestingly, as I've discovered while writing this book, 3½ ounces of Chinese wolfberries (*gay zee*) contain 18 mg of iron. Chinese yam (*wai san*) is said to be good for the kidneys.

20 slices dried Chinese yam (*wai san*)

One 1¾ pound black chicken (*zook see gai*)

1 teaspoon salt

2 tablespoons wolfberries (*gay zee*), rinsed

4 to 5 slices ginger

4 ounces pork loin, well trimmed

Rinse the Chinese yam in several changes of cold water. In a medium saucepan, bring 2 cups cold water to a boil over high heat. Add the Chinese yam, cover, reduce heat to low, and simmer 2 hours, or until yam is just tender when pierced with a knife.

Remove any fat pockets from the chicken and rub it all over with the salt. Rinse the chicken under cold water.

Place the Chinese yam and its cooking liquid, black chicken, wolfberries, ginger, pork loin, and 4 cups cold water in a Chinese-style tureen (or a deep heatproof bowl) and cover with an airtight lid.

Place about 2 inches cold water in a pot (such as a canning kettle or lobster pot) that is large enough to fit the tureen *without touching the sides of the pot*. Place a cake rack on the bottom of the pot, and carefully place the tureen on the rack. Cover the pot and bring water to a boil over medium-high heat. Steam on medium-high heat 4 hours. Check the water level often, and replenish with boiling water, never letting the depth of the water fall below 2 inches. Remove from the heat and carefully remove the tureen from the pot. Serve piping hot (no more than 1½ cups per person). A serving includes everything in the pot, although the chicken and pork will be tough. Be aware that the wolfberries have small, sharp pits.

Makes 4 servings as a tonic.

Gai Zul

Chicken Wine Soup

The Cantonese serve Chicken Wine Soup, a blood tonic soup, with rice to new mothers during the first ten days after birth, when it is believed that absolutely no vegetables or fruits should be eaten because they are too cooling to the body. My Auntie Ivy's mother says this soup also cleanses the reproductive system and strengthens weak legs. The wood ears (*mook yee*) and lily buds (*gum tzum*) are said to remove dead blood (*san hoot*), and the ginger and rice wine help to rejuvenate and warm the body. Chinese dried mushrooms are reputed to revitalize the body. Recently, Scientists have identified a molecule in the mushrooms, called lentinen, that may boost the body's immune system.

Sometimes, in the winter, when I've complained of having cold hands and feet, Mama will suggest that I make this. It is also beneficial for women to drink this following their menstrual cycle. My Uncle Sam recalls that in China, Popo, my grandmother, made Chicken Wine Soup on a regular basis for this purpose. One shouldn't make this in the summer, as it would warm the body too much. Again, this may be too invigorating for some women and not beneficial. The traditional glutinous rice wine, *hock mai zul,* is found in Chinese supermarkets or liquor stores. The amount of ginger used depends on your tastes and, of course, the heat of the ginger you buy. Never add salt, because it is said to make the wine bitter.

1 ounce wood ears (*mook yee*), about 1 cup

16 Chinese dried mushrooms

¼ cup lily buds

4 pounds chicken, cut up

10 ounces ginger

½ cup raw, skinless peanuts

2 ounces pork butt, julienned

One 750-ml bottle *Tung Kiang* glutinous rice wine

In a medium bowl, soak the wood ears in cold water to cover for about 2 hours to soften. Drain and discard the water. Remove any hard spots from the wood ears, and carefully rinse under cold water to remove any dirt. Roughly cut the wood ears into 1½-inch square pieces.

In a medium bowl, soak the mushrooms in 1 cup cold water for 30 minutes, or until softened. Drain and squeeze dry, reserving the soaking liquid. Cut off and discard the stems, leaving the caps whole.

In a small bowl, soak the lily buds in ½ cup cold water for about 30 minutes to soften. Drain and discard the water. Remove the hard end from the lily buds and tie each lily bud into a knot.

Set aside the chicken wings. With a meat cleaver, chop the chicken through the bone into bite-sized pieces (or disjoint into serving pieces). Using a paring knife, scrape the ginger to remove all the peel, and cut the ginger into ¼-inch-thick slices.

In a large pot, combine the wood ears, lily buds, chicken wings, ginger, peanuts, pork, the reserved mushroom soaking liquid, and 6 cups cold water. Bring to a boil over high heat. Add the mushrooms and return to a boil. Cover, reduce heat to low, and simmer 10 minutes.

Uncover the pot and increase the heat to high. Add the chopped chicken and rice wine, and return to a rolling boil. When the chicken is just cooked, remove from the heat. Serve immediately, piping hot (no more than 1½ cups per person). Be advised that the ginger is very spicy, but a serving includes everything in the pot.

Makes 10 to 12 servings as a tonic.

Pickled Pig's Feet

In Cantonese tradition, a new mother eats Chicken Wine Soup (page 236) for the first ten days after giving birth. Then, for the rest of the month, the mother-in-law makes *Zhu Kurk Geung Cho* (Pickled Pig's Feet), which are said to help the mother produce more milk for the baby. The eggs in this dish are a symbol of birth and life, and the ginger helps to reinvigorate the new mother's body. To make this correctly, you most peel the ginger, which takes incredible patience.

All the relatives and friends who come to visit the new baby are also treated to the pig's feet, for pots and pots of this are prepared. I distinctly recall having it many times as a child and loving it. The black vinegar (*hock naw mai cho*) and sweetened black vinegar (*teem ding teem cho*) are found in Chinese supermarkets. If these vinegars are not available, white distilled vinegar can be used, but it is not as restorative, and more sugar must be added.

There are two types of pig's feet used here: the front trotters (*zhu sul*) have the most meat; the back trotters (*zhu kurk*) give the best flavor. Both are plentiful in Chinese butcher shops.

If making Pickled Pig's Feet for after childbirth, you want the full strength of the ginger. If not, the ginger should be blanched in 6 cups of boiling water for 15 minutes and then drained; this removes some of its heat. Do not have more than 1½ cups a day.

My friend Grace Choi says that this was too rich for her after she gave birth. She was not able to have this or the Chicken Wine Soup because her body generally does not need restorative foods.

2 pounds ginger

4 pounds pig's feet, front trotters (*zhu sul*)

1 pound pig's feet, back trotters (*zhu kurk*)

One 20-ounce bottle black vinegar (*hock naw mai cho*)

Using a paring knife, scrape the ginger to remove all the peel. Place the ginger in a large bowl and cover with cold water. Set aside.

Bring a large pot of water to a boil over high heat. Add all the pig's feet and return to a boil. Drain and rinse the pig's feet under cold water and drain. Using a disposable plastic razor, shave off any visible hairs on the skin. Rinse the feet under cold water and drain well. With a meat cleaver, chop the pig's feet into smaller pieces.

Drain the ginger, discarding the water. With the side of a cleaver, smash the ginger, and then cut into 1-inch-thick chunks.

One 21-ounce bottle sweetened black vinegar (*teem ding teem cho*)

4 large eggs

3 slabs brown candy (*peen tong*), about 6 ounces

1½ cups distilled white vinegar

In a large nonreactive (such as enamel-coated) pot, combine the ginger and 6 cups boiling water. Bring to a boil over high heat. Add the pig's feet and the regular black vinegar, and return to a boil over high heat. Cover, reduce heat to medium-low, and simmer, stirring the pot occasionally, until the pig's feet are just tender enough to be poked easily with a knife, about 1 hour. Add the sweetened black vinegar and return to a boil over high heat. Cover, reduce heat to medium-low, and simmer 20 minutes. Remove the pot from the heat and cool. Refrigerate and, the following day, remove the hardened fat on the top. The flavor is always better after 24 hours.

Hard-boil the eggs and remove the shells. Add the hard-boiled eggs to the pig's feet, and marinate 4 hours at room temperature. Cut each slab of brown candy into 3 to 4 pieces.

Bring the pot to a boil over medium-high heat. Add the brown candy and white vinegar, and cook, stirring, until the candy is dissolved and mixture is heated through, about 5 minutes. Serve piping hot (no more than 1½ cups per person). A serving includes everything in the pot; be advised the ginger is very spicy.

Makes a large batch that will last 2 to 3 days for a young mother.

牛腩蘿白湯

Beef and White Turnip Soup

It is rare that the Chinese use beef to make stock, preferring to use pork. The beef and ginger bring warmth to the body, which makes this soup especially good to have in the winter. The tangerine peel (*guo pay*) harmonizes the ginger and star anise, and the Chinese white turnip (*law bock*) is a cleansing vegetable. The beef used here is outside flank (see Braised Beef, page 54), not to be confused with flank steak.

1 piece dried tangerine peel (*guo pay*), about 3 inches wide

2 pounds outside flank (*gnul nam*)

One 1-inch slice fresh ginger, smashed

1 piece dried ginger (*sa geung*)

1 star anise (*bot guok*)

2 pounds Chinese white turnip

½ teaspoon salt

In a small bowl, soak the tangerine peel in ¼ cup water 30 minutes, or until softened. Leave softened tangerine peel whole and discard the water.

In a 5-quart saucepan, bring 2 quarts cold water to a boil over high heat. Add the beef, and return to a boil. Drain and rinse under cold water. Cut the beef into 2-inch squares, using a very sharp meat cleaver or knife, as it will be difficult to cut.

Return the beef to the pot and add 2½ quarts cold water. Add the fresh and dried ginger, star anise, and tangerine peel, and bring to a boil over high heat. Cover, reduce heat to medium-low, and simmer 3 hours.

Meanwhile, wash the turnip in several changes of cold water. Peel and cut the turnip into 3-inch chunks. Return the broth to a boil over high heat. Add the turnip and return to a boil. Cover, reduce heat to medium-low, and simmer another hour. Stir in salt. Serve piping hot (no more than 1½ cups per person).

Makes 8 to 10 servings as a tonic.

SHOPPING LIKE A SLEUTH

Shopping for Chinese ingredients requires patience, persistence, and excellent deductive skills. The first place to master is the Chinese grocery store. Before you enter, it is important to understand that often you cannot rely simply on the English name of a Chinese ingredient as it appears in a recipe. There is, unfortunately, no rule for English names on Chinese package labels, which means that an ingredient like lily bud, for example, can be labeled golden needles, lily flowers, tiger lily bud, or lily stem. The Cantonese know it only by its Cantonese name, *gum tzum*. If you request it by any one of the English names, the clerk may or may not know how to help you. And, to make matters worse, because there are no standards for English names on labels, completely different products can occasionally share the same name. I have found packages of snow fungus, cloud ears, and black moss all vaguely labeled "dried vegetable." For an added challenge, there are manufacturers in China who misspell names or come up with creative new names, such as star ani-seed for star anise.

One of the most frustrating ingredients to find using English is salted turnip. One manufacturer sells three different turnip products, but labels all of them "salted turnip." The packages are correctly differentiated with Chinese characters, but if you cannot read Chinese and do not know how the ingredient should look, you will not be able to tell the packages apart. Also, peeled almond seeds come in two completely different varieties, but this is never indicated in English on any package. When purchasing peeled almond seeds (*nom hung* and *buck hung*), salted turnip (*chung choy zack* and *teem choy poe*), Chinese red beans and adzuki beans (*hoong dul* and *zeck siu dul*), and white and red wet bean curd (*fu yu* and *nom yu*) seek out a Chinese clerk for assistance.

That said, try not to become frustrated with the Chinese clerk who looks at you blankly when you request an ingredient in English. This lack of standardization for labeling often makes it difficult for anyone to make sense of what you want. Also, Chinese grocers, butchers, and produce vendors can seem slightly aloof. There are exceptions, of course, but for the most part, food sellers do not see themselves as cultural ambassadors. Their role is not to assist you in deciphering the maze of exotic groceries, educate you in the differences in quality, or explain how to select produce. The task of demystifying Chinese ingredients is a complex undertaking compounded by the fact that many vendors do not speak English well, and most non–Asian shoppers cannot speak Chinese; it is no wonder many clerks seem unhelpful. Try to remind yourself: If you were a foreigner unable to speak English looking for a particular pasta in an American supermarket, how helpful would a typical clerk be at explaining why bow-tie pasta is also called butterfly or farfalle, depending on the manufacturer?

In Chinatown take the same approach you would if you were going abroad. Be self-sufficient and be aware of a rough lay of the land. Educate yourself with as much information as you can about the ingredients you seek. This will save you the frustration of having to constantly ask for help. Every Chinese grocery store is set up differently but there are some common threads: Just as in an American supermarket, once you locate the cottage cheese, you'll find the cream cheese, and know that the yogurt cannot be far away. Approach a Chinese market as if you were a sleuth. It is imperative that you read the descriptions in the Glossary (page 246) and note the physical characteristics of the ingredient and the kind of package it generally comes in. Check to see if the ingredient matches the photo identification (see the ingredients photos in the photo insert). And, when absolutely necessary, show the Chinese character of the ingredient to the shopkeeper and try to say the ingredient based on the Cantonese phonetic pronunciation provided.

When you enter a Chinese grocery store, notice that the most expensive ingredients, the great delicacies like shark's fin, dried scallops, dried mushrooms, ginseng, and XO Sauce, are generally behind the check-out counter, sometimes in boxes with plastic covers and, occasionally, in a locked glass cabinet. Though you can find inexpensive mushrooms on the regular store shelves, behind the checkout counter you'll find a variety of more expensive mushrooms at a range of prices. It goes without saying that the more expensive the mushrooms, the better the quality; the flavor will always be more intense. This is true of the dried oysters, scallops, tangerine peel, *dong quai*, and ginseng too. For everyday cooking, use the less expensive ingredients, but for special occasions it's nice to treat yourself. And, because the flavor is so much more concentrated, you can use less. If you would like more information about the differences in quality of herbs like ginseng (and why they vary so widely in cost), there are herb shops where English is spoken, but understand that the selection of herbs is an art in itself and no one can provide a quick understanding of how to shop for them. In general, more clerks speak Cantonese than any other Chinese dialect.

HERE ARE SOME BASIC GROUPINGS OF INGREDIENTS IN CHINESE GROCERY STORES:

- the refrigerator section carries fresh egg noodles (except fresh broad rice noodles, which are sold in bakeries, stores that sell fresh tofu, or at the checkout counters of some grocery stores), won ton skins, spring roll wrappers, firm tofu, silken tofu, five spice tofu, fried bean curd, soy milk

FREQUENTLY SHELVED TOGETHER:

- white sesame seeds, black sesame seeds, green mung beans, yellow mung beans, Chinese small red beans, adzuki beans, peanuts, dried chestnuts, soybeans
- thin soy sauce, black soy sauce, sesame oil, oyster flavored sauce, Shao Hsing rice cooking wine
- red rice vinegar, sweetened black vinegar, black vinegar
- rock sugar, packages and open bins of slab brown candy
- hoisin sauce, plum sauce, ground bean sauce
- tapioca starch, pearl tapioca, glutinous rice flour, rice flour
- skinless lotus seeds, whole blanched lotus seeds, foxnut, barley, peeled almond seeds, lily bulb
- rice vermicelli, cellophane noodles, water chestnut starch
- dried oysters, dried shrimp
- chili garlic sauce, chili sauce, chili oil
- *ching bo leung* (herb soup mix), dried sweet potato, wolfberries, dried yam, *dong quai,* ginseng
- five spice powder, star anise, licorice, cinnamon bark, Sichuan peppercorns, dried ginger
- cans of whole baby corn, straw mushrooms, bamboo shoots
- salted turnip, Sichuan preserved vegetable
- dried red dates, dried brown dates, dried black dates

- dried tangerine peel, Chinese dried black beans, stick dried bean curd, sheet dried bean curd, seaweed, wood ears, cloud ears, snow fungus, dragon eye, dried figs, gingko nuts, sweetened red bean paste, red wet bean curd, white wet bean curd, black moss, bamboo leaves

As you approach a Chinese produce stand, you may be overwhelmed by what at first glance seems to be an unfamiliar and unusual array of vegetables. But, in fact, if you look more closely, you'll see familiar produce like peppers, carrots, and cabbage scattered among the water chestnuts, water spinach, and lotus root. And for the rest, the photograph ("Fresh Vegetables" in the photo insert) illustrates every vegetable mentioned in this book except for amaranth. Look carefully at the items photographed and use the illustration as a reference when shopping for produce. Sometimes you will encounter produce not pictured in this book, such as jicama or small taro roots; most Chinese people do not use these vegetables daily so I have not included them. There are indeed at least four different kinds of bok choy that are available. However, I have chosen the most common and popular variety to show. Undoubtedly, you will also see exotic fruits, such as finger bananas, fresh lychee nuts, fresh dragon eye, or maybe even the king of fruits, the durian; be adventuresome and try them.

Knowing in which shops to find the ingredients is also critical. Many of the ingredients mentioned in the Glossary that follows can be found in both Chinese grocery stores and herb shops. This is because the Chinese consider many mild herbs to be basic food ingredients: for example, peeled almond seeds, black moss, cinnamon bark, cloud ears, dried dates (brown, red, and black), dragon eye, dried figs, dried ginger, licorice root, lily bulb, lotus seeds, pearl barley, snow fungus, tangerine peel, wood ears, *dong quai,* foxnut, ginseng, dried sweet potato, wolfberries, and dried yam. The quality in an herb shop is generally better. Again, use the photograph ("Foods with Medicinal Attributes" in the photo insert) and read the Glossary description carefully.

In America, I have only been in the Chinatowns of San Francisco, Chicago, and New York, and there are slight differences in how basic grocery items are sold in each city. In New York, fresh broad rice noodles are sold in shops that specialize in tofu and fresh noodle products. In San Francisco, you'll only find broad rice noodles in Chinese bakeries or at the checkout counter of some supermarkets. Chicago has the noodles at the checkout counter in a few markets. My Uncle Sam tells me that in Los Angeles every large supermarket carries fresh rice noodles. In New York and San Francisco, Chinese butcher shops carry Smithfield ham steaks, Chinese sausage, Chinese bacon, and black chickens, in addition to fresh meat and poultry. In Chicago, Chinese butcher shops and fish markets are less common, so supermarkets seem to carry a little of everything, from dry ingredients and herbs, to meat, fish, and Chinese vegetables. Of course, it's better to buy these items in a butcher shop than in a Chinese grocery store.

There are a few cuts that you can only find in a Chinese butcher shop. Pork spareribs that have been cut into one-inch pieces for steaming, Smithfield ham steaks, Chinese sausage, Chinese bacon, outside flank, black chickens, and beef tendons are abundant in Chinese butcher shops and are definitely not available in a Western butcher shop. Black chickens, also known as silky chicken or black meat chicken, is, in fact, a game bird and is only found in some Chinese butcher shops; American butchers are totally unfamiliar with them. Outside flank is a popular item in all Chinese butcher shops. Do not attempt to buy this in an American butcher shop; it is *not* flank steak. Ground pork butt is another common ingredient in a Chinese butcher shop, while an American butcher will probably have to specially grind this for you. If you have access to a Chinese butcher shop, the meat and poultry are generally very fresh and less expensive. In New York, Chinese butcher shops often carry salted duck eggs, fresh egg noodles, and won ton skins; in San Francisco, butcher shops only carry meat and poultry. Fish markets, whether Chinese or American, are the same on both coasts except for the variations of local fish. The only exception is that fresh frog is available in Chinese fish markets on both coasts; American gourmet fish markets will only occasionally have frog legs.

Chinese liquor like rice cooking wine is available in Chinese grocery stores but for more specific liquors such as *Mei Kuei Lu Chiew* liquor or Tung Kiang Glutinous Rice Wine, go to a Chinese liquor store. Some recipes call for cooked foods like barbecued pork, salt roasted chicken, soy sauce chicken, roast pork,and white cut chicken, which are readily available in Chinese delis, and at some restaurants, where you'll often see them hanging in the windows. If you do not live near a Chinatown, the recipes provided in "Dutiful Daughter Returns Home" (page 170) will help you make these dishes at home.

Don't forget to look for specialty dishes and pots and pans while you're in Chinatown, as they are very inexpensive. Most Chinatowns have hardware shops and specialty cookware shops that carry a large selection of dishes, bamboo and metal steamer pots, soup tureens, sandpots, bamboo chopsticks for cooking, and cast-iron and carbon-steel woks. Larger Chinese supermarkets will have a smaller selection of the same merchandise.

The popular shallow bowls with the painted fish used for steaming (see "The Art of Steaming," page 33) are found in various sizes next to rice bowls, noodle bowls, platters, and condiment dishes. Here you'll also find bamboo steamers in all sizes and the 10¼-inch-wide metal steamer pot with two tiers and a domed lid. Don't forget to look for an ingenious tool—a three-pronged plate lifter for removing a hot plate from the steamer. There are also Chinese-style tureens, which are ceramic

1. 3-cup individual tureen with double lid

2. 7-cup tureen with porcelain spoon and lid

3. 14"-skillet with rack, shallow bowl for steaming, and plate lifter

4. Bamboo steamer with lid in stainless-steel wok

5. 10¼" aluminum double-tier steamer

6. 14" flat-bottomed carbon-steel wok with cleaning brush

7. 14" flat-bottomed cast-iron wok with metal ladle

8. 2-quart sandpot with lid

9. 5-quart sandpot with lid

pots with a lid specifically designed for double-steaming such dishes as Dragon Eye and Lotus Seed "Tea" (page 206), Double-Steamed Black Chicken Soup (page 235), and Korean Ginseng Soup (page 232). Western-style tureens cannot be substituted because the tureen must have a tight-fitting lid that prevents vapors from escaping. The standard Chinese-style tureens come in different sizes starting at about seven cups. The smaller tureens have about a three-cup capacity and even have a second, interior lid in addition to the domed lid to ensure that no flavor escapes. This interior lid is also useful because it prevents the smell of herbs like *dong quai* or ginseng from lingering in your kitchen.

Sandpots are available in a variety of sizes, from two quarts to six quarts, and are used for braised dishes (Sandpot Braised Lamb, page 62, and Seafood Sandpot, page 60) and for cooking soups (Homemade Chicken Broth, page 234). The pots are cream-colored ceramic with a rough, unglazed exterior (sort of sandy textured, hence

1. Chinese chef's knife
2. Meat cleaver
3. 8" cook's knife
4. 7" Santuko/Japanese cook's knife

the pot's name) and a dark brown, glazed interior; some sandpots have a large wire mesh on the outside. Be sure to examine the interior of the pots for any cracks to avoid a pot that will leak.

In specialty cookware shops in Chinatown, you'll find a large variety of cleavers. The traditional Chinese cleaver is carbon steel, but there are now high-carbon stainless-steel vegetable and meat cleavers, which are much easier to care for. However, it is not necessary to use a Chinese cleaver. There is a huge variety of high-quality chef knives and meat cleavers available in American specialty cookware shops. These knives ("Shreds of Ginger Like Blades of Grass," page 47), generally from Europe, are hand-forged high-carbon stainless steel, and I feel they are of better quality than the knives from China.

Finally, there are the traditional twelve- and fourteen-inch Chinese cast-iron and carbon-steel woks that are available with flat and round bottoms. They require seasoning and special care in washing (see "The Breath of a Wok," page 20, for more information on types of woks and the care of a traditional wok). However, do not forget that there are fabulous cast-iron and stainless-steel woks available in American specialty cookware shops. Although carbon-steel woks are better conductors of heat, they are more trouble to take care of. Look for a flat-bottomed wok with sides that flare out and be sure to buy a lid, too. Never buy the round-bottomed woks, as they cannot get hot enough on a home stove. Next to the woks in Chinatown, you'll also find metal spatulas, shallow strainers, Chinese ladles, plate lifters for steaming, extra-long bamboo chopsticks perfect for deep-frying, and brushes for cleaning a cast-iron or carbon-steel wok.

As you wander about Chinatown in pursuit of your ingredients and equipment, enjoy the assignment of hunting down your treasures. Let your curiosity lead you and follow your instincts, for you never know what will turn up. I never tire of going to Chinatown; there are streets I have walked down hundreds of times, but I am always on the alert for an unusual ingredient, a freshly opened box of fragrant mangoes, a new restaurant, or a treasure to be unearthed.

GLOSSARY

赤小豆

Adzuki Beans (*zeck siu dul*): Small, elongated red beans, about one-fourth inch long, with a tiny line. Do not confuse these with Chinese small red beans, which are the same color and also have a little line, but differ in having a rounder shape. In a Chinese grocery store the two beans are generally labeled red beans, but you can always tell them apart by the distinguishing oblong shape. Adzuki beans are sometimes available in gourmet and health-food markets. They are mainly used in soups in Chinese cooking. Store in an airtight jar in a cool, dark, dry cupboard.

莧菜

Amaranth (*yeen choy*): This vegetable resembles a bunch of young spinach, except for a splash of burgundy color in the center of the flat leaves. It is sold in bunches and is best in the spring to early summer. By midsummer, the stems are tough. Use in stir-fries or in soups. Amaranth is rich in iron. Store in the refrigerator vegetable crisper bin for up to two days.

細粟米

Baby Corn (*sai sook mai*): This canned baby corn is two to three inches long. The corn should be drained and rinsed before using. Store unused portion in the refrigerator in a plastic container, covered with cold water, for up to three days.

竹葉

Bamboo Leaves, dried (*jook yeep*): These leaves are sold bundled in twelve-ounce packages, about fifteen to eighteen inches long. They are used to wrap Savory Rice Tamales (page 152) and Sweet Rice Tamales (page 154). Store in a cool, dark, dry cupboard for up to one year.

竹筍

Bamboo Shoots (*jook soon*): Fresh bamboo shoots are sometimes available, but canned are more convenient to use. The vegetable is pale yellow and is available in cans whole, sliced, or shredded. Rinse or blanch the bamboo shoots for one minute to remove the metallic canned taste before cooking. Unused portion should be stored in the refrigerator in a plastic container, covered with cold water, for up to one week; change the water daily.

薏米

Barley, Job's Tear (*yee mai*): A different variety than Western barley, this is sold in eight-ounce packages. However, if it is not available, use regular barley. Mainly used in soups. Store in an airtight jar in a cool, dark, dry cupboard.

Bean Curd. *See* Fried Bean Curd, Sheet Dried Bean Curd, Stick Dried Bean Curd, Tofu, and Wet Bean Curd.

芽菜

Bean Sprouts (*gna choy*): There are two varieties of Chinese sprouts: mung bean sprouts, which are more commonly available, and soybean sprouts. For either, choose fat, plump sprouts no more than two-and-one-half inches long. Avoid long, stringy, brown, and limp sprouts, indications that they are old. On page 80 you will find a recipe for sprouting your own soybean sprouts at home; you can use the same method for mung bean sprouts.

芽菜
Mung Beans Sprouts (*gna choy*): These have a head that is the size of a grain of barley, about one-fourth inch wide. Traditional Cantonese cooks like to remove the head and tail before cooking.

大豆芽菜
Soybean Sprouts (*dai dul gna choy*): These are more nutritious, being high in protein. The head, which is the size of a small jelly bean, about one-half inch, is the most nutritious part of the sprout. Do not eat raw soybean sprouts, as they are toxic. Store in the refrigerator vegetable crisper bin for no more than one day.

涼瓜
Bitter Melon (*leung qwa* or *foo qwa*): Popular in the summer, this vegetable is light or dark green and about eight to ten inches long. The melon is, in fact, bitter in taste because it contains quinine. The light-colored melon is milder than the dark-green bitter melon, and is best paired with strong flavors like Chinese dried black beans, beef, pork, or chicken. Some cooks like to blanch the melon to reduce the bitterness before cooking. Halve the melon, remove the seeds, and blanch the cut halves. Note that some melons have a creamy white pulp while others have a bright orange pulp, but they will taste the same. Choose melons that are fat at the bottom and taper slightly. The skin should have thick ridges. Store in the refrigerator vegetable crisper for three to five days.

發菜
Black Moss (*fat choy*): Also known as *seaweed hair, dried black moss,* or *hair vegetable,* because it looks like very fine black hair. This ingredient is primarily used around Chinese New Year's in the vegetarian dish *Jai* (page 126). The name of the ingredient, *fat choy,* is the same as the greeting for New Year's, *"Gung hay fat choy,"* and, therefore, has auspicious meaning. It is found in Chinese grocery stores or herb shops in plastic packages or in bulk. Soak in water with a little oil before using. Store in an airtight jar in a cool, dark, dry cupboard.

白菜
Bok Choy (*bok choy*): This member of the cabbage family is available in several varieties, and is popular for stir-fries. The most common variety found in Chinatown (see "Fresh Vegetables" in the photo insert) is sold in bunches about eight to eleven inches long, with white stalks and unblemished dark green leaves. The best bok choy is called *choy sum,* or heart of bok choy, and is more delicate. American supermarkets always seem to carry bok choy that is large, up to twenty inches long and, therefore, much older and tougher. Other varieties that have begun to appear in the last few years are Shanghai spoon bok choy, oil seed rape vegetable (*yul choy*), and *tatsoi*. Choose bok choy with tightly closed buds. Avoid any open flowers, yellow leaves, or stems that are beginning to brown, all signs that the vegetable is old. Bok choy is available all year round but is best in the winter months. It is rich in calcium. Store in the refrigerator vegetable crisper for up to three days.

片糖
Brown Candy (*peen tong*): These slabs of sugar are not a confection, but a type of sugar. They are available in one-pound plastic packages, sometimes called *brown sugar,* and are also sold loose in bins in some markets. The slabs are about five inches long, one-and-one-fourth inches wide, and a scant

one-half inch thick, with three different-colored layers. It is used mostly for desserts and sweet soups, and is said to remove toxins from the body. Store in a cool, dark, dry cupboard.

合掌瓜

Chayote (*hup cheung qwa*): Also known as mirliton, this pale green, flat, pear-shaped squash is about five to seven inches long and three-and-one-half inches at its widest point. It is in season from fall to spring. This squash must be peeled before cooking. Halve the squash and remove the seed if there is one. Chayote is excellent in stir-fries, braises, and soups. Store in the refrigerator vegetable crisper bin for up to one week.

栗子

Chestnuts (*loot zee*): Chestnuts are available both fresh and dried.

Fresh Chestnuts: These are available from about November until the end of December. Choose dark mahogany-colored shells that are shiny, heavy, and do not feel hollow. Make a slash in the chestnut skin with a paring knife, and soak the chestnuts in cold water for four to six hours. Chestnuts can either be boiled or roasted until they are tender when pierced. Cool the chestnuts before removing the shell and peel. If fresh are unavailable, use dried chestnuts, but these have less flavor. Store fresh chestnuts in the refrigerator in a paper bag in the vegetable crisper bin for up to one week.

Dried Chestnuts: These are available in Chinese and Italian markets all year round in plastic bags. They are an adequate substitute when fresh are not available, from January until November, and are far superior to canned or jarred chestnuts. Dried chestnuts that have been sitting around for a long time are not worth using. Sometimes they have an off smell, indicating that they are not fresh and that the flavor has diminished. Dried chestnuts are always shelled, but oftentimes the inner, thin peel has not been thoroughly removed. The chestnuts are about one inch wide and look wrinkled. Try to choose chestnuts that have very little peel. The chestnuts must be soaked until softened and then simmered for forty to fifty minutes, or until tender, before they can be added to a recipe. After they are simmered, any remaining peel can be removed with a paring knife. Store chestnuts in an airtight jar in a cool, dark, dry cupboard for up to one year.

蒜蓉辣椒醬

Chili Garlic Sauce (*shoon yong lat ziu zheung*): Also known as *chili bean sauce* or chili garlic paste, this reddish-brown sauce with flecks of red is made of chili pepper, salt, rice vinegar, and garlic. The sauce is very fragrant, spicy, and hot. I prefer Lee Kum Kee brand, which is available in eight-ounce jars and keeps in the refrigerator for several months.

辣油

Chili Oil (*lat yul*): This oil is a reddish-orange color, and is flavored with dried red chilies. It is a favorite table condiment, but add sparingly, as the oil is fiery hot. Store in a cool, dark, dry cupboard for up to six months, or refrigerate.

臘肉

Chinese Bacon (*lop yok*): Also known as *winter-cured pork,* this is pork belly that has been dry cured. When asking for this in a Chinese butcher shop or market, you must say the Cantonese name; do not ask for Chinese bacon. It is available in Chinese butcher shops and in some grocery stores; it can also be made at home in the winter (page 182). Although it is bacon, it is much drier and harder than Western bacon and is never sold thinly sliced. Sometimes it is steamed briefly to soften it before chopping or slicing because it is so hard. It has an earthy, smoky flavor. It is also found in Cryovac packages in Chinese markets, but try to buy it fresh in a butcher shop. Store in the refrigerator in a plastic bag for up to two weeks.

芥蘭

Chinese Broccoli (*gai lan*): Also known as *Chinese kale,* the individual stalks are most commonly sold all year round in two-pound bundles, but are best in the winter months. This broccoli bears no re-semblance to Western broccoli. The entire vegetable is dark green, and the stalks are ten to four-teen inches long and one-half to three-fourths of an inch in diameter. The leaves on one stem can be as big as a lettuce leaf and as small as a petal; there are tiny, pale-green buds hidden in the leaves. When selecting Chinese broccoli, never choose broccoli with thick stalks, open flowers, or yellow leaves, for these are signs of age. The best method of preparation is to cut the stalks in half length-wise, then cut the stalks and leaves into two-inch sections, and stir-fry. Store in the refrigerator veg-etable crisper bin for up to five days.

豆豉

Chinese Dried Black Beans (*dul see*): These beans are also known as *salted black beans, fermented black beans,* or *preserved beans.* The small black beans are fermented with salt and spices, and are a popular seasoning with meat, seafood, and poultry. The beans are sold in plastic bags or in a small, round, cardboard container. Before using, the beans must always be rinsed in several changes of cold wa-ter. Most of the time they are crushed with the handle of a cleaver (or a wooden spoon) and com-bined with soy sauce, garlic, or ginger before cooking. A favorite brand is Yang Jiang Preserved Beans, which are packaged in a cardboard box smaller than but similar to an oatmeal box. They keep indefinitely in a cool, dark, dry cupboard or in the refrigerator.

茄子

Chinese Eggplant (*ke zee*): The best eggplants are lavender, firm, and blemish free with a silky skin. They are about eight to nine inches in length and two inches wide. Because they are smaller than the Western variety they are much more tender with almost no seeds and are said to be less bitter. Never select a wrinkled eggplant, or one that is soft to the touch or light in weight. Store in the re-frigerator vegetable crisper bin for up to one week.

冬菰

Chinese Mushroom, dried (*doong qwoo*): Also known as *black mushroom, golden oak mushroom, dried win-ter mushroom,* or *shiitake,* as they are called in Japan, these dried fungi are brownish, gray-black mushrooms and vary greatly in quality depending on weather conditions, season of harvest, and the type of logs they are grown on. The Chinese dried mushroom caps can be about one-eighth inch thick to a scant three-eighths inch thick and one to three inches in diameter. They vary in price from about three dollars per pound to well over fifty dollars per pound. (See "Chinese Staples" in the photo insert to see the difference between the two types.) Mushrooms are sold in cellophane packages, boxes, and in bulk in Chinese grocery stores or herb shops. Pale, thick mushroom caps with lots of cracks are the most prized and expensive and are called *fa qwoo.* The flavor of these mushrooms is more robust and concentrated with an almost meaty taste. Thicker mushrooms also require more time for soaking: one to two hours versus fifteen to thirty minutes for less expensive mushrooms. The thinner, browner caps are less expensive. Remove the woody mushroom stem from either type and discard. Always reserve the soaking liquid, for it is very flavorful and can be added to other dishes to add flavor. Do not use the last teaspoon or so of the soaking liquid, as there is often grit that is released as the mushrooms soak. Dried mushrooms have a significant amount of protein, iron, and calcium. Store mushrooms in an airtight jar in a cool, dark, dry cupboard.

臘腸

Chinese Sausage (*lop chong*): This dried sausage is made of pork, pork fat, sugar, soybeans, and spices. It is sold in Chinese butcher shops, where it is generally hung behind the counter in pairs, connected by a thick cord. The sausages are available extra-lean and "regular"; I generally select the extra-lean for cooking. They are also sold in the refrigerator section of Chinese grocery stores in Cryovac packages or loose in open bins. The sausages look like skinny salami; the links are about six to seven inches long and one-half inch in diameter. Like Chinese bacon, the sausages are very hard, and can be difficult to slice if not steamed briefly. Sausages are used in stir-fries and are a favorite for flavoring rice. Store in the refrigerator.

蘿白

Chinese Turnip (*law bock*): This turnip is a daikon radish, but the Cantonese word for this vegetable translates as *turnip*. It is eight to twelve inches long, cylindrical, and three to four inches wide. It is often confused with Japanese daikon, which tastes and looks very similar. The Japanese type tends to be a creamy white color with perfect smooth skin; the Chinese turnip is a dirtier cream color and has rougher skin. The best Chinese turnips are heavy and firm, with slight cracks on the surface. The stem end should have fresh green shoots and not dry, brittle stems. If Chinese turnips are not available, the Japanese daikon can be used, but it is not as flavorful. Chinese turnip is cooked in braises, soups, and the famous Turnip Cake (page 128). Store in the refrigerator vegetable crisper bin for up to one week.

清補涼

Ching Bo Leung: This is a specific group of herbs that can be cooked throughout the year with pork and water to make a *yun* soup (page 214). The herbs for the soup come premeasured in a soup mix sold in six-ounce plastic packages. The label is sometimes written in English, but mainly is only in Chinese. It is a special combination of seven Chinese herbs: Job's Tear barley (*yee mai*), lotus seeds (*leen zee*), dried dragon eye (*longan*), lily bulbs (*bock hup*), foxnut (*chee sut*), Solomon's Seal (*yook jook*), and Chinese dry yam (*wai san*). Although the packages are good, the quality of herbs is always better if you buy them individually. *Ching bo leung* is sold in grocery stores and some herb shops, and will keep for up to one year.

Chives: The Chinese have three varieties of chives:

韭菜

Chinese Chives (*gul choy*): These look like hearty Western chives or very young scallions. The stem end has about one inch of white before the chive turns dark green. This vegetable is sold in small to medium bunches ranging from ten to sixteen inches in length. Chinese chives are popular in stir-fries, and are known for removing the metallic taste of a new carbon-steel wok (page 23). Store in the refrigerator vegetable crisper bin for up to five days.

韭菜花

Flowering Garlic Chives (*gul choy fa*): These chives have a tiny one-half-inch-long, pale-green bud rather than flowers. The chives are dark green and are eight to twelve inches long. Store in the refrigerator vegetable crisper bin for up to five days.

韭王

Yellow Chives (*gul wong*): Also known as *blanched garlic chives,* they are in fact pale yellow to almost white, because they are grown in the dark. They are the most delicate, fragrant, and expensive of the three chives. They are generally sold loose and are eight to thirteen inches in length with tips that can have a hint of brown. They require careful washing to remove dirt. These chives are popular in stir-fries, especially paired with pale ingredients like bean sprouts. Store yellow chives in the refrigerator vegetable crisper bin no more than two days.

芫茜

Cilantro (*yeem sai*): Also known as *fresh coriander* or *Chinese parsley,* it is more fragrant than parsley. Cilantro has delicate leaves and a strong flavor, and is best when sold with its roots. In addition to being a seasoning, cilantro is often used as a garnish. Select green, fresh leaves with thin stems, avoiding yellow, wilted leaves. Wash carefully in several changes of cold water to remove dirt before using. Place roots in a glass of water, cover the leaves with a plastic bag, and store in the refrigerator for up to five days.

肉桂枝

Cinnamon Bark (*yok quai zee*): Also known as *cassia bark* or *Chinese cinnamon,* it is unlike Western cinnamon in color and thickness. Chinese cinnamon is thicker, gray, hard, brittle, and looks like tree bark. The cinnamon is sold in plastic bags in grocery stores or in bulk in herb shops and is about six inches long and about three-fourths of an inch in diameter. Never use Western cinnamon as a substitute. This is a key ingredient in five-spice powder. Store in an airtight jar in a cool, dark, dry cupboard, indefinitely.

雲耳

Cloud Ears (*wun yee*): Also known as *tree ears, dried vegetable,* or *black fungus,* these dried fungi are gray-black. Cloud ears look like delicate, paper-thin, crinkled, one-inch leaves, which crumble easily. They must be rinsed and soaked in cold water before using, and will expand to two to three times their size. Remove the hard knob before cooking. Rinse well after soaking, as dirt is often lodged in the cloud ears. Once cooked, the cloud ears are almost flavorless, and the texture is both silky and crunchy. They are sold in plastic bags in Chinese grocery stores; they should be transferred to a jar and stored in a cool, dark, dry cupboard for up to one year. Do not confuse with wood ears (page 268), which are much bigger.

枣

Dates, dried (*zoe*): There are three main Chinese dried dates: black, brown, and red. The red date is the most readily available but all are typically found in plastic bags in a Chinese supermarket, and are also sold in bulk in Chinese supermarkets and herb shops. None of them resemble Western dates; I am told that they are technically not dates.

黑枣

Black Dates, dried (*hock zoe*): Mainly used for medicinal purposes, they are sold in herb shops and some grocery stores. They look like prunes that have lost all their moisture. They are most commonly used with *dong quai* for a female tonic (page 230).

蜜棗

Brown Dates, dried (*mut zoe*): Also known as *dried sweetened dates,* or *honey dates,* these dates are sold in twelve-ounce plastic bags. They are about one and one-fourth inches long and one inch wide. The skin is deep brown and not smooth; there is a fine pit inside that does not need to be removed before cooking. These are never eaten raw but are mainly cooked in soups. Store in an airtight jar in a cool, dark, dry cupboard.

紅棗

Red Dates, dried (*hoong zoe*): Also known as *jujube,* these dates have leathery skin. The dates are red and about the size of a large, cylindrical olive, about three-fourths inch long and one-half inch in diameter. They have a fruity fragrance like that of raisins. They are never eaten raw but are added to soups, braises, steamed dishes, desserts, and as a decoration. Dates are said to be good for circulation and contain significant amounts of potassium, iron, and calcium. Red dates, unlike the brown or black variety, must always be pitted before cooking; soak the dates in cold water to soften in order to remove the pits. Red dates are also sold pitted. Store in an airtight jar in the refrigerator indefinitely.

當歸

Dong Quai: Also known as *angelica* or *Angelicae sinesis, dong quai* is sold in plastic bags, in boxes, or in bulk in Chinese grocery stores and herb shops. It is said to be a blood tonic and particularly beneficial for women (page 230). *Dong quai* is available in two forms and both are equally good. One form is ivory-colored knobs with brown veins that are about one ounce each and one and one-half inches long and three-fourths inch in diameter. The second form is thin slices about one-eighth inch thick with a fat pear shape. Store in an airtight jar in a cool, dark, dry cupboard, or in the refrigerator indefinitely.

龍眼

Dragon Eye, dried (*longan*): This dried fruit is covered by a light brown, brittle shell, and is a one-inch ball. The shell is very thin and is easy to break. The longan meat is deep red to dark brown. The flesh is only about one-fourth inch thick, very sweet and meaty, and surrounds a one-half inch dark pit. Dragon eye is also available pitted and shelled, but this product is generally in a different place in the store. This dried fruit is often eaten raw as a snack or used in soups. In the shell, it is sold in plastic bags in grocery stores, and pitted in little boxes. In July and August, the fresh fruit, which is delicious, is available, but it cannot be substituted for the dried in recipes. Store fruit in an airtight jar in a cool, dark, dry cupboard.

無花果乾

Figs, dried (*mo fa guo gawn*): Chinese dried figs look like Western dried figs, except that they are ivory-colored. They are sold in cellophane packages in Chinese grocery stores and in some herb shops. They are mainly used in soups and are never eaten raw. Although they are dried, they are often only available during the autumn and winter. Store in an airtight jar in a cool, dark, dry cupboard for several months.

五香粉

Five Spice Powder (*nmm heung fun*): This is a ground spice made up of Chinese cinnamon, cloves, fennel, peppercorns, and star anise. It is sold in plastic bags or in a small jar. It is sometimes available in Western supermarkets in the spice section. Store in an airtight jar in a cool, dark, dry cupboard.

茨實

Foxnut (*chee sut*): Foxnuts are about a scant one-half inch in diameter, and have a reddish skin with a white center. They are considered a mild herb, used mainly in soups throughout the year. They are sold in plastic bags in grocery stores and in bulk in herb shops. They are one of the primary herbs in Ching Bo Leung Soup (page 214). Do not confuse with halved lotus seeds with skins; lotus seed skin is closer to burgundy in color, with a cream-colored center.

豆腐角
Fried Bean Curd (*dul foo gock*): Also known as fried gluten (a misnomer), bean curd puffs, or fried tofu, these golden bean curd puffs are available in the refrigerator section. They are triangles, squares, or cubes of tofu that have been deep-fried. They are sold in plastic bags, about twelve to a bag, and are added to braises because they absorb the flavors of the sauce in which they are cooked. Store in the refrigerator for one to two weeks.

節瓜
Fuzzy Melon (*zeet qwa*): This green squash ranges in length from four to ten inches. Select a fuzzy melon that has very fine prickly hairs. Once the squash is smooth, it is overly mature and not worth cooking. The flavor of the squash is mild: It is popular in soups and braises, but it must be peeled before it is used. Fuzzy melon can also be stuffed (Stuffed Fuzzy Melon, page 98); for stuffing, choose long skinny squash. The best season for them is the summer. Store in the refrigerator vegetable crisper bin for up to one week.

薑
Ginger Root, fresh (*geung*): This rhizome is available year-round and is fundamental to Chinese cooking. In the spring and summer, young ginger (*zee geung*), sometimes called *spring ginger,* is available and is milder in flavor; it is pale yellow with a tender skin that does not require peeling, and has pink-tipped shoots. The more common ginger (*low geung*) has a browner, drier skin. Select ginger that is heavy and firm. The best ginger is knobby, with rough rather than smooth skin. Ginger that is smooth-skinned has more fibers and is tougher with less flavor. However, even though the skin should be rough, it should not be wrinkled. Ginger is a yang food, which means that it counteracts foods that are yin, or cooling. It is said to aid digestion and improve circulation. Dried or ground ginger is not a suitable substitute. Store in the refrigerator vegetable crisper bin in a brown paper bag placed inside a plastic bag for up to two weeks.

沙薑
Ginger, dried (*sa geung*): Also known as *spiced dried ginger,* this ginger is sold in small plastic bags in Chinese grocery stores, and in bulk in herb shops. The ginger is sliced about one-fourth inch thick and one-half inch in diameter. The flesh is a pale cream color with light-brown skin. Fresh ginger is completely different and cannot be substituted. Store in an airtight jar in a cool, dark, dry cupboard.

白果
Gingko Nut (*bock guo*): Available fresh in San Francisco almost all year round, they are only available in New York from about late November until April. Gingko nuts or gingko seeds are grown in America, but the majority of product comes from China, where the gingko tree is the oldest living tree species. These nuts look like closed pistachio nuts. The hard shell must be cracked with a hammer. Blanch the shelled nuts in boiling water to remove the skin, before cooking in braises, desserts, or rice porridge. Gingko nuts are said to be beneficial for coughs and removing phlegm. This should not be confused with gingko biloba, derived from gingko leaves, and said to help memory. Place the gingko in a jar and store them for up to one month in the refrigerator. Do not use canned gingko nuts.

人參
Ginseng (*yen sum*): Ginseng is available in Chinese grocery stores and herb shops, in plastic bags, in boxes, or in bulk. The purchase and selection of ginseng is a fine art. It comes in many different grades, forms (whole, sliced, chopped, powdered, capsules, and in extract form), and prices. Depending on the variety of ginseng, the herb is said to cleanse toxins, stimulate, relieve stress, or build blood. The three principal varieties are American (page 225), Chinese, and Korean (page 232). Purists always cook ginseng in a porcelain Chinese-style tureen or a nonreactive saucepan. Metal is said to interfere with the positive effects of ginseng. Ginseng should be consumed in moderation. Store in an airtight jar in a cool, dry, dark cupboard, indefinitely.

花旗參
American Ginseng (*fa kay sum*): This is completely different from the Chinese and Korean types and cannot be used interchangeably. It comes in two forms: wild and cultivated. The wild is more potent, is a stimulant in addition to being able to clear toxins from the body, and is extremely expensive. The cultivated is much milder and more affordable.

吉林參
Chinese Ginseng (*gut lum sum*): This is similar to Korean ginseng, and can be used as a substitute for it, although it is considered inferior in quality. The most expensive form of this ginseng resembles the form of the human body; the sliced is much less expensive.

高麗參
Korean Ginseng (*ko lay sum*): This is known for its restorative qualities. Whole Korean ginseng has a distinct look; the ginseng is mahogany-colored and looks like squarish cigars; it also is sold sliced. It is said to be a stimulant that replenishes *qi* energy, and helps to reduce stress and fatigue. Some studies show that it strengthens the immune system and builds blood. Korean ginseng is considered to be superior to Chinese ginseng and is much more expensive.

綠豆
Green Mung Beans, dried (*look dul*): These small jade-green beans are not perfectly round. They are a scant one-eighth inch in diameter with a small line, and are sold in fourteen-ounce plastic bags. I prefer Golden Chef brand from Thailand. Do not substitute yellow mung beans (page 268) for green mung beans in recipes. They are the same bean but the yellow mung beans have been hulled. Green mung beans are also used for sprouting mung bean sprouts. Store in an airtight jar in a cool, dark, dry cupboard.

青蘿白
Green Turnip (*chang law bock*): This variety is about half the size of a Chinese turnip, six to eight inches long and two to three inches in diameter. The distinguishing feature is that two-thirds of the turnip is pale green. It is mainly used in soups, especially in the winter. Store in the refrigerator vegetable crisper bin for up to one week.

麵豉
Ground Bean Sauce (*meen see*): This chocolate-colored sauce is also known as *brown bean sauce, bean sauce, brown bean paste,* or *yellow bean sauce* and is sold in cans and jars. I prefer Lee Kum Kee brand in the thirteen-ounce jar. It is made from naturally fermented soybeans, flour, and sugar. Store in the refrigerator for several months.

海鮮醬

Hoisin Sauce (*hoisin zheung*): This chocolate-brown sauce is mildly sweet and smoky. It is made from sugar, soybeans, garlic, sesame seeds, chili peppers, and spices. It is very thick and is sold in cans or jars. I prefer Lee Kum Kee brand, which is available in a fourteen-ounce jar. Hoisin sauce is used in cooking and is a favorite condiment. Store in the refrigerator for several months.

香茅

Lemongrass (*heung mal*): This herb is sold as individual stalks about eighteen inches long. Select stalks with thick bottoms that are not dry or brittle. The majority of the stalk should be pale green, and almost cream colored at the stem end. Remove all the outer leaves and use only the base or soft core, which is about three inches long, for cooking. The leaves can be used to brew tea. Store in the refrigerator vegetable crisper bin for up to one week.

甘草

Licorice Root, dried (*gum cho*): Chinese licorice root looks like small dried branches and is fragrant with the scent of licorice. The skin is brown and the flesh tan. It is used mainly in braised dishes, but is also used in herbal tonics, as it is said to benefit all organs. It is sold in small cellophane bags or in bulk in herb shops in two-and-one-half-inch-long pieces that are about one-fourth inch wide. Store in an airtight jar in a cool, dark, dry cupboard.

金針

Lily Buds (*gum tzum*): Also known as *golden needles, lily flowers, tiger lily buds,* or *lily stems*. Lily buds are a dried ingredient comprised of three-inch flexible strands that are honey colored to dark brown. Select the honey-colored strands, as the brown lily buds are old. They should be soaked in cold water in order to remove the knob, which feels like a little bump at the stem end. The tradition is to then tie the lily bud in a knot (for aesthetic reasons) before cooking. Lily buds have an earthy taste and add texture to stir-fries and soups. They are most often sold in plastic bags. Store in an airtight jar in a cool, dark, dry cupboard.

百合

Lily Bulbs, dried (*bock hup*): These ivory-colored, petal-shaped bulb pieces are slightly curved and about three-fourths inch long, one-half inch wide, and a scant one-eighth inch thick. They are hard and firm with no scent. Lily bulbs are considered both a food and herb, and are sold in fourteen-ounce plastic bags in grocery stores or in bulk in herb shops. They are mainly used in soups. Recently, fresh lily bulb from China has occasionally been available in produce markets; it is sold in small Cryovac bags and can be used in soups or stir-fries. Store the dried lily bulb in an airtight jar in a cool, dark, dry cupboard.

豆角

Long Beans (*dul gock*): Also known as *yard-long beans,* these beans are available in two varieties: dark green beans (*chang dul gock*) and light green beans (*bock dul gock*). The dark green beans are crisper and the light green less crunchy. Both can be eighteen to thirty inches long. Even when farm fresh, the beans are limp, and can have tiny brown blemishes. They are available all year and are said to be the only "neutral" vegetable a woman can eat after childbirth. Long beans are rich in iron. Trim the ends and cut into one-fourth-inch to two-inch sections before stir-frying. Store in the refrigerator vegetable crisper bin for up to five days.

蓮藕

Lotus Root (*leen gnul*): This is one of the most distinctive vegetables one will see in Chinatown. Lotus root is ivory colored, is about sixteen inches in length, and has three sections (although some markets separate the sections) with little root hairs between each piece. Each section requires careful washing to remove the mud in which it is grown. Once the root is cut, rinse it again to make sure all the mud has been rinsed off. Cut off any dark spots. The longest section is best for stir-fries; the two shorter sections are best for soups. Lotus root season is September, October, and November, but you can find it at other times of the year. Never select lotus root that has been wrapped in cellophane; you must be able to smell the lotus root to make sure it has a clean smell. Select roots that are heavy, firm, and blemish free. Peel the lotus root and cut into thin slices to reveal a beautiful pattern of holes. Store in the refrigerator vegetable crisper bin for up to five days.

蓮子

Lotus Seeds, dried (*leen zee*): Lotus seeds are available in two forms: whole blanched (skinless) or halved, with paper-thin burgundy skin and cream-colored center. The packages often have no English written on them. Both varieties are sold in sixteen-ounce plastic bags or in bulk in Chinese grocery stores and herb shops. Blanched lotus seeds sometimes have a small green stem that must be removed, because it is bitter. To do this, soak the lotus seeds in cold water to soften briefly, before removing the stems. Lotus seeds are used in sweet and savory soups, desserts, and some braised dishes. Do not confuse with foxnuts, which have a reddish skin and a white flesh. Store in a jar in a cool, dark, dry cupboard indefinitely.

絲瓜

Luffa (*see qwa*): Also known as *angled luffa, Chinese okra,* or *silk squash,* luffa is dark green with thin, sharp ridges about one-half inch apart, and is ten to twenty inches long, two inches in diameter, with a slight curve. Choose squash that is firm, but has a soft skin and gives slightly when squeezed. Rough, hard skin indicates the squash is old. Peel just the ridges if the squash is young, but if it is old all the peel must be removed. Cut the squash into small chunks before using in stir-fries or soups. If the squash is dried in the sun, it becomes a luffa bathing sponge. Store in the refrigerator vegetable crisper bin for up to three to four days.

芥菜

Mustard Greens (*gai choy*): Available starting in October and November, this is a popular vegetable for soups and braises in the autumn. Mustard greens are pale green and are usually available in big bunches with wide, firm, curved stems and broad, frilly-edged leaves (*dai gai choy*) or smaller bunches with skinny stems and more delicate leaves (*gai choy sum*). The larger bunches are sweeter in flavor, and the skinny variety is more bitter and pungent. Mustard greens have a significant amount of calcium, folate, and beta carotene. Store in the refrigerator vegetable crisper bin for up to one week.

黃芽白

Napa Cabbage (*wong gna bock*): Also known as *Peking cabbage,* this vegetable grows in two varieties; neither resembles Western green cabbage. *Wong gna bock,* which is short and squat, is more commonly found. *Siu choy* is longer and narrower. Both are available year-round, but are best eaten in the winter. Some cooks feel *siu choy* is the sweeter of the two. Choose cabbage with pale white to yellow crinkly leaves and creamy white stems. Select cabbage that is blemish free, with no tiny brown or black spots. Napa cabbage is well suited for stir-fries, braises, dumplings, and soups. It is available in all Chinese produce markets and often found in American supermarkets. Store in the refrigerator vegetable crisper bin for up to ten days.

麵

Noodles (*mein*): Fresh and dried noodles are used in Chinese cooking.

河粉

Broad Rice Noodles (*haw fun*): These are made from ground rice powder, wheat starch, and water, and are sold in long sheets that have been steamed, lightly oiled, and then folded to roughly the size of a folded kitchen towel. They are soft and flexible until they have been refrigerated. Do not refrigerate them if you are planning to use them the day of purchase, especially for Stuffed Noodle Rolls (page 164). Broad rice noodles are also used for stir-fries and soups. They are sold in bakeries, stores that sell fresh tofu, or at the checkout counters of some grocery stores. Store in plastic bags and refrigerate for three to four days.

粉絲

Cellophane Noodles (*fun see*): These are also known as *glass noodles, bean thread noodles, green bean thread,* or *vermicelli,* and are available in a variety of package sizes, from 1.7 ounces to 17.6 ounces. Cellophane noodles are made from ground mung beans, and must be soaked in cold water for five to ten minutes, until softened, before cooking. Once cooked, they are almost translucent and slightly gelatinous. They are bland and take on the flavor of the seasonings they are combined with, especially in braises and soups. Cellophane noodles are sold in plastic bags in Chinese grocery markets. Store in an airtight jar in a cool, dark, dry cupboard.

新鮮全蛋麵

Fresh Egg Noodles (*sun seen choon dan mein*): These come in two varieties: *won ton* or *lo mein* (won ton are thin, *lo mein* are thick) and have a golden egg color. They only require about one to three minutes of boiling. The noodles are available in the refrigerator section of most grocery stores. Be aware that *lo mein* noodles are available cooked and uncooked; both can be used for Lo Mein Noodles (page 97). Store in the refrigerator for up to one week.

米粉

Rice Vermicelli, dried (*mai fun*): These are also known as *rice sticks* or *rice noodles,* and are superthin, white noodles that are very brittle. The noodles must be soaked for ten to fifteen minutes in cold water, never hot or boiling water, until softened, before using in stir-fries. For soups, they can be added dried to boiling water or broth and cooked until softened, about five minutes. The noodles come in a big rectangular block in a plastic bag: Simply pull off what you need. Store the unused portion in a plastic bag in a cool, dark, dry cupboard indefinitely.

蠔油

Oyster Flavored Sauce (*hoe yul*): A thick, brown sauce that is sold in bottles and used in cooking and as a condiment. Oyster flavored sauce varies greatly in quality. The brand I like is Lee Kum Kee and has a woman and boy in a small boat pictured on the label. Its founder invented the sauce in 1888. It is made from oyster extracts, sugar, and salt. Store in the refrigerator for up to one year. Vegetarian oyster sauce is now available and is made from mushroom extracts rather than oysters.

蠔豉

Oysters, dried (*hoe see*): Dried oysters are golden to reddish to dark brown colored, and are two to three inches long and one-half to one inch wide. They are sweet, flavorful, and fragrant. They are sold in loose bins in most grocery stores. The oysters must be rinsed and soaked in cold water at least two hours (and sometimes up to four hours, depending on the quality) before using. Always reserve the soaking liquid, for it is very flavorful and can be added to other dishes. Do not use the last teaspoon or so of the soaking liquid, as there is often grit that is released as the oysters soak. Use dried oysters sparingly, as they have a strong flavor. Store in a jar in a cool, dark, dry cupboard indefinitely.

杏仁

Peeled Almond Seeds (*hung yen*): Also known as *dried almonds, dried almond seeds,* or *apricot seeds,* Chinese almond seeds bear no resemblance to the Western variety and are, in fact, apricot kernels. They are also sold unpeeled, which makes them look more like Western almonds. Never eat them raw. They are sold in plastic bags or loose in grocery stores or herb shops. There are two varieties, but they are not labeled differently in English, so ask a clerk for help. Both almonds are creamy white and are almost heart shaped. They are used primarily in soups.

北杏

Buck hung: This is the smaller almond and slightly bitter, but is said to bring out the sweet flavor of the *nom hung;* only a few almonds are ever added to a dish. Store in an airtight jar in a cool, dark, dry cupboard for up to one year.

南杏

Nom hung: This is the larger almond, sweet in flavor, and used most frequently in recipes.

酸梅醬

Plum Sauce (*shoon moy zheung*): This honey-colored sauce is available in cans or jars. The plums are cooked with sugar, plum, salt, ginger, and chili pepper, to make a thick, sweet-and-sour sauce. Store in the refrigerator several months.

梘水

Potassium Carbonate Solution (*gan soy*): Sold in five-and-one-half-ounce bottles. A favorite brand is Koon Chun. It is used for Sweet Rice Tamales (page 154). Store in a cool, dark, dry cupboard.

紅豆

Red Beans, dried (*hoong dul*): These small red beans are about one-fourth inch wide and have a thin line. They are often confused with the elongated adzuki beans, which are also labeled red beans in Chinese markets. These beans are used in soups, red bean paste, and desserts. They are sold in plastic bags and should be transferred to an airtight jar and stored in a cool, dark, dry cupboard.

米

Rice (*mai*): There are two main varieties of rice used in Chinese cooking, long grain and sweet rice. Store all rice in a cool, dark, dry place.

米

Long Grain Rice (*mai*): This is long and slender and is about three times longer than it is wide. This is the most popular form of rice in the Chinese diet. The grains, when cooked, are light and fluffy. Some cooks prefer jasmine with its aromatic flavor and nuttier texture.

糯米
Sweet Rice (*naw mai*): This is also known as *glutinous, wax,* or *sticky rice;* the grains are short and pearly white. It should be soaked briefly in cold water before cooking. When cooked its texture is sticky and rich. The flavor of the rice is not sweet, but it may be called sweet because it is a popular ingredient in Asian desserts. This rice has a higher amount of amylopectin, a type of starch that makes the rice stickier than long grain rice.

米粉
Rice Flour (*mai fun*): There are two forms. They are not interchangeable in recipes.

糯米粉
Glutinous Rice Flour (*naw mai fun*): This is flour milled from glutinous rice. It is mainly used in dim sum, New Year's Cake (page 132), and desserts, and is prized for its chewy texture. It cannot be substituted for rice flour. The brand I prefer is from Erawan Marketing Co., Ltd., of Thailand, and is sold in sixteen-ounce plastic bags. Store as you would flour, in a cool, dark, dry cupboard.

粘米粉
Rice Flour (*zeem mai fun*): This is also known as rice powder. It is flour made from long grain rice. It cannot be substituted for glutinous rice flour. The brand I prefer is from the Erawan Marketing Co., Ltd., of Thailand, and is sold in sixteen-ounce plastic bags. Store as you would flour, in a cool, dark, dry cupboard.

冰糖
Rock Sugar (*bing tong*): Also known as *rock candy,* rock sugar is crystallized sugar that comes in very big to small chunks that range in color from amber to clear. If small pieces are needed, tap the larger chunks of sugar with a hammer to break off what you need. Rock sugar is available in plastic bags and small boxes. It is used in sweet soups and also in braised dishes, where it adds a sheen to the food. Store in an airtight jar in a cool, dry, dark cupboard.

咸蛋
Salted Duck Egg (*hom dan*): These eggs have been preserved in brine and ash for forty days. They are cured in America; some are also imported from China. The eggshells are generally white but can be slightly grayish, and are more difficult to crack than regular eggs; the raw egg white is cloudy and the dark orange yolk is very firm and looks cooked. The egg white is the saltiest part of the egg, so some recipes omit the egg white (Savory Rice Tamales, page 152), while others use the whites sparingly (Steamed Pork Cake with Salted Duck Egg, page 38). The eggs are sold loose or in rectangular Styrofoam containers in Chinese grocery stores. Store at room temperature in a cool and breezy room for up to one month.

咸蘿白
Salted Turnip (*ham law bock*): There are a number of different types of salted turnips, and each has a distinctly different taste and appearance; they are only available in Chinese grocery stores. In purchasing salted turnip, you must really make an effort to show the Chinese character and to say the Cantonese name to make sure you have the correct product. I provide the Cantonese pronunciation, but this does *not* appear on the package. The only English you are likely to see is "salted turnip." Always transfer the vegetable to an airtight jar and store in a cool, dark, dry cupboard. Always soak salted turnip in cold water for at least thirty minutes to remove some of the salt before cooking. I have only used two varieties in the recipes:

沖菜扎

Chung choy zack: This is sold in thirteen-ounce packages and is a combination of turnip, salt, and water. The vegetable is khaki colored and has been rolled tightly to form one-inch-wide bundles.

甜菜甫

Teem choy poe: This has been preserved only in salt and water, but it also has a sweet flavor. The vegetable is sold in seven-ounce packages and is khaki-colored; the pieces are three to five inches long, one-half inch wide, and one-fourth to one-half inch thick. The slices are pliable.

葱

Scallions (*chung*): Also known as *spring onions* or *green onions,* this vegetable is often paired with ginger. Although the entire scallion can be cooked, for more delicate dishes only the white portion is used. Store in the refrigerator vegetable crisper bin for up to one week.

江瑤柱

Scallops, dried (*gawn yu chee*): Dried scallops look like fresh scallops, except for their golden color. They are very expensive but very flavorful. Dried scallops are sold in boxes or loose from large bins in grocery stores or herb shops. Quartered or broken scallops are less expensive and can be equally flavorful. Choose scallops that resemble sea scallops in size, rather than bay scallops, which are less flavorful. They should be fragrant, golden, and shiny. They require rinsing and about two hours of soaking in cold water to soften sufficiently before cooking. Remove the hard knob on the side of the scallop before cooking, then shred the scallops. Always reserve the soaking liquid, for it is very flavorful and can be added to soups. Store in an airtight jar in a cool, dark, dry cupboard.

紫菜

Seaweed (*zee choy*): Also known as *nori, roasted seaweed,* or *kizunori,* it is sold in flat cellophane packages. I prefer the Japanese product to Chinese or Canadian seaweed, as it is always clean and does not require any rinsing or cleaning. There are about ten sheets of dark green to purple-black seaweed per .075-ounce package; the sheets are about seven by eight inches. Seaweed is available in Asian markets and in health-food stores. Once opened, store in an airtight container free from moisture.

麻油

Sesame Oil (*ma yul*): A seasoning oil made from toasted or roasted sesame seeds, it is golden brown, fragrant, and aromatic. It is sold in bottles. Only a small amount is needed to enhance the flavor of foods. Some cooks prefer black sesame oil, which has a fuller flavor. Choose a pure sesame oil rather than one that has been blended with another oil. Sesame oil is also available hot with chili flavor. Store in the refrigerator for up to one year.

芝麻

Sesame Seeds (*zeema*): There are black and white sesame seeds, and they are sold in plastic bags in Chinese grocery stores. Store in an airtight jar in the refrigerator to prevent the seeds from becoming rancid. Before using, always smell the seeds to make sure the seeds are not spoiled.

黑芝麻

Black Sesame Seeds (*hock zeema*): These are also labeled *dried sesame seeds*. These seeds look like sesame seeds except for their black color. They are available from Thailand, China, and Japan. The Thai and Chinese seeds often have little tiny stones, grit, or tiny twigs in the package. The Japanese seeds cost a little bit more, but the quality is worth the extra money, because they are totally clean and without grit. Black sesame seeds taste similar to white sesame seeds, except for a little bitterness that comes from their hulls. They are available in Asian markets and, sometimes, in American gourmet and health-food stores.

白芝麻
White Sesame Seeds (*bock zeema*): These are tiny hulled sesame seeds that are mainly used for pastries. The seeds develop flavor after they have been roasted in a skillet. These are available in Chinese and American markets.

紹興酒
Shao Hsing Rice Cooking Wine (*siu hing zul*): Also known as *rice wine,* this wine is made by fermenting glutinous rice. It is available in most Chinese grocery stores or in Chinese liquor stores, and is inexpensive. If unavailable, use pale dry sherry, but never use sake. Store at room temperature.

魚翅
Shark's Fin (*yu chee*): This is available canned, dried, or frozen. The canned and frozen products are not as delicious as the dried variety, which is sold in a rectangular five-by-seven-inch block weighing about five to seven ounces, and also as a whole dried fin; the heavier the block the better. Both dried forms require soaking and blanching several times before using (page 114), which takes time. The block form, which is blond colored, is more common, and is easier to work with. Shark's fin is a highly prized delicacy, and is served braised or in soups at banquets and on special occasions. Store the dried in a cool, dark, dry cupboard.

扁腐竹
Sheet Dried Bean Curd (*bien foo jook*): Also known as *dehydrated bean curd* or *dried bean thread,* these ivory-colored sheets are sold next to the stick dried bean curd (page 263). The packages are often labeled identically, but the sheets are about seven-and-one-half-by-thirteen-inch rectangles and a scant one-eighth inch thick. They are made from soybean starch and water. Store in plastic bags in a cool, dark, dry cupboard for up to one year.

蝦米
Shrimp, dried (*ha mai*): These dried baby shrimp are one-half to one inch big, and are very flavorful. They are sold loose in big bins or in plastic packages. Choose bright orange shrimp; avoid shrimp that look flaky. Dried shrimp are cooked in dumplings, soups, and stir-fries; use sparingly. Store in an airtight jar in a cool, dry, dark cupboard for up to one year.

花椒
Sichuan Peppercorns (*fa ziu*): Sichuan peppercorns are reddish brown and resemble peppercorns but are, in fact, berries. They are always sold in plastic bags and have tiny twigs included. The peppercorns must be dry-roasted in a wok or skillet to bring out their fragrance and flavor, then crushed before being cooked. Peppercorns do lose flavor with time but most people keep them indefinitely. Store in an airtight jar in a cool, dry, dark cupboard.

炸菜
Sichuan Preserved Vegetable (*cha choy*): Also known as *preserved mustard stem* or *preserved radish,* this is a pickled vegetable, which has been covered with chili paste and salt to preserve it. Sichuan preserved vegetable is sold in large open bins, in cans, and in Cryovac packages in Chinese markets.

The chili paste must be rinsed off just before using. The vegetable is then finely shredded or minced. It has a sweet, salty, pickled flavor. A two-ounce portion is about the size of a golf ball. Store the unrinsed vegetable in a jar and refrigerate for several months.

火腿

Smithfield Ham (*faw toy*): Also known as *Chinese Smithfield ham, sliced ham, peppered ham,* or *Virginia ham,* Smithfield ham is remarkably similar to a famous ham from the province of Yunnan in China. It is a dried and salty ham that, according to the USDA, must originate in Smithfield, Virginia. It is used sparingly in recipes, but adds a lot of flavor. It is sold in Chinese butcher shops whole or sliced into small steaks, about one-half inch thick, which always have a small bone. Slices are often two to four ounces and wrapped in Cryovac. Smithfield ham is sold in some American butcher shops whole, but never as small steaks. Most recipes call for boiling the ham steaks in water to remove some of the saltiness before adding to a dish. Store it in the refrigerator for several months in a sealed container.

雪耳

Snow Fungus (*shoot yee*): Also known as *silver fungus, white fungus,* or *dried vegetable,* these are feather-light, yellow puffs that look like dried flowers. Snow fungus is about two to three inches in diameter, with a rounded top and flat bottom that have a slightly darker color. Choose yellow or light golden snow fungus rather than white. It must be soaked in cold water before cooking, during which the snow fungus will expand two to three times its original size. After soaking, remove the hard spots and break into smaller pieces. Commonly cooked in soups, it is silky and gelatinous. Some people prefer snow fungus barely cooked and crunchy, while others like to cook it until it nearly melts in your mouth. It is available in the dry-goods section of a Chinese market. Store in an airtight jar in a cool, dark, dry, cupboard for up to one year.

荷蘭豆

Snow Peas (*haw lan dul*): These flat pods are sweet and crunchy, and best in stir-fries. Select bright, shiny, green pods with smooth, unblemished skin. Remove the stem ends and string along the straight side before cooking. Snow peas are available all year round and are a good source of vitamin C. Store in the refrigerator vegetable crisper bin for up to one week.

豆苗

Snow Pea Shoots (*dau miu*): One of the more expensive vegetables, these delicate shoots from the snow pea are a cold weather vegetable; as the weather warms up, the shoots toughen. They are pale green, with small, delicate leaves, tendrils, and stems. The leaves are matte and the shoots appear slightly limp even when fresh, but should never be yellow. Once cooked, they are slightly reminiscent of spinach, with a more delicate flavor. There is a hothouse variety sometimes available in gourmet stores year round; it has uniform dark green sprouts with no tendrils and it is inferior in taste. Stir-fry snow pea shoots in season, and avoid the hothouse variety. Store in the refrigerator vegetable crisper for up to two to three days.

黃豆

Soybeans, dried (*wong dul*): Also known as *yellow soybeans,* these are sold in plastic bags in Chinese markets and health-food stores. They are used to make soy milk, soups, and for sprouting soybean sprouts. Store in an airtight jar in a cool, dry, dark cupboard for up to six months.

豆漿

Soy Milk (*dul cheung*): This looks like dairy milk, but has a completely different taste and texture, with no creamy characteristics. It can be made at home from dried soybeans and water (page 209). Soy milk is also available in Chinese markets and health-food stores, but the two products are generally different. Soy milk available in Western health-food shops and supermarkets often has malted-cereal extract, barley, and kombu added; therefore, it is not advisable to use in Chinese recipes. Soy milk from Chinatown has none of these ingredients and is available sweetened or plain. Be sure to check before buying, as the sweet version is very sweet and should not be used for cooking. Soy milk from Chinatown and homemade soy milk should be stored in the refrigerator no more than three to five days.

豉油

Soy Sauce (*see yul*): There are many varieties of soy sauce, but the two most essential for cooking are thin and black. The sauces are made from soybeans, wheat flour, sugar, salt, and water, and are naturally brewed. Store soy sauce at room temperature. Also available are mushroom flavored soy sauce, seasoned soy sauce for seafood, and chili soy sauce.

老抽

Black Soy (*low zul*): This is also known as *soy superior sauce* or *dark soy sauce.* It is darker, thicker, and richer in color and slightly sweeter in taste. This sauce is aged longer than thin soy sauce.

生抽

Thin Soy (*sang zul*): This is also known as *superior soy, premium soy sauce,* or *light soy sauce.* It is available in large bottles, and has the most flavor. This is not to be confused with "lite" or reduced-sodium soy sauce. Thin soy is most often used in cooking, and is saltier than black soy sauce and lighter in color. The soy sauce sold in Western markets is generally thin.

春卷皮

Spring Roll Wrappers (*chun guen pay*): Also known as *egg roll wrappers,* these are found in the refrigerator section of Chinese grocery stores. They are about eight by eight inches and are sold in packages of ten to twenty-five wrappers. Select wrappers that are paper-thin and translucent. Spring roll wrappers are sometimes available in Western supermarkets, but these tend to be thicker and therefore tougher. When using spring roll wrappers, cover the wrappers with a damp kitchen towel to prevent the dough from drying out. Keeps one week refrigerated or can be frozen.

八角

Star Anise (*bot guok*): Also sold as *star ani-seed,* each star anise is made up of an eight-pointed star that is hard, reddish brown, and about the size of a quarter. Sometimes it has a one-and-one-half- to two-inch stem. Star anise is very fragrant, and has a distinct licorice flavor. It is used in braises and stews, and is one of the spices in five-spice powder. It does lose flavor with time but most people keep it indefinitely. It is sold in plastic bags that should be transferred to an airtight jar and kept in a cool, dark, dry cupboard.

腐竹

Stick Dried Bean Curd (*foo jook*): Also known as *dehydrated bean curd* or *dried bean thread,* stick dried bean curd is ivory colored, about twelve inches long, and shaped like a giant horseshoe. It comes in a large twelve-ounce package, and must be soaked in cold water to soften for ten minutes to twenty-four hours (depending on the quality of the bean curd), or blanched in boiling water one to two minutes before cooking. Choose bean curd that is slightly translucent. Store in plastic bags in a cool, dark, dry cupboard for up to one year.

草菇
Straw Mushrooms (*cho qwoo*): Available in cans, they must be rinsed before using. Store unused portion, covered with cold water, in a plastic container in the refrigerator for up to four days.

豬仔薯
Sweet Potato, dried (*zhu zai shu*): These are oval slices that are white in the center with a faint tan skin. They are about one-fourth inch thick and three inches in length. They are sold in seven-ounce plastic bags, and should be transferred to an airtight jar and stored in a cool, dark, dry cupboard for up to one year.

豆沙
Sweetened Red Bean Paste (*dul sah*): This thick red paste is made of mashed red beans and sugar. It can be homemade (see page 139), which is superior in taste, or purchased in an eighteen-ounce can. The best brand is Companion. Once opened, the bean paste can be stored in a plastic container in the refrigerator for up to one week.

果皮
Tangerine Peel, dried (*guo pay*): Sometimes called *orange peel,* it is in fact the peel from tangerines that has been dried in the sun until quite hard. The peels become dark brown on the outside and pale tan on the pith side; some people dry the peels themselves. The peels are sold in plastic bags in grocery stores or loose in herb shops and are about one-and-one-half to three inches wide. Tangerine peel that is aged for at least one year is called *chun pay,* and is more expensive; the older the peel, the better the bittersweet citrus flavor and fragrance. The peel must be soaked in cold water before cooking, but do not soak for more than thirty minutes or it will lose flavor. Some cooks scrape off the pith before cooking. Store in an airtight jar in a cool, dry, dark cupboard, indefinitely.

西米
Tapioca, Pearl, Small (*sai mai*): Available in fourteen-ounce plastic bags, this tapioca is much bigger than Minute tapioca, found in Western supermarkets. The tapioca looks like small, white pearls, and is typically used in desserts. Store in an airtight jar in a cool, dry, dark cupboard.

菱粉
Tapioca Starch (*ling fun*): Also known as *tapioca flour,* this starch is available in fourteen-ounce packages, and is used in marinades and to thicken sauces. It has a similar appearance to cornstarch, which can be used as a substitute if tapioca starch is unavailable. The Chinese feel it is more stable than cornstarch. The best brand is from Thailand, from Combine Thai Foods Co., Ltd. Store in an airtight jar in a cool, dark, dry cupboard for up to one year.

芋頭
Taro Root (*woo tul*): This starchy root vegetable is six to ten inches long, four inches wide, and cylindrical. The skin is dark brown, hairy, and very dusty. The taro root should be firm and heavy. Never choose taro root that has been sliced on either end. Check the root carefully for mold spots. The texture is starchy and reminiscent of a potato. It is used in braised dishes and in Taro Root Cake (page 130). Raw taro root is said to cause itchiness when touched with bare hands, so many people wear rubber gloves when handling it. The flesh is potato-colored with fine flecks and occasional blush spots; it turns a pale lavender color once it is cooked. Store as you would a potato and use within one week.

豆腐
Tofu (*dul foo*): Also known as *bean curd,* tofu is made by combining soybean milk and a coagulant; the resulting curds are pressed together to form cakes of tofu, which come in several different

forms. Tofu is high in protein, cholesterol free, low in saturated fats, and rich in phytochemicals. Studies have shown that tofu can lower cholesterol levels and may help in preventing some forms of cancer. It is mild in flavor and is used in braises, soups, and stir-fries. Always select tofu that has a clean smell and is creamy white (except for five spice tofu); check the expiration date if in a sealed package. Store the unused portion, covered with cold water, in a plastic container. Refrigerate and change the water daily for up to three days.

豆腐
Firm Tofu (*dul foo*): This comes in three-inch squares, one-half inch thick. It can be diced, cubed, or sliced, and is used in stir-fries, braises, and soups. It is made fresh daily in Chinatown, where it is kept in large tubs or in sealed packages in the refrigerator section of Chinese grocery stores, supermarkets, and health-food stores. There is also extra-firm tofu, which has a drier and less silky texture.

五香豆腐乾
Five Spice Tofu (*nmm heung dul foo gawn*): Also known as *spiced tofu* or *flavored bean curd,* this is pressed tofu flavored with soy sauce and five-spice powder, which colors the tofu a light nut brown. It is typically used in stir-fries, and has a drier, firmer texture (even firmer than extra-firm tofu). It is sold in small eight-ounce rectangular packages in the refrigerator section of Chinese grocery stores. Store in a plastic bag in the refrigerator but never cover with water.

滑豆腐
Silken Tofu (*wat dul foo*): This is custardlike and is more delicate. It is mainly used in soups, and is available in sealed packages in the refrigerator section of Chinese grocery stores, supermarkets, and health-food stores.

油
Vegetable oil (*yul*): Chinese cooks have typically cooked with vegetable or peanut oil. Today, many families, adapting to the latest health information on fats, are using mild or light olive oil for stir-fries and deep-fat frying. Olive oil, rich in monounsaturated fats, offers many health benefits, and it is now stocked in many Chinese markets. Never use extra virgin olive oil, as the fruity taste of olives would not be appropriate for Chinese cooking.

醋
Vinegar (*cho*): Chinese vinegar is primarily made from glutinous rice. Store at room temperature in a cool, dark, dry cupboard for up to one year.

黑糯米醋
Black Vinegar (*hock naw mai cho*): This is also known as *black rice vinegar sauce*. It is mainly used for Pickled Pig's Feet (page 238) and is sold in twenty-ounce bottles. Store at room temperature.

大紅浙醋
Red Rice Vinegar (*dai hoong zeet cho*): This is mainly used as a dipping sauce.

添丁甜醋
Sweetened Black Vinegar (*teem ding teem cho*): This is also known as *sweetened black rice vinegar.* It is mainly used for Pickled Pig's Feet (page 238) and is sold in twenty-one-ounce bottles. Store at room temperature.

馬蹄

Water Chestnut, fresh (*ma tai*): A bulblike dark brown vegetable, lightly covered in dirt, water chestnuts are about one-and-one-half inches around and are about one inch high. They are grown underwater in mud, and have a thin skin. Choose water chestnuts that are heavy and firm. They must be peeled with a paring knife before cooking, which is labor intensive but worth the effort. Water chestnuts have a sweet flavor and a crunchy, crisp texture, like an apple. The flesh should be white and not yellow or ivory. They are excellent in stir-fries and dumplings and are delicious raw. They are extremely high in potassium. Never use canned water chestnuts, for they are inferior in taste. Store in the refrigerator vegetable crisper bin for up to one week.

馬蹄粉

Water Chestnut Flour (*ma tai fun*): Also known as *water chestnut powder* or *water chestnut starch,* it is sold in small eight-and-four-fifths-ounce boxes. The best brand is Pan Tang Brand, although high-quality water chestnut flour is difficult to find; it is often stale and sometimes black if the water chestnuts were not thoroughly peeled before being made into flour. Store in an airtight jar in a cool, dry, dark cupboard for up to one year.

通心菜

Water Spinach (*toong sum choy*): These are sold in big one-and-one-half-pound bunches. The entire stalk is about eighteen inches in length, and is pale green with slightly darker green leaves. Most of the stalk is made up of a hollow stem with skinny, pointed leaves. Water spinach is always broken into two-inch lengths and cooked with garlic and wet bean curd (*fu yu*) in stir-fries. It is most popular during the summer. Once cooked, the leaves taste a little like spinach. Store in the refrigerator vegetable crisper bin for no more than two days, as water spinach wilts easily.

西洋菜

Watercress (*sai yeung choy*): One of the most popular vegetables for soups, watercress is available year-round in Chinese and American markets. Choose dark green bunches, about six inches long, with young, delicate leaves and tender stems. Watercress has a distinct mustard flavor and a significant amount of beta carotene and calcium. Store in the refrigerator vegetable crisper bin for up to four to five days.

腐乳

Wet Bean Curd (*fu yu*): Also known as *fermented bean curd,* and sometimes *bean sauce* (although this is different from ground bean sauce, page 254), wet bean curd comes in two main varieties and, as with certain other ingredients, the English labeling will not help you. You have to know what they look like: One is beige-colored and the other red. They are both sold in jars in Chinese grocery stores. Wet bean curd is cheeselike, because it has been fermented and is very flavorful; no more than a few cubes are ever used in one dish. Once opened it must be refrigerated; it will keep indefinitely. A favorite brand is Chan Moon Kee.

白腐乳

Wet Bean Curd, white (*bock fu yu*): These are one-inch beige-colored cubes of fermented bean curd in liquid. The bean curd is made from fermented soybeans, salt, and rice wine and is mainly used in stir-fries. The jar is seldom marked "white." This also is available spiced with dried red chilies.

南乳

Wet Bean Curd, red (*nom yu*): These are one-inch red cubes of fermented bean curd in a thick red sauce. This bean curd is made from fermented soybeans, salt, rice wine, and red rice and is mainly used for braises. The jar is not always marked "red."

澄粉

Wheat Starch (*dung fun*): This looks like flour and is used to make the wrappers for shrimp dumplings. It is sold in fourteen- to sixteen-ounce bags; a popular brand is Man Sang FTY. Store as you would flour, in a cool, dark, dry cupboard for up to one year.

冬瓜

Winter Melon (*doong qwa*): This is about the size of a medium to large watermelon. Choose winter melon that is as old as possible; signs of age are a heavy white powder coating on the hard rind. If the melon is sold by the wedge, a mature melon will have seeds that pull away from the flesh. Most people buy a wedge weighing one to three pounds, but a small melon can be bought, carved, and filled with chicken broth and steamed (Fancy Winter Melon Soup, page 143). Winter melon rind, seeds, and pulp are said to have medicinal attributes, and are often cooked in soups. If the rind is to be cooked, it must be well scrubbed and rinsed. Choose cut winter melon that has a clean smell. Winter melon is mainly used for braises and soups. When cooked, the flesh becomes translucent. Store slices in the refrigerator vegetable crisper bin for up to three days. Whole winter melon will keep in the refrigerator one week.

杞子

Wolfberries, dried (*gay zee*): Wolfberries look like oval, red raisins, about one-half inch long and one-eighth inch wide. They should be a bright red color and not deep burgundy, which shows age. Wolfberries have a small pit that does not need to be removed before cooking. They have a significant amount of iron and calcium; Chinese people believe they are good for your eyes. They are used mainly in soups and are found in Chinese grocery stores in plastic bags, or sold in bulk in herb shops. Store in an airtight jar in a cool, dark, dry cupboard.

雲吞皮

Won Ton Skins (*wun tun pay*): The fourteen- to sixteen-ounce packages of paper-thin, silky dough are found in the refrigerator section of Chinese grocery stores. The dough, made of flour, egg, and water, is available in three-and-one-half-inch squares or rounds, about one hundred to a package. Square won ton skins are used for traditional Won Ton (page 158), the round skins are used for Pork Dumplings (page 156). The dough can vary in thickness: The thinner dough is used for boiled or steamed dumplings, the thicker skins for deep-fried won tons. When using won ton skins, cover the skins with a damp kitchen towel to prevent the dough from drying out. Refrigerate for up to five days or freeze.

木耳

Wood Ears (*mook yee*): Also known as *dehydrated vegetable* or *sea vegetable,* these fungi are three to four times the size of cloud ears, and much cruder in appearance. The pieces can be as big as two by three inches, and are black on one side and look like tan suede on the underside. The fungi are about one-eighth inch thick, and are woodier and harder than cloud ears. Wood ears are prepared like cloud ears, and require soaking in cold water before cooking. They, too, will expand to two to three times their original size. Wood ears are sold in large six-ounce plastic bags in grocery stores, and are also available in bulk in herb shops. They are used in braised dishes, in particular Chicken Wine Soup (page 236). Store in an airtight jar in a cool, dark, dry cupboard indefinitely.

XO 醬

XO Sauce (*xo cheung*): Relatively new, this condiment sauce has become the rage in Hong Kong, and is called the Caviar of the Orient. The XO in the name pays homage to XO brandy, which is revered by the Chinese (there is no brandy in the sauce, however). Made by Lee Kum Kee, it's a mixture of dried scallops, shrimp, shallots, shrimp roe, soybean oil, soy sauce, garlic, and seasonings, and is delicious as a condiment for dumplings or as a seasoning in stir-fries. It is also available in an extra-hot version.

淮 山

Yam, dried (*wai san*): Also known as *Chinese yam*, this is sold in creamy white slices, two to eight inches long and one-half inch thick. It is one of the primary ingredients used in the famous Four Flavors Soup (page 216) and is a mild Chinese herb that is used year-round for the spleen and stomach. It is sold in Chinese grocery stores in boxes and in bulk in herb shops. Store in an airtight jar in a cool, dark, dry cupboard indefinitely.

綠豆去皮

Yellow Mung Beans, Dried (*look dul hoy pay*): Also known as *peeled mung beans,* these beans look like small yellow split peas, and are sold in fourteen-ounce plastic bags. They are green mung beans that have been hulled, but green mung beans cannot be substituted for the yellow. They are used in Savory Rice Tamales (page 152). Store in an airtight jar in a cool, dark, dry cupboard for up to one year.

MAIL-ORDER SOURCES

I always prefer to shop for ingredients and equipment. You should only use mail order if nothing is available in your area.

CHINESE AMERICAN TRADING CO., INC.
91 Mulberry Street
New York, NY 10013
(212) 267-5224
Fax: (212) 619-7446

This is my favorite shop in Chinatown. The staff is helpful and they speak English. They carry every kind of ingredient called for in this book (including the herbs) except for fresh produce and meats. They also have a wide selection of traditional cooking equipment. It's best to send a check with your order, or orders can be sent by UPS C.O.D.

LIN'S SISTER ASSOCIATES CORP.
4 Bowery
New York, NY 10013
(212) 962-5417
Fax: (212) 587-8826

This is a fantastic herb shop where English is spoken. Visa and Mastercard accepted and they will ship UPS.

UWAJIMAYA
519 6th Avenue South
Seattle, WA 98104
1-800-889-1928
(206) 624-6248
Fax: (206) 624-6915

This shop carries an amazing selection of Asian produce–from fresh water chestnuts, to winter melon, gingko nuts, Chinese broccoli, and lotus root. They also have some Chinese ingredients, but specialize mainly in Japanese products. Ask for their brochure. Visa, Mastercard, and American Express accepted and they will ship UPS.

INDEX